Character Education

A Neo-Aristotelian Approach to the
Philosophy, Psychology and Education of Virtue

ISBN: 978-90-5972-702-1

Eburon Academic Publishers,
P.O. Box 2867, 2601 CW Delft, The Netherlands

Photographs Shutterstock
Cover design Sander Hermsen Visuele Communicatie, Nijmegen
Graphic design Sander Hermsen Visuele Communicatie, Nijmegen

© 2012. All rights reserved. No part of this publication may be reproduced, stored in a retrieval system, or transmitted, in any form or by any means, electronic, mechanical, photocopying, recording, or otherwise, without the prior permission in writing from the proprietor.

Character Education

A Neo-Aristotelian Approach to the
Philosophy, Psychology and Education of Virtue

Wouter Sanderse

Eburon
Delft 2012

To my parents

Acknowledgments

When I visited a PhD defence in the field of medical science some time ago, it struck me how the candidate never used the singular pronoun 'I', but referred to the research he defended in terms of 'we'. I tried to justify this by reminding myself that medical research is a collaborative enterprise, but remained a bit disappointed. The defence was excellent, but I expected him to claim ownership of his thesis, to make the PhD really *his*. I remember thinking that things were completely different in philosophy. However, I was mistaken. The distinction between what I have achieved by writing this thesis and what others have contributed to it, is not always easy to make. First of all, this thesis would not exist without the long and rich Aristotelian tradition, which I have tried to make useful for educational theory and practice. But many other wonderful people made the years that I worked on the thesis a valuable and pleasurable experience.

First, I would like to thank my supervisor Paul van Tongeren. He has been a mentor to me ever since I became an assistant at the Department of Ethics in 2004. He suggested the subject to me, was patient enough to let me acquire a feeling for it, always stimulating me to maintain close ties with educational practice. While he was critical about the potential value of studying the Anglo-Saxon philosophy of education, and remains sceptical about a fruitful cross-fertilisation of moral philosophy and empirical psychology, he endorsed my choices to follow these paths anyway. This also illustrates the more general trust he put in my ability to bring the project to a good end, which I found very encouraging. My colleague Marcel Becker has been an inspiring example of how to apply virtue ethics to several domains of professional practice, and he has made daily life at the faculty much more fun, too. I could always put my questions to him, he cheered me up with the jokes he stole from his son, and we share a passion for running.

Furthermore, I am grateful for three experts who hosted me on several stays abroad. In the beautiful city of Edinburgh, David Carr found time, despite an overabundance of professional commitments, to initiate me during the autumn of 2008 into the field of moral education, and the philosophy of education more generally. In the summer of 2010, I stayed a month in Reykjavik, where Kristján Kristjánsson did all he could to make my visit productive and pleasant, and found time to read and discuss a large part of my thesis. Finally, Randall Curren hosted me in Rochester (NY) during the winter of 2012. He made sure that I could concentrate on the last chapters of the thesis. For a month, he and his wife Christina were kind enough to involve me in their lives and take me to several concerts in the Eastman School of Music. In Rochester, I was also lucky to be able to interview Howard Kirschenbaum twice, one of the leading figures in the values clarification movement of the 1970s.

Parts of the thesis have been presented at international conferences and I would like to thank the people that attended my presentations for their questions and comments: the conference 'Understanding Conflict – Cross-Cultural Perspectives' in Arhus (Denmark), August 2008; the 3rd conference of the International Society for MacIntyrean Enquiry (ISME), Dublin (Ireland), March 2009; the 35th annual conference of the Association of Moral Education, Utrecht (The Netherlands), July 2009; the annual conference of the Philosophy of Education Society of Great-Britain, in Oxford (England), March 2010 and April 2011; the conference 'What Makes Us Moral?', Amsterdam (The Netherlands), June 2011. Moreover, the summer school on 'Contemporary Psychology and the Moral Point of View' of the Netherlands School for Research in Practical Philosophy inspired me to write the section on role modelling (§4.2). It has been accepted for publication by the *Journal of Moral Education*.

Furthermore, I received useful feedback from Pieter Mostert on the section on 'Socratic Dialogue'. Unofficially, he took me on as a student in order to learn how to supervise these dialogues, and I am very grateful that there have been many opportunities where I could watch him make teachers and pupils enthusiastic about philosophy. I thank Paulien Snellen, at that time research master student at the department, for her comments on the section about self-control and moral development. Especially during the first years, I was glad enough to know Frank Willems, who worked on a more empirically oriented PhD project on 'virtue ethics and moral education'. It was good to talk with somebody who was also trying to get a grip on the same subject.

However, I did not only receive philosophical support. For example, I learned a lot from people working in education. I would like to thank the teachers who participated in the courses I taught, for sharing their experiences and ideas with me. Furthermore, I would like to thank the members of the 'Moral Education Advisory Board', with whom I met twice a year to discuss the relevance of my research for educational practice over dinner. Besides Paul van Tongeren, this group consisted of Pieter Vos, Ans Buys, Herman van Rhee, Louis Engels and Ine Raangs. In addition, I would also like to thank Joan Alexandersen Coke for reading and carefully language-editing the whole manuscript. Finally, Toon and Jan, the faculty's 'coffee men' (the equivalent of 'tea ladies') provided me every single day with strong coffee, a joke and a chat.

I have been very fortunate to have a number of valuable friends, some of them deserve to be mentioned by name. It has been a pleasure for me that Tim Houwen, who was already a good friend, also worked on a PhD thesis in philosophy at the same faculty. For five years, we saw each other almost on a daily basis, and shared our private lives, day-to-day worries about our research, and philosophical ideas. I have good memories of the conversations we had during our numerous lunches, in particular, when historians Wim de Jong and Joris Gijsenbergh joined in. I want to thank another friend, Dirk Geurts, for sharing his excessive energy and vigorous mind with me. It was his idea to start walking the Pieterpad, a long distance route in the Netherlands, which occasionally provided us with a perfect excuse to spend a whole day talking about life and work. He also introduced me to *Senex Captiosus*, the academic society which broadens my academic horizons.

Hilde, on our first date, I subjected you to a barrage of Socratic questions to find out what you already knew about Socrates. The questioning did not work – but our relationship does. You are a great person, and you remind me that being a moral philosopher is not necessarily sufficient for being a morally good person. With you, life is better.

Wouter Sanderse
Nijmegen, July 2012

Content

Chapter 1: Introduction
The Virtue Ethical Approach to Moral Education 15
    1.1 Moral Education in Schools 15
    1.2 The Aim of this Thesis 17
    1.3 Problems with the Education of Virtue 18
    1.4 Contemporary Character Education 20
    1.5 Neo-Aristotelian Virtue Ethics 22
    1.6 Overview of the Book 25

Chapter 2:
The Alternatives to Character Education 27
    2.1 Introduction 27
    2.2 Values Clarification 29
        2.2.1 The Emergence of Values Clarification 29
        2.2.2 The Goal of Values Clarification 31
        2.2.3 Value Psychology and Development 34
        2.2.4 Values Clarification in Schools 36
    2.3 Cognitive Development Theory 39
        2.3.1 The Emergence of Cognitive Develpment Theory 39
        2.3.2 Piaget's Stages of Cognitive Development 41
        2.3.3 Kohlberg's Stages of Moral Development 43
        2.3.4 From Moral Judgment to Action? 45
        2.3.5 Justifying the Highest Stage 47
        2.3.6 Cognitive Development in Schools 51
    2.4 Care Ethics 54
        2.4.1 The Emergence of Care Ethics 54
        2.4.2 The Relationship between Justice and Care 55
        2.4.3 Natural and Ethical Caring 57
        2.4.4 The Psychology and Development of Care 60
        2.4.5 Care Ethics in Schools 63
    2.5 Challenges to Character Education 65

Chapter 3
Virtue Psychology and Development — 73

- 3.1 Introduction — 73
- 3.2 Aristotle's Moral Psychology — 77
  - 3.2.1 The Human Soul — 77
  - 3.2.2 Moral Virtue — 78
  - 3.2.3 Character Traits — 80
  - 3.2.4 Emotions and Actions — 82
  - 3.2.5 The Observance of the Mean — 85
  - 3.2.6 Practical Wisdom — 87
  - 3.2.7 Rival Moral Psychologies — 89
- 3.3 The Situationist Challenge to Virtue Ethics — 91
  - 3.3.1 The Situationism Debate — 92
  - 3.3.2 Practical Wisdom under Siege — 93
  - 3.3.3 The Solution: Virtues as Ideals? — 95
  - 3.3.4 Minimal Psychological Realism — 97
  - 3.3.5 Prospective Practical Wisdom at Last — 100
- 3.4 A Neo-Aristotelian Model of Moral Development — 102
  - 3.4.1 Categories or Stages? — 102
  - 3.4.2 Stage 1: Morally Uncommitted — 106
  - 3.4.3 Stage 2: Lack of Self-Control — 108
  - 3.4.4 Stage 3: Self-Control — 111
  - 3.4.5 Stage 4: Full Virtue — 114
  - 3.4.6 Towards a Virtue Ethical Alternative to Kohlberg — 116
- 3.5 Conclusion — 117

Chapter 4
The Education of Virtue in Schools — 123

- 4.1 Introduction — 123
- 4.2 Role modelling — 125
  - 4.2.1 Introduction — 125
  - 4.2.2 The Use of Modelling — 127
  - 4.2.3 Teachers as Moral Exemplars — 129
  - 4.2.4 Habituation as Imitation and Emulation — 132
  - 4.2.5 Improving Role Modelling — 135
  - 4.2.6 The Cross-fertilisation of Philosophy and Social Science — 136
- 4.3 The Moral Educational Use of the Arts — 137
  - 4.3.1 Introduction — 137
  - 4.3.2 Learning a Moral Lesson — 138
  - 4.3.3 Cultivating Compassion — 141
  - 4.3.4 Life as a Narrative Unity — 143
  - 4.3.5 Integrity and the Speed of Moral Development — 146
  - 4.3.6 Narrative Strategies in the Classroom — 148

4.4 Socratic Dialogue	149
4.4.1 Introduction	149
4.4.2 Plato and the Socratic Dialogues	149
4.4.3 Leonard Nelson's Approach	152
4.4.4 The Hourglass Model	155
4.4.5 Practical Wisdom's Regressive Movement	159
4.4.6 Teachers' Practical Wisdom	161
4.4.7 Practice-oriented Moral Enquiry	163
4.5 Conclusion	165

Chapter 5
Virtue and Human Flourishing — 169

5.1 Introduction	169
5.2 Teachers' Understanding of Virtue	170
5.2.1 Private Virtue and Public Morality	170
5.2.2 Beyond the Split Model	172
5.3 Aristotle on Human Flourishing	176
5.3.1 Eudaimonia	176
5.3.2 Some Vexed Questions	179
5.4 Interlude: Teaching 'Happiness'	180
5.5 A Common Human Nature	183
5.5.1 Biological Teleology	183
5.5.2 Feasibility Constraints	184
5.5.3 Wise and Experienced Judges	186
5.5.4 Mapping the Moral Terrain	188
5.6 A Variety of Ethical Worlds	189
5.6.1 Virtues in Practices and Life Narratives	190
5.6.2 Virtues and Moral Enquiry in Traditions	191
5.6.3 Educating Virtue in a Plural Society	195
5.7 Conclusion	198

Chapter 6: General Conclusion
Problems, Questions and Prospects — 201

6.1 Aristotelian Character Education	201
6.2 Six Aristotelian Fusions	204
6.3 Implications for Education, Psychology and Philosophy	206

References	209
Summary	227
Samenvatting (Dutch summary)	232
Curriculum Vitae	237

Chapter 1: Introduction
The Virtue Ethical Approach to Moral Education

1.1 Moral Education in Schools

The moral concerns of teachers working in secondary education are diverse. Some teachers address explicit moral themes because they teach religious or civic education. As the goal of these subjects is often to introduce pupils to important religious, political and ethical traditions, they involve the transfer of certain authoritative values (such as justice, freedom, equality and tolerance) and the clarification and evaluation of the values that pupils already cherish. These values can be discussed during critical classroom discussions about a topical issue in which these or other values are at stake. Other teachers, whether they teach history, biology or English, also frequently stumble upon moral issues that somehow need to be addressed. For example, topics such as eugenics, the Holocaust, child labour, slavery or animal welfare are often part of the curriculum. Furthermore, there are all kinds of 'morally critical situations', in and outside the classroom, e.g. when a pupil suddenly makes a discriminating or sexist remark. In an instance, need to decide whether to ignore the remark, show their disapproval non or take the pupil aside.

Sometimes they will appeal to school rules to deal with a problematic s Without some of these rules, for example about school hours, lunch arrangements, absence, homework, dress and appearance, etc. teachers and pupils could easily be distracted, and not much teaching or learning would occur. Other rules do not only create optimal conditions for learning, but have a more explicit moral nature, in the sense that they concern other people's well-being. For example, schools often have rules that forbid pupils to pester, use abusive language, use violence and that oblige them to keep off other children's property. In a more positive vein, there are rules that encourage children to listen to each other and be respectful. Such rules are imposed on children when they enter a school or a new class, and teachers usually spend a considerable amount of time reminding recalcitrant adolescents of these rules. When rules are violated, teachers will sometimes be forgiving and will sometime punish pupils when they think that this will improve their attitude or behaviour.

Besides transferring values in separate subjects, enforcing school rules and encouraging critical thinking, there is another moral concern that most teachers usually recognise as important, but which is at risk of being neglected since it happens in very subtle ways. It is educating pupils' virtues. While the term 'virtue' is not part of our everyday vocabulary, our speech is interspersed with virtue terms, such as honesty, patience, generosity, care or justice, and many of our actions show whether we have 'character'. In particular, teachers consider respect, justice, reliability, love, joy and care to be important virtues (Van Oudenhoven et al., 2007, p. 16). Educating for virtue is a subtle and sometimes invisible affair since it is connected to teacher's 'manner', i.e. to how their character is revealed through all kinds of small decisions and emotional reactions (Fallona, 2000). For example, if the distribution of scarce resources over a number of people is a matter of justice, the way a teacher divides his attention over a group of pupils tells us something about how (un)just he is. If courage is the virtue that one needs in dangerous situations, the way a teacher reacts to an aggressive pupil denotes something about his (lack of) courage. Likewise, teachers will be more or less patient when a pupil does not immediately grasp an explanation, and they can react compassionately or coldly when a pupil receives a phone call that his grandmother has just passed away.

When we look at the place of moral education in schools from a virtue perspective, we see that it is not something optional that can easily be left out. School rules can be kept to a minimum, classroom discussions can be done without, and the more value-laden subjects can be removed from the curriculum. However, teachers cannot be forced to leave their character at home and act out some kind of professional role that is unrelated to who they are and what they value as a person. As long as teaching is a form of normative interaction between human beings, teachers do not only transfer subject-relevant knowledge and skills to pupils, but also influence their development through the moral strengths and weaknesses they exhibit. Moreover, as teachers' moral characters are likely to be affected by their teaching, educating for virtue offers opportunities for self-cultivation, too (Higgins, 2010). When we look at this aspect of the practice of moral education, the moral dimension of teaching is all about morality in a basic sense: it does not mean 'teaching morality', but 'being a moral teacher', which means extending everyday morality into the nuances of teaching.

1.2 The Aim of this Thesis

The problem with the cultivation of pupils' virtues is not so much that those working in middle and high schools are completely unaware of this less visible part of their moral educational task. Veugelers & De Kat (1999) and Klaassen (2002) have shown that teachers realise that moral education is not a supplementary task, but part and parcel of secondary education. When teachers are asked to express their ideas about what it means to be a teacher, they seem to attach great importance to moral developmental goals and see their pedagogical and moral task as an intrinsic part of teaching. Most teachers think that the moral aspects of teaching are an important part of their everyday task. To some, they even belong to the more meaningful and satisfying aspects of their profession. However, t' self-identity as moral educators has not led to a real *understanding* of their role corresponding responsibilities (Carr, 1991, p. 8). While teachers realise that have a moral educational task, this still superficial awareness has not culmin in a more profound grasp of why moral education is desirable or how it can best be achieved. This lack of proper understanding and the associated competences to improve educational practice would be less inconvenient if teachers did not care about moral education. However, as they indicate that they do want to contribute to children's moral development, teachers' lack of understanding is poignant.

Klaassen (2002) empirically investigated the views that teachers have on their pedagogical responsibilities. After having interviewed almost fifty Dutch primary and secondary school teachers, he concluded that many teachers refrain from mentioning the intrinsic educational merit of values and norms, do not want to teach moral virtues explicitly and generally avoid moral discussions in class. Teachers shy away from talking about norms and values explicitly, and try to serve as a model in a predominantly non-verbal manner. The difficulties on the level of educational practice are also reflected in the curricula of colleges for teacher training and a 'blank spot' in the literature on (and empirical research about) the moral aspects of teacher education (Lunenberg, Korthagen & Swennen, 2007). The existing theoretical discourse on moral education has not found its way into the curriculum. A comprehensive review of studies on teaching strategies for moral education made clear that there is a lack of conceptual clarity about the central issues in moral education (Schuitema, Ten Dam & Veugelers, 2008). Secondly, hardly any attention is paid to the specific skills and attitudes that pupils need if they are to be morally educated. Finally, it is unclear how values, which are generally considered to be an important objective of moral education, are taught.

When teachers feel that they are responsible for moral education but do not have an answer to questions concerning the nature, desirability and implementation of moral education, it can lead to feelings of incompetence, insecurity and stress – which can together be labelled as 'moral embarrassment'. The aim of this thesis is to take this embarrassment away by contributing to a better theoretical understanding of an education in the virtues, which will hopefully lead to the improvement of educational practice too. Teachers' understanding can become more 'theoretical' in the sense that they acquire a rational understanding of what they are doing (Carr, 2000, p. 63). The enquiries in this thesis aim at the moral justification and theoretical foundations of character education, and not at the production of a collection of concrete strategies for moral educators. However, philosophy can improve educational practice, if we treat theory as necessary for intelligent practice. As John Dewey famously put it: there is no question of theory *versus* practice, but rather of intelligent practice versus uninformed practice. The philosophical theory that I hope to develop is an abstraction from direct experience, but must ultimately return to it to make practice more intelligent.

We know now that there is a gap between the importance that teachers attach to moral and character education, and their understanding of them. However, what we do not know yet is what constitutes the gap. What are precisely the things that teachers need to know if they are really to understand what they already cherish? In this thesis, three central questions will be investigated in order to help teachers understand what the 'education of virtue' entails. Firstly, we need to know what a virtue is, and how it develops. Secondly, we need to find out what schools can contribute to this development of virtue. And thirdly, we are looking for an answer to the question why an education in the virtues is morally desirable.

1.3 Problems with the Education of Virtue

One reason why the moral aspects of teaching are under threat has to do with the way in which 'morality' is understood in Western societies. The current understanding has a long and complicated history, to which we will return in Chapter 5. This history has culminated in the widespread belief that the truth of moral values and judgments depends on subjective preferences or arbitrary cultural conventions. When this sinks in with teachers, they realise that they run the risk of bothering or even indoctrinating adolescents with their own [views] about right and wrong, preventing them from thinking for themselves and [develop]ing their burgeoning autonomy. While teachers in denominational schools [a]re committed to teaching something like traditional religious virtues, public schools generally treat the education of the virtues as a private affair (of the home) with which teachers should not interfere. With regard to the content of anything that goes beyond a bare moral minimum, an attitude of neutrality is adopted (Carr, 1999). Symptomatic for this neutrality is the invocation of the value of 'respect', which can be found in virtually all mission statements that schools have formulated. While 'respect' could refer to the awareness that each person has its own viewpoint on the world, it is often reduced to an attitude of indifference towards other people's moral ideas. The popularity of the value of 'respect' suggests that the contents of moral education, i.e. the virtues that can be communicated through teachers' words and deeds are still a controversial subject. Teachers agree upon the value of respect to conceal the inconvenient truth that there is not much else to agree on.

Besides the dominant ideas about moral education in the more encompassing ethos of our particular culture and age, there are also some more recent problems, at least in the Dutch context, that have contributed to the controversial nature of moral education. A first problem is the tension between 'schooling' and 'education' that teachers provide. The task to 'school' children involves equipping them with the knowledge and skills that enable them to become productive and financially successful members of society. As schooling is a social institution that is provided for public funds, taxpayers and their democratic representatives will want to know whether the educational budget had been well-spend. However, many parents will also want that teachers educate their children, i.e. that they help them to acquire an understanding of themselves, others and the world, and pursue interests and projects of intrinsic value, even when these activities are not 'useful' (Carr, 2003a, pp. 15-16). Especially in hard times, policy makers tend to stress the vocational and socio-economic aspect of teaching. Pupils should mainly learn how to read and write, be able to do mathematics, and acquire other skills that prepare them for the labour market. This technical-instrumental approach leaves little room for moral education or reduces it to a political instrument, which is in sharp contrast to the idea that all major approaches to moral education subscribe to, i.e. that being morally educated is also valuable in itself.

A second problem is that many of the traditional sources that had provided an answer to the question what children should be morally educated for have gradually lost their influence. For example, Catholic schools traditionally stress the importance of moral education and have always provided a distinct alternative to (and interpretation of) the kind of citizenship education promoted in public schools. Nowadays, many Catholic institutions have difficulties articulating what it means to contribute to a child's education from a Catholic perspective. They lack a critical mass of educators, parents and pupils who can embody the professed moral goals of the school (Rymarz, 2010). As a consequence, teachers and teacher educators have to think for themselves through some very complex questions about what, why and how pupils should be morally educated. This is difficult because they are simultaneously faced with a pressure not to pay attention to 'soft' topics that are difficult to measure and do not guarantee competitive examination results. The absence of a personal and rational conversation about what it means to be 'morally educated' is not typical of secondary schools, but can be found in colleges for teacher training, too.

Chapter 1

hird problem is related to the type of schooling that will be focused on in esis. The moral education in secondary schools (children who are roughly n 11 and 17 years old) is essential because teachers who have a restricted interpretation of professionalism tend to interpret their job as transferring subject-relevant knowledge and skills (Klaassen, 2010, p. 1). In secondary schools, teachers are experts in a particular subject, such as history, geography or biology, while such institutional constraints are less limiting in primary schools. Especially when there is much time pressure, middle and high school teachers will fall back on the idea that they are trained, licensed and hired to focus on the instruction of their academic specialities (Lockwood, 2009, p. 88). They are not used to reflect on the moral aspects of teaching in a professional way. Even when they say they value the moral aspects of their work, they are mainly oriented towards the instructional and cognitive aspects of their work. This orientation is fostered by the school's structure. While school days are organised for coursework in subject areas, the education of virtue is a dimension of all teaching. If no attention is paid to moral education in separate subjects, it runs the risk of not receiving the attention it deserves – even if teachers take it to be worthwhile.

1.4 Contemporary Character Education

One approach that could help us answer the three central questions of this thesis is called 'character education'. In the late 1980s and early 1990s, a number of educationists started to address issues about educating pupils for virtue and character. While character education had always been influential in the United States (see §2.2.1), it re-emerged at the end of the twentieth century. The aim of this contemporary character education was to find a solution to social problems in the United States, which had been caused by people's materialistic and individualistic attitudes (Ryan & Lickona, 1992, p. 4). The educationalists believed that these attitudes had led to a 'moral decline' of the youth, resulting in increased levels of vandalism, stealing, cheating, disrespect for authority, bigotry and bad language (Lickona, 1992). Equally, because institutions that had traditionally looked after the moral education of the youth, such as families and churches, gradually lost their importance, the character education movement invented programmes that were supposed to turn schools into moral communities which offered children the opportunity of a full human development (Ryan & Lickona, 1992, p. 3). School-directed programs designed to pay direct and systematic attention to the cultivation of children's virtues would bring about good behaviour among youth and diminish socially destructive behaviour (Lockwood, 2009, p. 12). Today, there are a large number of commercial character education programmes and websites, especially in the United States. For example, the *Character Counts*

---

1   Such as Ryan (1989), Lickona (1992), Ryan & Lickona (1992), Bennett (1992), Kilpatrick (1993) and Wynne & Ryan (1997).

programme, which promotes 'consensus ethical virtues' (trustworthiness, respect, responsibility, fairness, caring and citizenship), claims to be the most widely implemented moral education programme in the world, reaching ten percent of all school-age children (7 million a year) in the United States.[2]

Character educationalists were not only driven by social and political concerns, but also promised to provide an alternative to three other approaches to moral education that were influential in post-war educational theory: values clarification, cognitive development and care ethics. Chapter 2 explains that values clarification was enormously successful with teachers, and that Kohlberg's cognitive development theory dominated research about moral development and education for decades. Character education joined feminist proponents of the ethics of care (Gilligan, 1982; Noddings, 1984) in their critique of these two approaches, which both presupposed a liberal ethical framework. Unlike the other two theories, character educationalists did not focus on the *process* of valuing or moral reasoning. Cognitive development and values education had been very irresponsible by leaving it to individuals to decide what they wanted to value or reason about. Character educationalists believed that these two other approaches had failed to deliver what moral education is really all about, i.e. turning children into good people. They took it as their task to emphasise the *content* of moral education again and set out to formulate substantial criteria to determine the soundness of moral values and good character. It highlighted the need for the formation of children's characters, which would ideally accommodate a whole range of virtues, understood as reliable dispositions to do and feel good (Lickona, 1992, p. 51). By seeing cognitions and emotions as components of virtue, and by treating 'care' and 'justice' as two elements of a virtuous character, they tried to solve the philosophical and psychological issues that arose during the so-called Kohlberg-Gilligan debate in 1980s.

However, the interest of these American character educators remained largely practical. While some character educationalists have drawn theoretical inspiration from psychological research, the movement as a whole remained a "philosophically undiscerning and underdeveloped movement" (Carr & S 1999, p. 242; Kristjánsson, 2007, p. 2). It has been criticised for having ' simplistic" philosophical views of values because it did not discuss the meaning or the development of virtues (Lockwood, 2009, ch. 2). For example, the proponents of character education have produced lists of character traits that appear desirable, but which are also too uncontroversial to be meaningful. Who does not prefer justice to injustice or courage to cowardice? As handbooks are also filled with countless classroom exercises, we can expect character education to be helpful when dealing with our second question, i.e. of how schools can contribute to the development of virtue. With regard to the philosophical and psychological questions about how we should conceive of the development and justification

---

2   Retrieved from http://charactercounts.org/pdf/charactercounts_brochure.pdf at July 28, 2012.

of virtue, the American character education proponents do not have much to offer. However, all character education advocates mention a single philosophical source of inspiration: Aristotle, the father of virtue ethics – a discipline which has received renewed scholarly attention. Especially Lickona (2004, p. 11; 1992, p. 50; 1991, p. 67) is sympathetic to an Aristotelian way of thinking about morality and moral education. While Aristotle is referred to several times, his ideas are never elaborated. This raises the question of whether Aristotelianism can contribute to teachers' understanding of educating for virtue. What would 'character education' look like if it had the full weight of Aristotle's moral thinking behind it?

1.5 Neo-Aristotelian Virtue Ethics

Turning to Aristotle's moral theory for help involves two things. Firstly, we want to know what an Aristotelian approach can make clear about moral education. However, I am not an Aristotle scholar or an expert in Greek. My aim is not so much to provide a new interpretation of classical texts, but instead to treat Aristotle's philosophy as containing interesting suggestions for educational theory and practice. So this is not a thesis in the history of philosophy but in the *philosophy of education*. I will rely on my own unsophisticated reading of Aristotle, and when necessary on the interpretations provided by Aristotle scholars. For example, Ackrill and Kraut will be consulted to understand what Aristotle considered to be the best life for human beings (see §5.3), and Burnyeat and Curzer will be referred to when discussing the development of virtue (see §3.4). Secondly, there is no guarantee that Aristotelianism will meet all of our expectations when we apply it to contemporary moral education. While we specify an Aristotelian way of thinking on contemporary educational issues, we will also have to assess the strengths and weaknesses of Aristotle's pre-modern heritage. We have to acknowledge from the start that a virtue ethical approach will have some difficulties of its own.

When dealing with these two tasks, we do not have to start from the very beginning. A seminal essay by Elizabeth Anscombe led to a renaissance of virtue ethics in the 1970s and 1980s. During these decades, a significant number of influential philosophers became interested in the Aristotelian notions of virtue, character and flourishing. This revival was so successful that it is now commonplace to list virtue ethics together with utilitarianism and deontology as the three dominant approaches to ethics. While many found renewed inspiration in ancient Greek theories of virtue, there are nevertheless profound disagreements that make 'virtue ethics' a somewhat misleading category (Nussbaum, 1999; Steutel & Carr, 1999). While 'virtue' plays a role in deontology and utilitarianism, *all* ethical theories are somehow 'virtue ethical'. It would therefore be more precise to refer to a 'neo-Aristotelian approach to virtue ethics', instead of using the more general label 'virtue ethics'. But as this thesis will not expound any non-Aristotelian virtue accounts, 'virtue ethics' will be used throughout this thesis as shorthand for 'neo-Aristotelian virtue ethics'. The same strategy will be applied to the notion of 'character education'. In theory, educating pupils' characters could be justified by pointing at the positive consequences this will have to people's well-being, or by explaining that people with character are disposed to act according to the categorical imperative. However, as utilitarian or deontological interpretations of 'character education' are not discussed in this thesis, 'character education' is generally equated with the 'Aristotelian education of the virtues' or the 'Aristotelian education for virtue'. A few times, 'character education' is used to refer to the American-style approach just mentioned, but this will be clear from the context.

In Anscombe's wake, some academics significantly interested in the historical aspects of virtue ethic investigated Aristotle's ideas about moral education and development (e.g. Sherman, 1989; Verbeke, 1990; Curren, 2000), while educational philosophers tried to make a more or less Aristotelian way of thinking useful to moral educational issues. In this thesis, we will draw in particular on the work of such neo-Aristotelians authors, such as Alasdair MacIntyre, Martha Nussbaum, David Carr and Kristján Kristjánsson. Each of them has dedicated a number of books to the link between Aristotle and moral education. Importantly, they have emphasised different aspects of Aristotle's theory to illuminate something about the moral problems and concerns involved in educating children, and they have also appealed to the ideas of different philosophers, such as Thomas Aquinas, Hegel or J.S. Mill to re-interpret Aristotelianism. Therefore, it will not come as a surprise that there are also disagreements between those who consider themselves to be 'neo-Aristotelian virtue ethicists'. To do justice to this diversity, the question of what an 'education of the virtues' entails will be addressed in greater detail by comparing the answers of different virtue ethicists in the following chapters.

What a neo-Aristotelian approach to moral education has to offer cannot be explained in this Introduction. It will be apparent in chapters 3, 4 and 5 – where the development, education and justification of the education of virtue will be discussed in much more detail – whether it can provide the philosophical foundations that the popular but theoretically poor American-style character education is currently lacking. In the next chapter, a discussion of the three rival approaches to character education (cognitive development theory, values clarification and care ethics) will improve our understanding of a number of perceived weaknesses of character education's theory and practice. The alternative interpretations of moral education and their criticism of character education will enable us to refine and explicate an improved version of character education in the rest of this book.

For example, the other three approaches are concerned about whether people's moral behaviour really can be explained in terms of virtuous character traits. Do people's character traits not change too much over time to be reliable? Do people really have character in the sense that they are virtuous in a large number of different situations over a lifetime, or are their lives actually much more fragmented? As character education is commonly associated with mindless habituation, it is also unclear whether character education has the potential to contribute to children's independent rational judgment. Does it merely inculcate certain character traits that are considered to be morally significant by a particular community? A third issue is whether virtues can be educated in societies in which there is a plurality of conceptions of the good life. Does the education of virtue have to be pluralised too, as MacIntyre suggest, or is it possible to explain in what way virtues enable people to flourish as human beings, regardless of cultural context and historical time? If a neo-Aristotelian approach is to be successful, we can expect it to explain how character traits and virtuous action are related, in what sense moral habituation is a critical practice, and what its influence can be in a plural society.

There is one extra challenge that an Aristotelian approach must face. While this thesis will focus on the contribution that Aristotelianism can make to a better understanding of an education in the virtues, this requires more than conceptual analysis. Moral education has always been a multidimensional domain, in the sense that it includes questions about the goal, development and education of virtue. When reading the *Nicomachean Ethics*, it becomes clear that Aristotle does not only provide a philosophical argument in favour of a virtuous life. For example, he also writes about the origins and nature of emotions and character traits, suggests a virtue ethical developmental model and mentions several ways in which people can acquire excellences of character, e.g. through enforcing laws, habituation and explicit teaching. Aristotle was a 'philosopher' in a much more encompassing sense than we conceive of philosophy today. Until the 19th century, such 'philosopher-scientists' wrote about what we now consider to be the psychological and pedagogical aspects of moral education.

When psychology and pedagogy became social sciences in the 19th century, moral educational issues were discussed more and more in separate academic fields: moral philosophy studies the ultimate goals of moral development, psychology explains the mental conditions that have to be met before these goals can be achieved, and pedagogy presents the educational means to achieve them (Kristjánsson, 2007, p. 1). If a morally justified and psychologically realistic account that make clear how virtue may be taught in schools is our aim, we will have to step across some imaginary barbed wire between these disciplines. Particularly when discussing the situationism debate (§3.3) and the use of role-modelling (§4.2), we will evaluate whether the social sciences have recently increased our understanding of a virtue ethical approach to moral education.

1.6 Overview of the Book

Before a virtue ethical approach is specified, Chapter 2 starts with a discussion of three other approaches to moral education that have been influential in educational theory and practice: values clarification, cognitive development theory and care ethics. For each of these approaches, it is examined what their main proponents take to be the goal of moral education, what people go through when they morally develop, and what schools can do to stimulate moral development. The chapter enables us to see more clearly the distinctive features and limits of a character educational approach, and it culminates in a number of challenges that virtue ethics will have to meet if it is to be successful in the eyes of the other approaches.

Chapter 3 introduces Aristotle's moral psychology and discusses claims of a number of 'situationists', who argue that an Aristotelian understanding of the moral and intellectual virtues is empirically flawed. An evaluation of this criticism reveals certain meta-ethical assumptions about how psychologically realistic moral concepts should be. The plausibility of these assumptions is discussed by drawing on the work of Flanagan (1991), who defends a principle of minimal psychological realism. It is argued that the virtue ethical ideal of practical wisdom is not too far removed from what psychological research has revealed about the human cognitive make-up. In order to show that results from social psychological experiments do not have to be taken for granted, a neo-Aristotelian account of moral development is developed. This model shows that and how children, who are uncommitted to virtue or lack self-control, can make moral progress. In order to understand how people can morally develop, four levels of moral development are distinguished, each involving a specific relationship between moral emotion, reason and action.

Chapter 4 focuses on the educational means that schools can use to stimulate pupils' moral development. By discussing three 'methods', it is shown that an education in the virtues is continuous with everyday teaching. Character education is presented as a more deliberate and systematic approach to a dimension of teaching that normally remains implicit, even though teachers engage in it all of the time. When we understand character education as a sophisticated attempt to contribute to the development of pupils' virtues through teachers' manner, role modelling turns out to be all-important. It is investigated what it really means to 'model' certain virtues and what teachers should be a model of. A second method is the moral educational use of the (narrative) arts. It is argued that reading books can be an extra means to make children better people, because stories and life share a narrative structure. However, children can also practice (moral) imagination by doing compassionate things in real life. Finally, it is suggested that Socratic dialogues, and more in particular the method of 'regressive abstraction' advocated in the tradition of Jakob Fries and Leonard Nelson, are a suitable way for teachers to practice the cardinal virtue of practical wisdom.

After the development and education of virtue have been discussed, the question why the education of virtue is morally justified is addressed in Chapter 5. This why-question is saved for last, because it is in line with the idea, discussed in this thesis, that knowledge of the 'why' can be acquired best after one has mastered the 'how' and 'what'. Despite a pervasive subjective understanding of morality in Western plural societies, it is argued that it can still make sense to understand virtues as objective moral qualities that are essential to people's well-being or happiness. After Aristotle's natural teleology is discussed, it becomes clear that the idea that human nature has an intrinsic purpose (*telos*) has to be abandoned. However, a discussion of the work of MacIntyre and Kristjánsson makes clear that Aristotle's pre-modern heritage can be interpreted in such a way that the education of virtue can still be objectively justified. While these two neo-Aristotelians advocate a different kind of Aristotelianism, their oeuvres show that virtue ethics places some limits on what can be regarded as a system of *human* morality, while it accepts that there is no direct route from nature to morality.

In Chapter 6, some of the conclusions of the preceding chapters are assembled and elaborated on. The challenges formulated in Chapter 2 are revisited to determine what a neo-Aristotelian approach makes clear about *moral education*, and what the themes explored in this thesis disclose about the viability of an *Aristotelian* approach. The book ends with some recommendations for a virtue ethical approach to pedagogical, psychological and philosophical research.

2.2 Values Clarification

In this section, the values clarification approach to moral education will be discussed. However, a discussion of this approach is complicated by a number of factors. Values clarification quickly became the "reigning fashion in moral education" in the 1970s but was never argued for well philosophically and psychologically (Hunter, 2000, p. 74). As a consequence, there are dozens of handbooks filled with practical classroom strategies, but hardly any critical investigations of the theoretical presuppositions and implications of this approach. Moreover, values clarification was a relatively short-lived phenomenon, which only existed for about a decade. Although there were some 'leaders' in the movement, several rival accounts flourished at the same time. The 'discussion' of values clarification is therefore also an attempt to relate different authors who contributed to this approach to each other and to make sense of its educational, psychological and philosophical tenets. A final complication is that it is not beyond doubt that values clarification really *is* an approach to moral education, because some of its proponents fiercely rejected anything that is associated with the inculcation of traditional values. More on this issue in due course.

The first section offers a closer look at the time in which values clarification emerged and (temporarily) flourished. In section 2.2.2, the emphasis will be on the goal of values clarification, and the ways in which this goal is justified. Questions that will be dealt with are, e.g.: Why should one's values be clarified? When are values 'clarified'? Are some values better than others? What does this have to do with morality? Section 2.2.3 discusses the psychology and development of values. What is a 'value'? What does somebody experience when his values are clarified? Finally, section 2.2.4 highlights the strategies that teachers can employ to clarify pupils' values in the classroom.

2.2.1 The Emergence of Values Clarification

In order to understand the point and purpose of values clarification, a closer look at the circumstances in which it emerged is called for. During the late 1960s and 1970s, the United States were in the embrace of the Vietnam War, there was a threat of nuclear war, and economic prospects were poor. There had been some major scientific and technological breakthroughs, such as the manned space missions to the Moon. American family life was changing rapidly too. The sixties are generally regarded as a period in which many young people demanded greater individual freedom, and wanted to break free from the social constraints of previous generations, sometimes through extreme deviation from the norm. In general, people had more freedom to live the kind of life that they wanted. At the same time, however, many people did not know how to deal with the uncertainty that accompanied the freedom of choice. Religions had lost much of their influence, 'culture' had turned out to be a relativistic notion, and science was value-free. People were deeply uncertain of their orientation in life, and seemed unsure and troubled as to the goals they held in esteem (Rogers, 1972, p. 75).

It was believed that especially young people would have difficulties adapting to the new kind of society that emerged: "...students in today's classrooms are confronted with more choices than any previous generation, and the bewildering array of alternatives open to these students is staggering." (Creamer & Creamer, 1978, p. 110). Others drew the more menacing conclusion that "[a]ll of us, young and old, often become confused about what we value in this rapidly changing world." (Pozdol & Pasch, 1976, p. 202). It is exactly this sense of being confused by the availability of alternative perspectives in a complex and changing society that explained the emergence of values clarification. Proponents of values clarification believed that 'values' formed the foundation of people's choices, and that (re)discovering these values would enable them to know what to do and who to be. With clear values, children would be able to pull themselves together and live a purposeful and satisfying life. Schools, as well as, parents, could help children to develop a set of values on which they could base their lives.

Values clarification was successful in the 1960s and 1970s because it adopted a child-centred perspective in a time that most education was authoritarian (Griffin, 1976, p. 194). It offered an alternative to traditional approaches to moral education that had treated children as primitive, ignorant, and immature people who needed instruction and guidance (Hall, 1978, p. 43). These traditional approaches had been occupied with inculcating values and virtues in the hearts and minds of children by means of 'setting an example', 'persuasion', 'setting rules', 'giving rewards and punishments' or 'appealing to conscience' (Pozdol & Pasch, 1976, p. 202). In the decades after World War II, values clarification proponents believed that it was neither possible nor desirable to ask of pupils uncritically to adopt the value system of their ancestors or community. In this 'new world', they let go of the hope that a single and unchanging traditional value system could be vindicated and passed on to a new generation. Moral education should be nothing more and nothing less than helping children to discover what they already valued. By paying attention to pupils' beliefs, their preferences and their choices, based on their value system, values clarification stressed their freedom, choice and autonomy.

The anti-authoritarian spirit can be understood even better if we see values clarification as an approach that specifically dismissed the kind of character education that had always been very influential in the United States (Cunningham, 2005). In the 18th century, the doctrine of original sin was very influential, which led character educators to believe that children by nature were immoral, and that training a child's character involved overcoming wild, savage impulses through discipline. This would help them to move toward the 'good', interpreted as a Christian way of life. During the 19th century, the religious consensus governing character education fell apart for several reasons, including waves of immigrants, the ideas of Darwin and Marx, the brutality of the American Civil War (1861–1865) and industrialisation. At the end of the 19th century, 'character education' was very popular again, but for different reasons. Educators believed that 'character' was a rather neutral notion that could somehow "...mend the ideological and perspectival frictions of America's new pluralism" (Cunningham, 2005, p. 170). At the turn of the twentieth century, issues of moral education became more political as a diversity of groups fought for control over schooling. As disagreements emerged, the empirical sciences were seen as a means to settle the disputes. One question that exercised many minds was whether 'character' consisted of general traits or of habitual responses to situational stimuli. A massive empirical research project, the *Character Education Inquiry* (CEI), was carried out between 1925 and 1926 to settle these questions for good (see Fairchild, 2006, chapter 3). The main researchers, Hugh Hartshorne and Mark May (1930, p. 755), observed that children were quite inconsistent in reacting to psychological tests and they concluded that "...there is no such thing as a unified trait of honesty residing within an individual". Psychologists started to abandon the notion of 'character' and educators familiar with the CEI draw pessimistic conclusions about the possibility to educate children's character.

After a war-time drop in discourse about moral and character education, the 1960s and 1970s were a time of 'retrenchment', in which schools were fighting for the right to educate children's intellects and did, at that moment, not mind their characters (Cunningham, 2005, p. 192). At the time that there was hardly any discussion about the importance of moral and character education, and agreement on these matters was even more difficult to find, values clarification became an important educational factor. While Kohlberg's PhD thesis appeared in 1958 and his theory of moral development was about to become the 'theoretical centrepiece' for moral education, his efforts had yet hardly any practical effect in schools (Hunter, 2000, p. 74). In educational practice, values clarification was far ahead. It quickly became a very popular approach with teachers, partly because it consisted of a series of loosely related techniques that were easy to learn and easily accessible to teachers (Lipe, 1981, p. 5). Forty books on values clarification were published during the 1970s, and one of them, *Values Clarification: A Handbook of Practical Strategies for Teachers and Students*, sold more than 600,000 copies. At its peak, the values clarification boasted a network of over a hundred trainers who conducted workshops in the didactics of values clarification for more than two hundred thousand teachers, counsellors, and helping professionals, such as nurses (Lipe, 1981, p. 5).

2.2.2 The Goal of Values Clarification

Many educators and philosophers have been extremely critical of values clarification. They rejected the whole approach immediately because values clarification had a subjective understanding of values. On a superficial reading, values clarification only permits teachers to ask pupils questions in order to help them discover what their actual current values are. For example, a teacher can give pupils three or four alternative choices for responding to a question like 'How do you learn best?' and then ask them to simply rank these choices according to their own preferences (Simon, Howe & Kirschenbaum, 1972, p. 58). It is presupposed that, somewhere deep down, children have values, but that they are not aware of them yet, and that teachers' clarifying responses to what children say and do can help them get these values straight. This process would only succeed if teachers are accepting, non-judgmental and neutral with regard to the rightness or wrongness of pupils' opinions. With a more sympathetic reading, however, there is much more to values clarification. Teachers can be more critical towards children's values than some critics think, because there are certain formal criteria that a 'value' has to meet before a child can be said to have a value at all. When values clarification proponents refer to 'values', they have an idea of what counts as a *real* value and what does not. Louis Raths (1900-1978), the founding father of values clarification, developed a value theory that enabled teachers to question a child's understanding of *what a value is* and also teach him *how to value*.

Raths, a teacher and educational theorist from New York, argued that people had to follow a seven-step valuing process in order to do make their values 'clear'. Someone would only really value something (let's say x) if seven criteria were met (Raths, Harmin and Simon, 1966). Firstly, x should be chosen freely, i.e. not be determined by external influences such as authorities. Secondly, x should be chosen from alternatives; otherwise, there would not really be a 'choice' at all. Thirdly, x should be chosen after thoughtful consideration of the consequences of each alternative. 'Thoughtful' means that a value has a cognitive aspect to it, and is not the product of impulses alone. Fourthly, valuing x is something positive, and people are happy with their values. People prize and cherish their values. Fifthly, x is only a value if one is proud of it, wants to be associated with it and affirms it when asked about it. Sixthly, a value will give direction to one's life and influence one's actions. Only preaching a value, i.e. without acting on it, is not really valuing it at all. Seventh, when somebody really values x, he will not act on it occasionally, but it will appear in several different situations, at several times. Values have persistency and make a pattern in life. So it was posited that paying attention to value-related issues in the classroom, having pupils think about what they choose, what they prise and how they act, would eventually change their attitudes and behaviour too. People with values would "demonstrate more purposeful, proud, positive and enthusiastic behaviour patterns" (Raths, Harmin and Simon, 1966, p. 5).

Raths, Harmin and Simon (1966) justified the role that values had to play in moral education by appealing to psychological research that would show that behaviour is normally informed by values. They considered values to be part of a theory of action, according to which people's values were causally involved in producing actions. But are the seven criteria really 'scientific' and 'value-free'? If we examine the criteria more closely, the impression is that values clarification tried to eat a normative cake empirically. Contrary to what its advocates claim, values clarification presupposes a set of normative considerations, even though these are rather minimal. In this interpretation, a value is a *good* value when it has been freely chosen after deliberation from a range of alternatives, with which people identify and upon which people act. The adoption of clarification as the 'correct' approach to moral education carries within it, at least implicitly, an espousal of a clear, consistent, stable, active and reflective life. Values clarification trusts people's own rational abilities and emphasises their freedom to choose the direction of their own lives (Hall, 1973, p. 45). Much confusion could have been avoided if values clarification had acknowledged from the start that the seven criteria do not determine what a *value* is, psychologically, but what a *good value* is, in moral terms. Howard Kirschenbaum (1976, p. 122) was one of the few values clarification proponents who admitted in the mid-seventies that

> "If we urge critical thinking, then we value rationality. If we support moral reasoning, then we value justice. If we advocate divergent thinking, then we value creativity. If we uphold free choice, then we value autonomy or freedom. If we encourage 'no-lose' conflict resolution, then we value equality."

In 1992, he argued that values clarification had implicitly promoted "freedom, justice, rationality, equality, and other democratic and civic values" in its goals and methods. While values clarification did not explicitly teach moral values, such values were nevertheless part of the hidden curriculum (Kirschenbaum, 2000). Initially, Kirschenbaum was one of the leaders in the values clarification movement, but as he came to understand the strengths and limitations of the values clarification approach, he became active in the character education movement of the 1990s.

His turn to character education makes sense if we look at the options that values clarificationists have when the normative nature of values is acknowledged. One can either deny that assumptions are made about the 'correctness' of values such as autonomy or freedom, and that its educational theory and practice do not need a justification. In this case, no reason can be given for why pupils should be subjected to the process of clarification, and it becomes unclear why we should prefer values clarification to an approach that *can* provide such reasons (Schindler, 1992, p. 252). Alternatively, one can acknowledge the implied judgment of preference for certain values, and in that case, values clarification will have to show why some values such as autonomy or freedom are exempted from the neutrality and relativity that was assumed with regard to values generally. In addition, the very practice of value neutrality or value relativity carries within it a non-neutrality or non-relativity in another sense. For example, if no judgment is passed on whether it is good to steal or not in a particular case, one can ask on a second level whether it is good to be tolerant of different views regarding the goodness or badness of stealing. (Schindler, 1992, p. 252). It follows that the question of the warrants or foundations of morality will also arise for the proponents of values clarification. When dealing with these questions, Kirschenbaum realised that character education could provide him with better answers. Ironically, he turned to an approach to moral education that had fiercely been rejected at its start.

Initially, many value clarification theorists denied that they were involved in any kind of *moral* education, because they did not want to profess certain values and force children to adopt them. 'Morality' was associated with absolute, objective or universal moral virtues and values, and 'education' as transferring these values to, instilling or inculcating them in, or imposing them on children. For example, Smith (1977, p. 5) wrote: "In the past, philosophy and theology sought to understand and define values: objective, ontological, metaphysical, and moral values. Most of us still feel the effects of the Puritan and Victorian eras, when values were defined primarily in terms of moralistic 'shoulds' and 'should nots'." When values clarification had clarified its own theory, its proponents became increasingly aware of the moral values they presupposed. They realised that they did not reject moral education as such, but were mainly opposed to a *traditional* kind of moral education. Values clarification was after an alternative approach to moral education, one that didn't rely on the transfer of values or religious virtues, but which stressed the importance of children learning to think for themselves.

2.2.3 Value Psychology and Development

If the goal of moral education is to have values that meet the above-mentioned seven criteria, then what do children go through while their values are clarified by educators? What does the psychology and development of values look like? It is difficult to answer to these questions because value clarification proponents developed a large number of classroom strategies, but never gave the development of value much thought.

It will not come as a surprise that the psychological concept values clarification proceeds from is 'value'. What is it, psychologically speaking? The seven criteria mentioned before have generally been grouped in three categories: prizing, choosing and acting (Raths, Harmin & Simon, 1966; Simon, Howe & Kirschenbaum, 1972). However, Kirschenbaum (1973, pp. 105-106) drafted an even more encompassing account. He replaced 'prizing' by 'feeling', maintained 'choosing' and 'acting', and added 'thinking' and 'communicating' to the list. Unfortunately, none of the authors explained how the elements of this taxonomy are related, what their relative importance is, or why these seven criteria single out a 'value' (and not something else). The criteria make clear, however, that a 'value' is a very demanding notion. They are settled dispositions which involve of emotions and deliberation and which help to make choices, choices that constitute an integrated life (Raths, Harmin & Simon, 1978, pp. 5, 192, 295). If we realise this, it becomes clear that the meaning of a 'value' is very close to what is described as a 'virtue' in the next chapter. If this is what values clarification is after, simply *clarifying* values will not suffice. For example, children will also have to be taught what it is to choose freely, to evaluate alternatives, to think through the consequences of their choices, to prise values, to have the courage to speak up for them in public, and to help these values become dispositional. Can 'clarification' do all this? If Raths, Harmin and Simon stick to their definition of values, either 'clarification' is a (small) part of a larger educational programme that helps people acquire these values, or 'clarification' will have to be defined so broadly that it is closer to 'values *education*'.

Being demanding does not have to be an unattractive feature of an approach to moral education. However, values clarification runs into trouble because it completely lacks an account of what someone goes through when his/her values are clarified. Is it simply unclear whether it is possible for people to clarify their values. It is very peculiar that its proponents do not refer to theoretical or empirical work in psychology, since 'values' were a central topic in the social sciences at that time, especially because of the work of Milton Rokeach in the 1960s. Rokeach' challenge was to come up with a conceptual definition and empirical measures of values that could be used in research. Moreover, he wrote about the origins, functions, and phenomenology of values (Mayton et al., 1994, pp. 1-3). Rokeach and his colleagues conducted numerous studies employing experimental, survey and content analytic methods. The *Rokeach Value Survey* (RVS) became, and remains, a major measurement tool in social scientific research. One reason why Rokeach' work was largely neglected by the values clarification approach may have something to do with disagreements over the nature of values. They agreed that values are the main variables that determine people's attitudes and behaviour. However, Rokeach (1968, 1973a) took – contrary to values clarification – both form and content of values to be universal. He argued that there is a relatively small number of universal 'terminal human values', which are hierarchically arranged and function as internal reference points that help people to formulate attitudes and opinions, and that can be used to predict a wide range of behaviour.

Although Rokeach (1973b, 1977) contributed to some volumes on values clarification, he was extremely critical of it. For example, he writes that "I believe that the school should abandon the position of value neutrality advocated by values clarification proponents because such a position can be defended neither theoretically nor philosophically, nor substantiated empirically" (Rokeach, 1979, p.

268). He argued that society depends upon the educational institution to inculcate educational values successfully, that it is impossible for schools to remain value free and that the focus of values clarification on the pupils' own values is too egocentric. It seems that the psychologist who could have provided values clarification with its theoretical and empirical underpinnings turned his back on it.

When evaluating values clarification by the standards of psychological research in the 1970s, its account of the development of value is extremely poor too. At the same time, Kohlberg constructed a theoretically sophisticated and empirically substantiated theory of moral development. The fact that values clarification lacks such a theory makes it difficult to answer questions such as: What does a child goes through when its values are clarified? How can we distinguish between people who have clarified their values to different degrees? Which strategies fit which level of development? Raths, Harmin and Simon (1978, p. 46) maintained that a developmental model is not necessary if an approach to moral education is to be useful to teachers. Moral education could be effective without knowing the underlying psychological mechanisms (Cogan & Paulson, 1978, p. 24). The only clue about how values develop comes from Steele (1983, p. 5), who mentions in passing Rokeach' theory of cognitive dissonance in order to explain how people gradually move from confused to consistent and integrated values.

Can cognitive dissonance theory explain how values develop? Note how Steele wrongly assumed that the theory of cognitive dissonance was Rokeach' invention. It has to be ascribed to Leon Festinger (1957), who formulated the original theory in the mid-1950s. He argued that a state of discomfort, called 'dissonance', is created when an individual holds two or more beliefs that are inconsistent with one another. Moreover, he argued that the unpleasant state of dissonance will motivate people to reduce the inconsistency. For example, while most people want to live a long and healthy life, many people smoke, even though they know cigarettes can cause lung cancer. Health and longevity are here dissonant with the pleasure of smoking: the smoker desires a cigarette, but because his health is at stake, he finds the desired object unattainable and experiences discomfort. There are several ways to deal with the dissonance: one can reduce the importance of the conflicting belief, change the conflicting belief so that it is consistent with its other beliefs or behaviours or focus on more supportive beliefs that outweigh the dissonant belief or behaviour. When we apply this mechanism to education, teachers could contribute to the process of making children's beliefs more consistent by providing them with experiences that reveal inconsistencies, and stimulate them to integrate their values better.

2.2.4 Values Clarification in Schools

After the goal of values clarification is touched upon, most handbooks quickly move on to questions of how values clarification can be implemented in schools through a variety of classroom exercises. Whatever specific strategy teachers choose, Raths, Harmin & Simon (1978) recommend them to follow a sequence of three steps. Firstly, children are asked to pay attention to an everyday issue with which they have some personal experience, such as what to do with leisure time or how to maintain relationships with friends. Secondly, a teacher invites pupils to express their opinions about leisure, friendship or other values by stressing that all contributions are accepted. Handbooks explicitly ask teachers to be as open-minded to different opinions as possible. Thirdly, teachers are to encourage pupils to reflect further on the choices, prizings and actions that they have just disclosed. Raths, Harmin and Simon (1978) discuss three kinds of strategies that follow this sequence: the dialogue strategy, a writing strategy and a discussion strategy. These strategies can be realised in hundreds of different ways.

Of the three, the most important strategy is the dialogue strategy, at the heart of which is the so-called 'clarifying response'. This is "...a response a teacher makes to something a student has said or done when the purpose is to encourage that student to do some extra thinking." (Raths, Harmin & Simon, 1978, p. 54). For example, when a child tells the teacher that he is about to go on holiday, the teacher should not assume that holidays are something pleasurable by saying something like 'That's nice'. Instead, he can ask the child whether he is glad to go. This will start the child thinking, and he may find out that he is not glad to go on holiday at all, because he would rather, e.g. spend the time with friends at home. The teacher's response can be said to be 'clarifying', because it makes the child realise what he really wants. In another example, the teacher asks a child, who is said to be liberal in political matters, where his ideas come from. After he says that these ideas come from his parents, the teacher asks whether he is familiar with other positions than his parents'. When he child answers 'sort of', the teacher's reaction is simply 'I see', then returning to the general lesson. The basic idea of the dialogue strategy is "...to raise a few questions, without moralizing, leave them hanging in the air, and then move on." (Raths, Harmin & Simon, 1978, pp. 57-58). Good clarifying questions include 'Are you happy about that?', 'Did you consider any alternatives?', 'Was it a free choice?', 'What do you mean by....?' and 'Is that very important to you?'. Teachers are recommended to avoid why-questions, because they tend to make children defensive. Open-ended questions are preferable, because they prevent teachers from giving in to the temptation of asking leading questions that will guide children's thinking in a certain direction.

Two additional strategies are the 'writing strategy' and the 'discussion strategy'. When teachers use the writing strategy, they ask children to fill out a 'value sheet', which consists of a description of a social or scientific context and a series of eliciting questions (Casteel & Stahl, 1974). The context can be related to the subject-matter of the lessons. For instance, a history teacher can make her own value sheet about slavery during a lesson in which the American

Civil War is being discussed (Raths, Harmin & Simon, 1978, p. 93). After having stimulated pupils' thinking about slavery, she continues class. The teacher can also decide to read the answers, make some comments and return the sheets to the pupils. Alternatively, she can choose to pick out a couple of answers and read them aloud in class. She may also choose to discuss the answers with pupils in large or small groups, but this is not regarded as particularly effective, since "...a person needs quiet hard thought, and careful decisions to produce clear, persistent, and viable values." (Raths, Harmin & Simon, 1978, p. 116). Moreover, in group discussions, pupils tend to remain passive and their thinking may be threatened by a group's tendency to prefer consensus. The discussion strategy differs from the writing strategy in that there is no value sheet involved. If a large group discussion is to become a rich, reflective discussion on a values issue, teachers are advised to keep a number of things in mind: they have to select a topic, pupils have to be encouraged to think before they talk, the participants have to share a conversation structure and pupils need some help to extract results from the discussion. This last step consists of asking pupils to sit alone after the discussion, consider what they have learned from the discussion, and write this down in sentences like 'I learned that...' or 'I rediscovered that...' (Raths, Harmin & Simon, 1978, p. 136).

Interestingly, the discussion strategy resembles the classroom strategies that are recommended by the movement called *Philosophy for Children* (P4C), which emerged around the same time. While the classroom discussions that Matthew Lipman (1980, 2003) recommends have much in common with the above-mentioned discussion strategy, Lipman considered classroom discussion to be the *best* way to give children a (philosophical) education. In values clarification, discussions play a more marginal role: comparing your own ideas to those of others can help to clarify personal preferences, emotions and habits, but it is not so much a *critical* process because the question why children have these preferences, or whether their habits are morally justified is not asked. For advocates of P4C, however, teachers' aim is to foster a 'community of inquiry' in which pupils will not only express their preferences, but also support their beliefs with *reasons* and respond to the similarities and differences between their ideas and those of their classmates. The substantiation of preferences or values with reasons is completely absent from the values clarification literature. This is very unfortunate, as Lipman et al. (2003, p. 37) considered Raths to be a prime example of an educator who wanted to educate children along Deweyan lines for critical thinking and help them to distinguish between better and worse values. For example, Raths (1955, p. 147) argued that values clarification would lead to "clearer purpose, more consistent thinking, and an independence of thought and action". Lipman complains that when Raths' followers took over, they transformed his theory of critical thinking into 'values clarification', and no value was considered better or worse than any other.

2.3 Cognitive Development Theory

While values clarification was in fashion in the 1960s and 1970s, the cognitive developmental approach was initially something of an 'odd duck' within American psychology but would have a much longer lasting influence (Brown & Herrnstein, 1975, p. 307). The landmark publication of this approach was Kohlberg's PhD thesis, called *The Development of Modes of Moral Thinking and Choice in the Years 10 to 16* (1958), in which he published the results of his empirical research into children's moral development. In line with these results, Kohlberg constructed a normative theory about the goal of moral development. As his ideas became more popular in both educational theory and practice, they gradually attracted criticism too, most importantly from his Harvard colleague Carol Gilligan (see §2.4). By trying to rebut or incorporate this critique, Kohlberg's ideas developed further and culminated with the publication of two volumes in the 1980s, in which most of his ideas were assembled (Kohlberg, 1981, 1984; also see: Power, Higgins & Kohlberg, 1989). From the 1990s onwards, there have been a number of post-Kohlbergian initiatives, which faced the limitations of Kohlberg's model and attempted to build on it towards a more comprehensive or integrated model of moral development (Arnold, 2000, p. 369). In this chapter, six issues will be addressed. After the background is sketched against which Kohlberg's approach emerged, a discussion of Kohlberg's main source of inspiration, Jean-Piaget, will follow (§2.3.2). Next, an examination of Kohlberg's own research on the development of moral judgment is presented (§2.3.3), after which the relation between moral judgment and action becomes the focus (§2.3.4). Section 2.3.5 looks at the goal of moral development and Kohlberg's justification of it. Finally, our attention turns to how to stimulate pupils' moral development through education.

2.3.1 The Emergence of Cognitive Development Theory

Kohlberg's original study on the moral development of children appeared in the late 1950s, when people's memories of World War II were still fresh. Kohlberg (1981, p. 407) described the Holocaust as "...the event in human history that most bespeaks the need for moral education and for a philosophy that can guide it". Moreover, he stated that "[m]y own interest in morality and moral education arose in part as a response to the Holocaust, an event so enormous that it often fails to provoke a sense of injustice in many individuals and societies." But why did the Holocaust 'bespeaks the need for moral education'? A Jew himself, Kohlberg believed that the Holocaust could only have happened because millions of young people had come to believe horrible things about Jews. In his view, the German educational system was partly responsible for this, because it had initiated children into the conventional morality of the 1930s, without teaching them how to reflect critically on these conventions. Kohlberg saw it as his mission to formulate absolute moral criteria that could be used to criticise the ideas that morality is relative to culture, and that moral education consists in inculcating the young with arbitrary cultural conventions. He conceived of conventional morality as a *stage* in a developmental process in which a 'principled' understanding of morality is highest. The construction of a new theory of moral education was an even more urgent task, since Kohlberg (1981, p. 7) believed that the existing approaches were not able to offer an adequate solution to the kind of moral relativism that had made the Holocaust possible.

In particular, Kohlberg rejected four theories: 'socialisation', 'spiritual growth', the 'bag of virtues' and 'values clarification'. So what is wrong with these theories? First of all, socialisation ensures that children internalise the norms and standards of society. But since there is no external way to judge whether these standards are *really* just, socialisation has difficulties explaining how indoctrination can be avoided. Kohlberg (1981, p. 8) refers to the educational system of the Soviet Union, where teachers act merely as agents of the state, while the critical question whether this state is just is not asked. A second approach that Kohlberg disapproved of tries to build a foundation of sound moral and spiritual values, such as the programme advocated by Carr and Wellenberg in *Teaching Children Values* (1966). Kohlberg criticises their approach, because it refers to all kinds of 'positive values' without justifying why children should have them. Admittedly, the proponents of this approach refer to the Golden Rule and the Ten Commandments, but without explaining in turn why *these* sources are sound. Kohlberg (1981, p. 9) provokingly states that without further argument, it is unclear why the Ten Commandments would be better than the code of Hitler or the communist youth. The third theory Kohlberg rejects is the 'bag of virtues' approach. He traces it to Aristotle, but criticises particularly the kind of character education that was popular in the 1920s and 1930 (see §2.2.1). There are several problems with this approach: firstly, everybody has his own bag of virtues, which means that everybody can compose his own list of virtues and vices; secondly, character education pretends that there is consensus about the meaning of virtues, while Kohlberg claims that people are likely to interpret virtues differently; and thirdly, Kohlberg (1969, p. 369) points out that character traits are not stable enough over time in order to be of interest to developmental psychologists. Whether Kohlberg is right about this will be considered in Chapters 3 and 5.

Kohlberg (1981, p. 10) regards these three approaches as 'cops-outs' from the relativity problem, since they leave teachers stuck with their own personal value standards and biases to be imposed on pupils. The last approach, values clarification, is rejected as well, but not because it is a cop-out to the relativity problem, but because it *embraces* relativity. According to Kohlberg, proponents of values clarification believe that right or wrong do not exist in matters of values, so it is not up to teachers to impose particular values on pupils, and their only legitimate task is to assist pupils in clarifying the values that they already endorse. He regards this view as obviously mistaken. He argues that pupils who justify cheating by saying that it is part of their consistent value hierarchy should not be praised for being 'authentic' but be punished because they are utterly wrong. We should expect teachers to teach children that cheating and other forms of behaviour are unacceptable, because it becomes impossible to teach without these rules. Kohlberg's critique of these four approaches makes clear that he was looking for an approach to moral education that did not treat morality as a matter of personal preferences or conventional norms, but as a matter of absolute and universal standards. He believed that the validity of some moral principles was not limited to a given society if they are understood as the product of mature *rational* judgment. Kohlberg's cognitive stage theory can be understood as a description of the development of rational judgement from a juvenile to a mature state (Reimer et al., 1983, p. 44). Kohlberg, a psychologist himself, relied for his philosophical ideas on the works of a number of scholars, in particular those of Kant and three philosophers that were influenced in different ways by Kant's ideas on ethics and epistemology: John Rawls' theory of justice, Richard Hare's prescriptivism and Jean Piaget's structuralism (Carr, 1996, 1999).

2.3.2 Piaget's Stages of Cognitive Development

Kohlberg's ideas about the goal of moral development calls for an examination of the ideas of the famous Swiss child psychologist Jean Piaget (1896-1980). Pioneer Piaget rebelled against the dominance of behaviourism by investigating the nature and growth of human *understanding*. His research of children's intelligence was informed by epistemological views that are known as 'genetic epistemology'. This epistemology is indebted to Kant, who had argued against the British empiricists of the eighteenth century that some *a priori* categories (like time, space, causality and substance) have to exist, if our experience is to be intelligible at all. For example, to be able to think of the sun, we need to have the mental category of substance, without which all sensory input cannot be synthesised into an intelligible object. Piaget saw it as his task to discover how these categories develop over time. He effectively replaced Kant's notion of *a priori* categories with the idea that our mental categories are constructed through a long process, as we adapt to physical and social environments.

Piaget devised a number of tests and concluded from his experiments that children develop similar logical principles that enable them to make sense of the world they live in. For example, when children are asked whether the earth or the sun is larger, seven-year-olds answer this question differently to four-year-olds. The latter will conclude that the sun is smaller, because it looks smaller, whereas the former already 'know' that the sun is bigger, and that it just looks smaller, because it is further away. Piaget insisted that the difference is not simply a matter of a seven-year-old *knowing* more about the world than a four-year-old. The phenomenon had to be explained by a transformation of the child's *logic*. The difference in the two responses reflected their different developmental capacities to understand relations among and between things – in this case to use the logical principle of perspective. A seven-year-old has a qualitatively different way of understanding and interpreting and thus, responding to the question asked (Popp & Portnow, 2001, pp. 17-18). Younger children use a very consistent logic to arrive at an answer (the smaller an object looks, the smaller it is), which will, however, turn out to be inadequate later in life. Older children use another kind of logic: they have mastered the principle of perspective, with which they can differentiate between a body's perceived and actual size. Ultimately, Piaget proposed a global theory of cognitive developmental stages in which children exhibit certain common patterns of cognition in each period of development. According to this theory, cognitive structures are simply natural reflexes at a very young age, which are gradually organised in schemes and become internalised as patterns of thought until they develop into complex intellectual structures. Piaget assumed that the human mind has a tendency to systemise its processes into coherent systems (Reimer et al., 1983, pp. 24-25).

His empirical research showed that cognitive development can be divided into four periods, called sensorimotor (years 0-2), preoperational (years 2-7), concrete operational (years 7-11) and formal operational (years 11-adulthood) (Shaffer & Kipp, 2010, p. 249). During the sensorimotor period, children have innate reflexes and a drive to explore the world. As they grow up, these reflexes become increasingly differentiated, until habits, coordination and insight develop. During the preoperational years, children learn to use and represent objects by images and words. Their thinking is still egocentric, as they have difficulties assuming the perspective of others. The mental operations become more and more adequate until the child is able to use logic appropriately. For instance, the child will develop the ability to view things from another person's perspective. This can be shown by the Sally-Anne test, used in developmental psychology to measure a person's social cognitive ability to attribute false beliefs to others. In the experiment, a child watches a comic in which Sally puts a doll under a box and leaves the room. Then, Anne enters and moves the doll to a drawer. When Sally returns, the child is asked where *it thinks* that *Sally thinks* the doll is. A child in the concrete operations stage can distinguish between his own knowledge and Sally's, and will rightly conclude that Sally thinks it is under the box, even though the child knows it is in the drawer. The last stage starts at around 11 years of age. Characteristic of this stage is the ability to think abstractly, reason logically, draw conclusions from the information available or even understand logical proofs.

Although Piaget was primarily interested in epistemology, he also attempted to develop a similar stage model for the development of *moral* judgments. Piaget

(1983, pp. 7-9) decided not to investigate children's moral behaviour or emotions, and understood 'morality' as a system of rules and the respect which individuals acquire for these rules. He investigated the development of morality by observing how children use rules in the games they play in the street, such as the game of marbles. He concluded that up to the age of five, children hardly cooperate and tend to be egocentric when communicating with others. Seven- and eight-year-olds, however, watch carefully what other players do, and try to cooperate in order to win the game. Even older children can modify the rules when this is necessary, for instance, when they are short of one player. Piaget did not only observe the games, but also interviewed children to find out how they understood the rules of the game. He concluded that a six-year-old's respect for rules and laws is very partial and egocentric. Basically, the child believes that rules have to be followed because otherwise bad consequences will follow. Later, when the child depends less on the authority of adults and interacts more with peers, rules come to be seen as an agreement to ensure that everybody will act in similar ways (Reimer et al., 1983, p. 41). As Piaget only studied children up to the age of 12, his work remained incomplete.

2.3.3 Kohlberg's Stages of Moral Development

Kohlberg (1958) extended Piaget's research on moral development. His initial sample was comprised of seventy-two boys, aged 10, 13, and 16, from both middle- and lower-class families in Chicago. In his follow-up research, he added younger children, delinquents, and boys and girls from other American cities and from other countries to his sample (Kohlberg, 1963, 1970). He interviewed subjects after they had read three hypothetical dilemmas. The most famous dilemma is the Heinz-dilemma:

> "In Europe, a woman was near death from a very bad disease, a special kind of cancer. There was one drug that the doctors thought might save her. It was a form of radium that a druggist in the same town had recently discovered. The drug was expensive to make, but the druggist was charging ten times what the drug cost him to make the drug. He paid $200 for the radium and charged $2,000 for a small dose of the drug. The sick woman's husband, Heinz, went to everyone he knew to borrow the money, but he could only get together about $1,000, which was half of what it cost. He told the druggist that his wife was dying and asked him to sell it cheaper or let him pay later. But the druggist said: 'No, I discovered the drug and I'm going to make money from it.' So Heinz got desperate and broke into the man's store to steal the drug for his wife." (Kohlberg, 1981, p. 12).

The experimenter asked the participating children whether Heinz should steal the drug in order to save his wife's life, and if so, why. Kohlberg was not as interested in whether the subjects answered 'yes' or 'no' to the dilemmas as in their reasoning behind it. Table 1 shows the kind of answers that subjects gave to the Heinz dilemma, their ideas about what is morally right, and their arguments for these ideas.

At the pre-conventional level, "...the child is responsive to cultural rules and labels of good and bad, right or wrong, but interprets these labels in terms of either the physical or the hedonistic consequences of action (punishment, reward, exchange of favours) or in terms of the physical power of those who enunciate the rules and labels." (Kohlberg, 1981, pp. 17-20). At the conventional level, children perceive that maintaining the expectations of the individual's family, group, or nation "...as valuable in its own right, regardless of immediate and obvious consequences. The attitude is not only one of conformity to personal expectations and social order, but of loyalty to it, of actively maintaining, supporting, and justifying the order and of identifying with the people or group involved in it." At the post-conventional level – which Kohlberg also called the 'autonomous' or 'principled' level – "...there is a clear effort to define moral values and principles that have validity and application apart from the authority of the groups of people holding these principles and apart from the individual's own identification with these groups." It should be noted that that these three levels are not just 'categories', in the sense they only contain different collections of people who share certain characteristics that are of equal value. There is a relative position or rank on a scale, on which the post-conventional level is considered to be highest, in the sense that it is psychologically most complex and morally most praiseworthy.

A Piagetian spirit is clearly recognisable in Kohlberg's model of moral development. Kohlberg's stages of moral development are supposed to mirror the stages of cognitive development as described by Piaget. This is known as the 'parallelism' or 'isomorphism' of cognitive and moral development. Children on a pre-conventional moral level base their reasoning on pre-operational or concrete operations; adolescents on a conventional moral level use the kind of reasoning that is typical of beginning formal operations; and adults on the post-conventional level base their moral reasoning on full formal operations. The close link with Piaget's theory makes it clear that Kohlberg's model of moral development is primarily about the kind of *reasoning* underlying moral judgments. Kohlberg (1969, pp. 352-353) also follows Piaget in his definition of moral 'stages'. Stages imply qualitative differences in children's modes of thinking or of solving the same problem at different ages. These different modes of thought form an invariant sequence, order, or succession, regardless of culture or religion. Each of these different and sequential modes of thought constitutes a 'structured whole' that determines responses to tasks which might not be manifestly similar. Cognitive stages are hierarchically integrated: they form an order of increasingly differentiated and integrated structures to fulfil a common function. Furthermore, Kohlberg and Piaget have similar ideas about the driving force behind moral development. Progress from one stage to the next is neither the undisturbed unfolding of a child's natural abilities, nor the simple product of external stimulation. As a child explores its environment, it builds cognitive structures or 'habits'. These are new ways of dealing with the world, which influence, in turn, its future experiences. When we interact with others, we can be motivated to come up with new, more comprehensive positions when our moral views are questioned and challenged. Kohlberg believed that cognitive *conflict* between people who are on different development levels is crucial to moral development. When somebody is confronted with a kind of moral reasoning that is higher than his/her own, he/she will be motivated to change the existing form of reasoning into a qualitatively new one.

2.3.4 From Moral Judgment to Action?

While it will be clear by now that moral development goes hand in hand with cognitive reorganisations, it is not clear whether or how somebody's ability to justify moral judgments by appealing to certain principles is related to moral action. Can somebody who has reached the post-conventional level be expected to *do* morally praiseworthy things? Since Kohlberg hardly writes about moral action, there are two options: either Kohlberg assumes that moral action follows automatically from knowledge of how to articulate particular moral judgments, or he is not interested in moral action at all.

Neither the early nor the later Kohlberg ever seems to have embraced the second assumption. The difference between his early and more mature work is only that he came to realise that the connection between moral reasoning and moral action was not as straightforward as he had initially assumed, and that "...moral education must deal directly with action and not just with reasoning" (Kohlberg in the foreword to Reimer et al., 1983, p. xiii). If we follow the later Kohlberg and agree that moral development involves both reason and action, we are faced with the question of *how* the two are related. This question is difficult to answer, because Kohlberg offers only very vague guidelines for approaching this relation. He simply hypothesises a positive correlation between the two (Blasi, 1980, p. 1). Kohlberg (1981, p. 44) cites one study that would show that children on higher moral stages cheat less than those on lower stages, but in his review of seventeen studies about the relation between moral reasoning and honest or altruistic behaviour, Blasi (1980, p. 9) cites several studies that contradict this finding. This suggests that there is no empirical evidence to support the claim that "true knowledge, knowledge of principles of justice, does predict virtuous action" (Kohlberg, 1984, p. 44). By focusing on the reasons that people use at different

Table 1: Kohlberg's stages of moral development

Level and stage	Typical answers to Heinz dilemma[3]	What is right[4]	Reason for doing right[5]
I : Pre-conventional level			
Stage 1: The punishment and obedience orientation.	Heinz was wrong to steal the drug because 'It's against the law' or 'It's bad to steal'. Children usually respond in terms of the consequences involved. Stealing is bad 'because you'll get punished'.	To avoid breaking rules backed by punishment, obedience for its own sake, and avoiding physical damage to person and property.	Avoidance of punishment, and the superior power over authorities.
Stage 2: The instrumental-relativist orientation	Children point out that 'Heinz might think it's right to take the drug, but the druggist would not.' Since everything is relative, each person is free to pursue his or her individual interests.	Following rules only when it is to someone's direct interest; acting to meet one's own interests and letting others do the same. Right is also what is fair, what's an equal exchange, a deal.	To serve one's own needs or interests in a world where you have to recognise that other people have interests, too.
II: Conventional level			
Stage 3: Mutual interpersonal Expectation, Relationships and Conformity orientation	Heinz was right to steal the drug because 'He was a good man for wanting to save her'. Even if Heinz doesn't love his wife, these subjects often say he should steal the drug because 'I don't think any husband should sit back and watch his wife die'	Living up to what is expected by people. 'Being good' is important and means having good motives, showing concern about others. It also means keeping mutual relationships, such as trust, loyalty, respect and gratitude	The need to be a good person in your own eyes and those of others. Your caring for others. Belief in the Golden Rule. Desire to maintain rules and authority which support stereotypical good behaviour.
Stage 4: The 'law and order' orientation	Many subjects say they understand that Heinz's motives were good, but they cannot condone the theft. 'What would happen if we all broke the law whenever we felt we had a good reason?'	Fulfilling the actual duties to which you have agreed. Laws are to be upheld except in extreme cases where they conflict with other fixed social duties. Right is also contributing to society, the group, or institution.	To keep the institution going as a whole, to avoid the breakdown in the system 'if everyone did it' or the imperative of conscience to meet one's defined obligations.
II: Post-conventional level			
Stage 5: The social-contract legalistic orientation	Respondents make it clear that they do not generally favour breaking laws; laws are social contracts that we agree to uphold. But Heinz' wife's right to live is a moral right that must be protected.	Being aware that people hold a variety of values and opinions, that most values and rules are relative to your group. Some non-relative values and rights like life and liberty, however must be upheld in any society.	A sense of obligation to law because one freely entered upon the social contract. The aim is overall utility of all and for the protection of people's rights.
Stage 6: The universal ethical-principle orientation	Kohlberg concluded that his method was not useful for distinguishing between stages 5 and 6. Consequently, he has dropped stage 6 from his scoring manual, calling it a 'theoretical stage'.	Following self-chosen ethical principles. Laws or social agreements are valid when they rest on universal principles of justice, such as respect for the dignity of individual human beings.	The belief as a rational person in the validity of universal moral principles, and a sense of personal commitment to them.

3   This column is based on Crain, W. (1985), chapter 7.
4   This column is based on Kohlberg, L. (1976).
5   Idem.

stages of moral development, Piaget and Kohlberg have rightly emphasised the role of cognition in moral judgment. They believe that the consequences of an action – however beneficial it may be to others' well-being – is not the only criterion to determine the moral worth of an action. However, it is unclear whether people who use certain kinds of reasons to justify their actions retrospectively are also more motivated to act morally in future situations. Blasi (1980, p. 25) concludes that there is some support for a positive statistical correlation between reasoning and action, but that the relations between them are often low. This suggests that moral reasoning is often not the only determinant of moral behaviour.

Due to the influence of Piaget's rationalistic view of human nature and moral functioning, Kohlberg either neglected other factors, such as feelings, or considered them to be functionally dependent on cognitive processes. Kohlberg (1981, p. 57, pp. 139-141) regarded feelings and cognition as "parallel aspects of the structural transformations that take place in development" and as "different aspects, or perspectives, on the same mental events." While Kohlberg acknowledged in his later work that feelings are involved in moral judgments, he insisted that the moral *quality* of these feelings were still determined by its cognitive-structural development. Consequently, emotional dynamics as such never had a fair hearing in the cognitive developmental approach. Despite persistent and growing criticisms that he did not do justice to the affective aspects of moral development, Kohlberg always remained "steadfast in focusing primarily on the cognitive aspects of moral development, with the affective aspects receiving secondary treatment" (Pritchard, 1984, p. 36). Rival approaches to moral education, such as those developed by care ethicists and neo-Aristotelians, did try to bridge the gap between cognition and action by appealing to notions such as 'moral sentiments', 'moral virtue' and 'moral self'.

2.3.5 Justifying the Highest Stage

How does Kohlberg justify the goal of moral development? Kohlberg (1981, p. 25) claims that his empirical research shows that everybody moves through these stages, regardless of varying social, cultural or religious conditions. This would mean that there is a universal and invariant sequence of moral development. As people grow older, they accumulate (moral) experiences and will try to integrate them cognitively better, i.e. they try to make new distinctions and integrate these experiences into more comprehensive structures. Psychologically, a later stage is more differentiated, more comprehensive, and more integrated. But is it also the best stage from a *moral* point of view? Kohlberg's empirical work can only provide a partial answer to this question: it was merely supposed to prove that his theoretical view of morality is also practically the highest stage of moral development. Especially because it was hard to identify individuals who consistently operated at the post-conventional level, the highest stage still needs a separate philosophical justification.

A psychologist himself, Kohlberg depended for philosophical arguments on John Rawls (1971) and Richard Hare (1952, 1963). Hare's influence is clearly visible in the criteria that Kohlberg (1981, p. 135) uses to determine whether a judgment is moral: universality and prescriptivity. The theory of prescriptivism was developed by speech act theorists who were impressed by Ludwig Wittgenstein's later work. The application of his theory of meaning to problems of ethics was very influential on post Enlightenment liberal thinking about the nature of morality (Carr, 1991, p. 92; MacIntyre, 2003, p. 20). According to Wittgenstein, language does not only describe the world, but has all kinds of functions. For instance, when I say 'good morning', a response like 'no, it's not', would not be appropriate, since my utterance is not meant as a description of the morning, but as a greeting or a wish that one would have a good day. When I say that a person is 'good', I do not just describe this person, but I assess or evaluate him. Now, prescriptivists argued that in moral discourse, 'good' is used to *commend*. This raises the question of what kind of behaviour is to be commended. Carr (1991, p. 93) has pointed out that prescriptivism commends actions that we ought to perform. In turn, these 'oughts' can only be defined in terms of what is commendable. To break out of this circular reasoning, Hare appealed to the universalisation of prescriptions. This means that those actions are commended or called 'good' of which we can reasonably want that they are done by everyone in similar circumstances (Carr, 1991, p. 93).

Prescriptivism limits the moral domain in several ways. Firstly, it restricts moral language to commendations or prescriptions. In contrast, Aristotle's virtue ethics is evaluative, in the sense that it distinguishes between good and bad lives, without issuing any prescriptions, therefore, it does not tell people how they *ought* to act or live. It assumes that our desires and interests give us reasons to act morally, not prescriptions. Prescriptivism can be called an 'anti-naturalist' ethical theory, because it "...refuses to regard any statement of what is valuable or what ought to be done in moral terms as derivable from considerations about how things happen to stand in human individual and social affairs." (Carr, 1991, p. 97). Prescriptions are categorical, in that they demand absolute command, irrespective of someone's circumstances, while naturalistic moral theories issue only in 'hypothetical imperatives', which depend on human emotions and experiences (Foot, 2002, chapter 11).

Prescriptivism limits the moral domain further by making universalisibility the central property of moral prescriptions. Prescriptivists see it as a logical feature of moral terms: anyone who uses a word such as 'ought' would be logically committed to universalisability. While universalisability could be a feature of some moral judgments, prescriptivists do neither prove that *all* moral judgments are necessarily universalisable, nor that only judgments that can be universalised are moral judgments (Mackie, 1977, p. 86). Another problem with this universalisability criterion is that it is purely formal, i.e. it does not say anything substantial about what kinds of behaviour are to be commended. This leaves the moral *content* of the prescription a matter for decision by individuals. For prescriptivists, the utterance of any universal principle is in the end "an expression of the preference of an individual will" (MacIntyre, 1984, p. 20). Chapter 5 highlights that several virtue ethicists are afraid that this leaves no room for the idea that some moral content can be justified objectively, too.

Kohlberg (1981, p. 162) admits that a prescriptivist understanding of morality leaves the moral content entirely a matter for decision by the person, and he aspires to built and justify more substantial ethical principles that meet the formal criteria outlined above. On the post-conventional stage, there are three principles that competent moral judgments should take into account: (1) the principle of justice, (2) the principle of reversibility and (3) the principle of impartiality or respect for personality. In order to articulate these principles further, Kohlberg turns for help to Rawls. At the same time, Rawls (1971, chapter 8) turns for help to Piaget and Kohlberg to draft an account of the course of moral development as it may occur in a society that realises his principles of justice.

In *A Theory of Justice*, Rawls (1971) describes a social contract account of justice, called 'justice as fairness'. In the search for fundamental principles of justice, Rawls claims that our reasoning should adopt a fair and impartial point of view. He asks us to engage in a thought-experiment, in which we imagine ourselves to be in a position of free and equal people who jointly agree upon and commit themselves to principles of social and political justice. This is the 'original position'. In this position, the metaphorical 'veil of ignorance' blinds all parties involved, so that they are deprived of knowledge concerning their personal characteristics and social and historical circumstances. In this way, Rawls (1971, pp. 18-19) makes sure that "...particular inclinations and aspirations, and persons' conceptions of their good do not affect the principles adopted." The parties are then presented with a list of different conceptions of justice. Rawls (1971, pp. 302-303) has argued that it would be rational for all parties in the original position to choose two principles of justice. First: "Each person is to have an equal right to the most extensive total system of equal basis liberties compatible with a similar system of liberty for all". And second: "Social and economic inequalities are to be arranged so that they are both (a) to the greatest benefit of the least advantaged, and (b) attached to offices and positions open to all under conditions of equality and opportunity." What Kohlberg likes about Rawls' principles of justice is that they help to decide between competing claims of individuals, which perfectly matches Kohlberg's (1981, p. 200) ideas about morality, which he considers to be "the 'logic' for coordinating the viewpoints of subjects with conflicting interests".

Kohlberg's second principle is the 'principle of role-taking' (also called 'role-reversibility', 'ideal role taking' or 'moral musical chairs'). What this means can be best be understood in comparison with Rawls 'veil of ignorance'. According to Rawls, principles of justice emerge best under the condition that individual actors deliberate with 'impersonal' preferences: they have no information about their personal characteristics. Kohlberg asks us to imagine someone making a similar decision in the Heinz dilemma. What should you do? – not knowing whether you are to be assigned the role of husband, wife or druggist. "Clearly, the rational solution is to steal the drug; that is, this leads to the least loss (or the most gain) to an individual who could be in any role." (Kohlberg, 1981, p. 200). It makes sense to Heinz, and anybody else in the same situation, to steal the drug because chances are too high that you – after the veil has been lifted – will end up in the position of Heinz' wife, without the medical treatment. In this thought experiment, the druggist's claim to be paid for the drug is not reversible, because if he were to switch roles with the sick woman, he would realise that he would like to live too. Wanting to earn money at the expense of somebody else's life and choosing your own life when you are ill is inconsistent.

The third and last principle that Kohlberg commends is 'respect for personality'. In an interview with a (hypothetical) philosopher who is said to be on stage 6, it becomes clear what the principle of respect for personality involves. When the philosopher is asked whether Heinz should still steal the drug if the husband does not feel very close or affectionate to his wife, his answer is: "Yes. The value of her life is independent of any personal ties. [...] The decision of what to do in such a situation [...] must be made from a disinterested point of view that allows one to make a decision that can be justified and that is consistent with the decision of any rational agent in a similar situation." (Kohlberg, 1981, p. 163). This means that Heinz should not steal the drug from the druggist because he loves his wife, but because this sick person, who is also, incidentally, his wife, is a human being whose life is in danger, and because any rational being confronted with this situation ought to do so, regardless of his local or personal circumstances. Whether Heinz should still steal the drug has to be answered by the moral reasoning of an autonomous person who has stripped himself entirely of his earthly belongings. Respect for 'personality', i.e. for a human being as a rational being, means that all people have to be treated impartially.

The troubling consequence of this view is that Heinz acts morally *worse* if he steals the drugs because he loves his wife than because he knows that 'respect for personality' is a principle that can be universally prescribed. One difficulty with this principle is that in much of our lives the claims of people to whom one stands in special and particular relations, such as friends and family, oppose strict impartiality. This makes 'impartiality' seem more like a part of public morality than a private virtue (Blackburn, 2005, p. 181). It will not come as a surprise that this kind of ethics has been criticised by care ethicists like Gilligan whose interest in moral education has to do with a sympathetic and caring concern for

2.3.6 Cognitive Development in Schools

In Kohlberg's educational ideas, two major strands can be distinguished (Reimer et al., 1983, p. 113). When the insights from the strands are combined, we find a comprehensive picture of (1) what individual teachers can do to stimulate moral development through classroom discussions, (2) how the (official and hidden) curriculum can be used to encourage pupils' moral reasoning, and (3) how the school itself can become a just community.

Originally, Kohlberg aimed at enabling teachers to discuss moral dilemmas in the classroom. Moshe Blatt, one of Kohlberg's students, was the first to investigate empirically how children's moral reasoning could be stimulated (Blatt & Kohlberg, 1975). He hypothesised that their reasoning could be improved by offering a programme that exposed pupils to a kind of reasoning that was typical of one stage *above* their own. The programme consisted of twelve weeks of classroom discussions at a Reform Jewish Sunday school. The teachers presented pupils with a moral conflict situation, asked them to supply possible ways of resolving it, and wrote down pupils' suggestions on a blackboard. Next, pupils were asked to specify the standard or hierarchy of values implicit in each of the solutions. As these arguments developed, the teacher focused on arguments that were proposed by pupils who were one stage above the majority of their classmates. He clarified and supported these arguments until the teacher felt that the other children understood its logic. Blatt & Kohlberg (1975, pp. 137-138) concluded that the moral reasoning of children in the experimental group improved significantly more than those in the control groups. They recommended teachers to use the dilemma discussions used in the experiment instead of unstructured discussion or other didactic forms of moral education.

When teachers want to engage in the 'Socratic' classroom discussions that Kohlberg advocated, there are several things to keep in mind.[6] Firstly, teachers should understand the meanings that different age groups attach to moral problems, because moral education can only work if teachers know what constitutes a moral issue at a particular age. Secondly, they should understand two specific elements that promote moral growth, i.e. 'cognitive conflict' and 'ideal role taking'. Thirdly, they need the practical know-how to stimulate pupils' awareness of certain moral issues, using both hypothetical dilemmas and ordinary classroom discussions and to stimulate these discussions by using a number of questioning strategies. Fourthly, they should develop the ability to take the perspective of *all* children in the class and to highlight differences and similarities between their individual contributions to the classroom discussions. Fifthly, teachers should anticipate some difficulties that may appear in practice, such as peer pressure, which can

---

6 For a full discussion of the Socratic method, see §4.4.

cause pupils to conform to others' opinions instead formulating their own point of view. Sixthly, an important function of teachers is to foster an atmosphere of "trust, empathy, respect and fairness", without which children are less likely to disclose the kind of personal information about themselves that is necessary to discuss moral matters (Reimer et al., 1983, p. 179). This involves taking care of physical arrangements and modelling an attitude of acceptance. Finally, teachers should know that they are likely to experience cognitive conflict themselves as they help children morally develop. Teachers cannot be moral bystanders; through educating others morally, they will simultaneously educate themselves.

Some teachers may object that Kohlberg demands too much from teachers. Will contributing to pupils' moral development not be at the expense of teaching particular subjects? In Kohlberg's view, teachers can also contribute to pupils' moral education by giving the improvement of moral reasoning structures a place *within* the existing and more comprehensive school curriculum (Reimer et al., 1983, p. 208). The official curriculum and all other things that go on in the 'hidden curriculum' can be taken as a starting point for the kind of discussions that Kohlberg advocates. Take, for instance, the use of literature in all language classes. By taking the perspective of the characters in a book, Kohlberg expects pupils to learn how to reverse roles in real-life situations too.[7] When pupils focus on different aspects in a story, depending on their stage of moral development, it is the teacher's task to raise issues suitable to the pupils' stage. For example, the moral reasoning of Huck, the main character of *Huckleberry Finn*, wavers between stage 2 and stage 3, i.e. between his own needs and respect, loyalty and gratitude to Jim. As a classroom exercise, pupils can try to describe the conflicts that Huck goes through, and by doing so, they may recognise some of the difficulties Huck experiences. This is just one example. There are many ways to pay attention to moral questions within the context of a normal class.

Although Kohlberg remained committed to this cognitive-conflict model of moral development, he became more interested in other strategies from the early 1970s onwards. He realised that the hypothetical dilemmas used in classroom discussions did not mirror the moral situations people face in their daily lives. For example, he admitted that "...continuing work in the schools led me to a view closer to that of most of my critics, however, that moral education must deal [...] with 'real-life' situations and not just with hypothetical ones." (Kohlberg in the foreword to Reimer et al., 1983, p. xiii). Moreover, Kohlberg came to realise that some social and institutional conditions have to be met before individuals' moral judgments can fully develop. Schools could be regarded as democratic societies in miniature that offer a wide variety of moral learning opportunities. In a cluster school in Cambridge, Massachusetts, he started to investigate how schools at large could be turned into 'just communities' (Kohlberg, Wasserman & Richardson, 1975). With Kohlberg's help, a number of such schools were formed in the states

---

7   See §4.3 for a more extensive discussion on the moral educational use of the arts from a virtue ethical point of view.

of Massachusetts and New York. Just community schools were also established in a women's prison in Connecticut, in a programme for dropouts in a high school in the Bronx, New York, and in a high school in France. In addition, Snarey, Reimer & Kohlberg (1985) evaluated the effects of kibbutz culture and education on the development of adolescents residing on the kibbutz and examined the possible implications of kibbutz education for schools in the United States. After Kohlberg's sudden death in 1987, his students continued the research. For example, Power (1981, 1988) and Power & Kohlberg (1986) investigated the influence of the moral atmosphere and the hidden curriculum of the school on the children's cognitive development.

What did those 'just communities' look like? A school would be run democratically by both staff and pupils. Although teachers made decisions regarding the curriculum, and although the school had to adhere to certain regulations, laws and educational policies, all other aspects of school life were decided by the community as if it was a full participatory democracy, on a one-person, one-vote basis (Battistich, 2010, p. 118). Community meetings with all members were held every week. For example, the programme included a pupil-run disciplinary committee that determined fair punishments for pupils who violated community rules, mediated disputes, and counselled pupils with disciplinary problems (Battistich, 2010, p. 118). A spirit of community would be built within the school. Teachers were expected to establish an atmosphere of mutual respect, democratic processes and the rules of a fair morality in the community. They acted as "facilitators of democratic processes by encouraging perspective-taking, raising issues about fairness and morality, articulating 'higher-stage' reasoning, helping to ensure full participation, and advocating positions that help develop group expectations of and commitment to justice and community" (Battistich, 2010, p. 118). In order to be good facilitators, staff had to be taught about Kohlberg's theory of moral development. Schools had to be small, because it would be practically impossible for teachers and pupils to meet face-to-face on a regular basis. In larger schools, the small scale was accomplished by creating 'schools within school', i.e. by dividing the schools into clusters of 60 to 100 pupils and four or five teachers. The just community schools were successful, in the sense that they had positive effects on pupils' commitment to the values of democracy, fairness, and community, norms and values were more collectively shared, and higher scores on moral reasoning tests were achieved, compared to pupils in 'normal' high schools (Battistich, 2010, p. 118). Longitudinal research showed that over eight years, all *teachers* moved from conventional (stage 3 or 4) to post-conventional reasoning (stage 5) too. Many of these results, however, are in need of replication (Power & Higgins-D'Alessandro, 2008, p. 240).

2.4 Care Ethics

Care ethics emerged in the early 1980s as a reaction to Kohlberg's hegemony over the field of moral development and education. In this section, the roots of care ethics will be traced, especially to Gilligan's *In a Different Voice* (1982), an influential study that showed how the inclusion of women in experiments changed the traditional paradigm of psychology.

2.4.1 The Emergence of Care Ethics

Gilligan (2009) recalls two important experiences that would eventually lead her to develop the notion of 'care'. In 1970, she became a research assistant for Kohlberg at Harvard University. While she taught an undergraduate course on moral and political choice, she recounts how the issue of the Vietnam draft came up. What struck her, was that the students who would be facing the draft as seniors did not want to talk about it. According to Gilligan, they were used solving Kohlberg's hypothetical moral dilemmas, which were used by psychologists to measure moral development. Moreover, they did not want to talk about the draft, because they knew that what they were thinking did not fit the higher levels of the stages of development of the theories they were learning. They did not reason their way through their choices with the help of impartial principles that could be applied universally, but thought much about their relationships with the people they loved, such as their families. Gilligan concluded that these men were reluctant to discuss the draft, because they were afraid that they would sound like women if they said what they were in fact thinking. After the Vietnam War, Gilligan resumed her study about 'turning points' in people's lives with twenty-nine pregnant women who were considering having an abortion, which had become a legal practice in the United States in 1973. What struck her, in particular, was a dissonance between the voice of these women and the terms of the public abortion debate at that time, which was largely in terms of rights, such as a child's right to life and a women's right to choice. Gilligan did not present women with the standard Kohlbergian dilemma's, but asked them how *they* defined moral problems and what experiences *they* went through. She found out that the choice to have an abortion or not was not primarily an issue about rights, but about relationships and responsibilities.

These experiences made Gilligan realise that something was missing in the conversation about the moral aspects of decision making and development (Gilligan, 2009). The ideal of a morally educated person was not exhausted by the Kohlbergian picture of an autonomous person that could universalise impartial judgments. Gilligan began to shift her attention to the 'voice of care', which she considered to be a central notion to our moral experience as well, especially but not exclusively to the experiences of women. From *In a Different Voice*, it is not always clear what this 'different voice' amounts to or how it relates to Kohlberg's approach to moral development. The lack of argumentative clarity is, however, in line with Gilligan's critique of the detached, abstract and objectifying perspective on moral issues that Kohlberg and other psychologists had taken. Her interest was not in "philosophically oriented theorizing about moral judgment", but in telling an interpretive story about the concrete lives of individuals and their personal, actual dilemmas (Jorgenson, 2006, p. 190). The book is interspersed with excerpts from the interviews with people who participated in one of the three studies, because she took these stories to exemplify the 'missing' moral voice she was after. While Gilligan put 'care' on the psychological agenda, others elaborated on the consequences of this shift for the sphere of the political (Tronto, 1993), and for morality and moral education (Noddings, 1984, 2002a, 2003; Slote, 2007, 2010a, 2010b).

2.4.2 The Relationship between Justice and Care

Gilligan's ideas on moral development and maturity can best be understood in connection with the theory it is a reaction to: Kohlberg's cognitive developmental approach. There are roughly three ways to interpret the relationship between the two approaches (Flanagan & Adler, 1983).

The first option is a 'separate but equal' view. In this model, Kohlberg's and Gilligan's theories are about different topics and do not make any opposing claims. They simply propose alternative sequences that develop along different pathways with different endpoints: Kohlberg writes about justice and impartially, while Gilligan focuses on issues about the good life, such as friendship, relationships and concerns for intimate others. Although Gilligan's and Kohlberg's theories can be distinguished in this way for analytical purposes, a substantial separation is more problematic. For example, both approaches seem to have something to say about *the same* Heinz dilemma. One can look at the dilemma from an impartial point of view and ask what would be just for Heinz, or any autonomous person in the same situation, to do; or one can look at it from the perspective of the caring relationship between two particular persons. The two approaches may be equal, but they are certainly not completely separate. This interpretation of the relationship between cognitive development and care ethics can only be sustained through a very benign reading of Gilligan's metaphor of a *different* voice (Flanagan & Adler, 1983, p. 587).

A second option is to treat Gilligan's approach as a rival approach that is incompatible with Kohlberg's. Assuming that there is no third option, this interpretation presupposes that either one of the theories encompasses all there is to morality. Although it is theoretically possible that there is a single, unitary account of the moral point of view, neither Kohlberg nor Gilligan are willing to endorse this kind of monism. While Gilligan (1977, 1980) suggests a few times that her conception of morality and moral development is better than Kohlberg's, these claims are not representative of her final statement. Her goal was to "... expand the understanding of human development by using the group left out in the construction of theory to call attention to what is missing in its account" (Gilligan, 1982, p. 5). Gilligan expressed great admiration for Kohlberg's ideas, and her work on care should not be perceived as a radical critique, but as an *expansion* of Kohlberg's theory (Jorgenson, 2006). Kohlberg, however, was more pretentious if we interpret him as claiming that post-conventional morality is the only 'real' morality. While Kohlberg considered post-conventional morality to be the *best* morality, he does not deny that other, lower, ways of thinking about moral dilemmas count as 'moral' too. In this way, Gilligan's considerations of care can be seen as a conventional way of thinking about morality. For Kohlberg, justice must be part of any comprehensive theory of morality, but it does not cover the gamut of moral issues (Rest et al., 1999, p. 14).

The last and best option is to *integrate* the two approaches. In this interpretation, "...the morality of rights and the morality of responsibilities achieve a tense synthesis in each person." (Flanagan & Adler, 1983, p. 587). Both Gilligan and Kohlberg seem to be comfortable with the idea that 'morally educated' people should be both caring *and* just. Gilligan only wanted to correct the male bias in psychological and moral theory, and Kohlberg tried to accommodate Gilligan's views (Jorgenson, 2006, pp. 195-196). Integrating the two approaches may, however, be easier said than done. From the publication of *In a Different Voice* onwards, several authors have proposed ways to reconcile justice and care. For example, psychologist Martin Hoffman (2000, p. 3) has tried to show that both care and justice have a common pro-social origin in the feeling of empathy. Hume scholar Annette Baier (1985, 1986) suggested that 'appropriate trust' can bring male and female moral theories – which she describes as an 'ethic of obligation and contract' and an 'ethic of love' – together. Feminist philosopher Susan Hekman (1993, 1995) argued that the metaphor of 'moral voices' should be interpreted more radically. The voices of justice and care are only two in an even larger and pluralistic moral and epistemological domain (see also: Blum, 1988, p. 383). Finally, virtue theorists regarded care and justice as two *virtues* that would, together with a number of other virtues, ideally be integrated into what they called a 'character' (Flanagan & Jackson, 1987, p. 627). Ironically, Kohlberg's cognitive development approach started as a critique of character education, but in order to formulate a universal theory of moral development, Kohlberg restricted the moral domain to such an extent that Gilligan and others wanted to make room for the notion of care. When virtue ethicists joined the debate in the early 1990s, the moral domain was eventually broadened to such extent, that a new kind of character education emerged.

2.4.3 Natural and Ethical Caring

Gilligan introduced a 'different voice' to show that a male perspective on human moral development is incomplete, and that ideals of attachment, love, friendship, listening and responding give equal rise to moral concerns. While Gilligan's book was mainly a narrative stage for the women that she interviewed in her studies, Nel Noddings' books[8] on morality and moral education cover so much ground that they contain much more of an *ethic* of care than Gilligan's work. In *Caring* (1984), which followed close on the publication of Carol Gilligan's *In a Different Voice*, Noddings makes clear that she is opposed to a kind of moral philosophy that concentrates on moral reasoning governed by universal and prescriptive principles of justice and fairness. The problem is that all influential philosophers to date have been male: "Ethics so far has been guided by Logos, the masculine spirit" (Nodding, 1984, p. 1). Noddings does not mention Kohlberg, but it is evident that she wants to settle scores with the cognitive development approach. In Noddings' view, morality is about teaching people to *be* good, something that grows out of a longing for goodness that human naturally have. More specifically, this natural inclination is a longing for a caring relationship. This *relationship* always involves two parties: the one who cares (the 'one-caring') and the one who is cared for (the 'cared-for').

When is a relationship 'caring'? Noddings does not give a systematic exposition of criteria for caring because she claims to be doing some kind of 'informal phenomenology' (she asks 'what we are like' when we engage in caring encounters) but she suggests three requirements for caring. Firstly, the one-caring must be in a particular state of mind: he has a feeling that is very close to what is commonly known as 'empathy' or 'feeling with' somebody. Noddings (1984, p. 30; 2010, p. 145) is not very fond of the concept of 'empathy', because she associates it with an intellectual understanding of other people's feelings. She prefers the term 'engrossment', which (literally) means being 'occupied exclusively', being 'absorbed' or 'monopolised' by someone, like a reader who is engrossed in a novel. Likewise, Noddings (1984, p. 30) writes: "I receive the other in myself, and I see and feel with the other. I become a duality." Somebody who cares, is absorbed or invaded by another person, by his needs and desires, like a mother when she hears her baby cry. Why would people be engrossed? By referring to Kierkegaard, Noddings (1984, p. 14) explains that when we care, we apprehend another's reality as *possibility*. For example, when we see a friend being diagnosed with a terrible disease, we care since we are moved by the idea that this can happen to us too.

Understanding that another person's reality is a possibility for oneself can arouse the feeling that one *must* do something: "I am impelled to act as though in my own behalf, but in behalf of the other." (Noddings, 1984, p. 16). Being motivated to act *on behalf of the other* is what Noddings calls 'motivational displacement'. This second characteristic of a caring person matters to care since the understanding of

---

8   See, e.g. Noddings (1984, 1995, 2002a, 2002b, 2003, 2006).

another person's situation does itself not necessarily involve the motivation to act in the other person's interests. These two criteria show that an ethic of care does not want to make 'narrow' judgments about whether actions are right or wrong, but is after heightening people's moral perception and sensitivities (Noddings 1984, p. 90). Care ethics puts less emphasis on the consequences of caring acts and more on the "pre-act consciousness of the one-caring" (Noddings 1984, p. 28). "Everything depends, then, upon the will to be good, to remain in caring relation to the other." (Noddings, 1984, p. 103). If people are to become caring, ethical theory will have to pay attention to the cultivation of their perception, feelings, motivations and understanding.

Interestingly, Noddings also discusses a requirement that the *cared-for* must meet in order for a relationship to be really caring. In her view, caring requires some form of recognition from the cared-for that the one-caring is caring. If caring is not reciprocal, Noddings (1984, p. 73) is afraid that the caring-one will not respect the freedom of the cared-for, treating the cared-for as an object instead of a person. The contribution of the cared-for, therefore, guarantees that the caring relationship is one between *subjects*. When there is a recognition of and response to the caring by the person who is cared for, one can speak about caring "in the fullest sense", which is "completed in the other" (Noddings, 1984, p. 68). In cases when the caring-one exhibits a caring attitude that is not noticed by the cared-for, caring is only partly realised. In these situations, the caring-one must help the cared-for as much as possible to become freer, more creative, more authentic, more spontaneous.

Noddings founds her ethics of care on a natural longing for a caring. Almost everyone who is alive must have been cared-for as a child, and these shared experiences guarantee that all people will have a natural, initial impulse to care. However, caring for others or accepting other people's care will not always be easy. Indeed, the relationship between family and friends may be very problematic. But caring for fellow-citizens or complete strangers seems even more difficult. Can we be expected to *care* for them too, or would another attitude be more appropriate? Noddings (1984, pp. 46-47) describes four concentric circles of caring. In the inner, intimate circle, we care because we love. This love is often natural, but sometimes it is not, for example, when we are tired or busy. The second circle includes those proximate people for whom we have personal regard, such as colleagues. We normally act according to the rules of the group we are in, which tell us to treat others in a polite, acceptable fashion. The third circle consists of people that one has not yet encountered, such as a future husband, a child, or prospective students. These people are potential objects of care because they can immediately be linked to people in inner circles. The fourth and outer circle is 'the stranger', who does not have any connections to the people one already cares for. Although a caring person cannot care for all strangers at the same time, when a stranger presents himself, a caring person must accept his claim even if the strain is great (Nodding, 1984, p. 47). Noddings admits that caring can be very demanding, and that in order to expand the circles of care, natural caring should be cultivated as an ethical ideal.

However, what if people do not recognise this obligation? Noddings' (1984, p. 50) answer is that they *should* only care because they *want* to. This answer may seem rather unsatisfactory because it raises the question why we should want to care, but it reveals something significant about Noddings' approach. She does not look for justifications, because philosophical arguments will not help people to become interested in ethical conduct (Noddings, 1984, p. 94). Moral philosophers have mistakenly tried to justify moral norms and ideals from a 'view from nowhere', but they forgot that the moral viewpoint is *prior* to any justification. We can only explain to a moral sceptic *why* he should be moral if he has some interest in becoming it. If a sceptic continues to reject the idea that he has a natural longing for caring and a motivation to be moral, he runs the risk of being separated from human relations, the membership of human communities and ideals of what his life could be like. What can motivate people to care is the memory of our own best moments of caring and being cared for. When care does not arise naturally, consulting this *ethical ideal* can help to maintain or enhance a caring attitude:

> "When I encounter an other and feel the natural pang conflicted with my own desires – 'I must – I do not want to' – I recognise the feelings and remember what has followed it in my own best moment. I have a picture of those moments in which I was cared for and in which I cared, and I may reach towards this memory and guide my conduct by it if I wish to do so." (Noddings, 1984, p. 80).

When it is difficult to accept care, e.g. because it is difficult to accept that one depends on others, this ethical ideal can also be helpful to the cared-for. He will have to cultivate the virtue of 'magnanimous receptivity' (Noddings, 1984, p. 76). A cared-for can achieve this state in two ways: either by being as receptive as he can, trying to make the encounter with the one-caring genuine, or the cared-for can give up his/her role and become a one-caring himself by responding to the needs of the one who was originally supposed to care. This can place a high burden on the one-to-be-cared for, who now has to help the one-supposed-to-care to care for the one-who-was-supposed-to-be-cared-for. The attribution of moral responsibility to the cared-for has been criticised, because it seems somewhat odd to say, e.g. that we morally praise a child's receptivity to and need for his mother's love (Slote, 1999). Michael Slote has argued that there is a fundamental difference in moral admirability between the one-caring and the cared-for, and that an ethic of care would be better based on the caring qualities of the caring-one than on the quality of the caring relationship between both parties. In Slote's view, an ethic of care would be better based on virtues.

Although Noddings became more interested in virtue ethics through the years[9], she maintains that caring is not a virtue. In *Caring*, her rejection of virtues was influenced by a Humean critique of virtue. For example, she writes that virtue carries with it the danger 'to withdraw from the public domain' (p. 85) or to 'turn inward' (p. 96). Moreover, she associated virtues with the qualities of a 'hermit monk on the mountains', such as celibacy, fasting, penance, mortification, self-denial, humility, silence and solitude. Even after Noddings became acquainted with Aristotelian virtue ethics[10], she emphasised that an ethics or care that promotes virtues runs the risk of stimulating people to perfect their own caring attitudes, without much regard for the other party in the caring relation. Noddings recognises that caring attitudes are necessary for a caring relationships, but she stresses that an ethic of care seeks to maintain and enhance a relationship. Care is primarily a quality of relations, not of agents (Noddings & Slote, 2002). Furthermore, because a relationship also includes a cared-for, who has to receive the caring, a caring person depends on the cared-for for his virtues to be completed.

2.4.4 The Psychology and Development of Care

Care ethicists have not only criticised the moral goal of development that cognitive stage theorists advocate, but also the psychology that is believed to be typical of a morally mature person. According to advocates of cognitive development, moral functioning is primarily a cognitive matter. Care ethicists, however, claim that reasoning has a very limited role to play in care. Being caring involves first of all getting in touch with moral sentiments.

Just as Kohlberg's moral psychology is, via Piaget, indebted to Kant, is much of the care ethical moral psychology derived from Hume. Although Noddings (2010, p. 146) denies a Humean influence on the first feminist formulations of care, she acknowledges the historical connection. Prior to a closer look at Hume's moral psychology, it is worth noticing the historical irony in care ethicists' turn to Hume for help. In the 18th century, Kant criticised Hume for offering a false picture of morality and reason. In the 20th-century debate on moral education, these roles are reversed: care ethicists use Hume to criticise a Kantian-based cognitive developmental approach. Hume argued against the rationalists of his time (Hobbes, Locke, Clarke) that reason is incapable of yielding a judgment that an act is right or wrong, or a character trait virtuous or vicious. It can only discover matters of fact in concrete situations or determine the general social impact of a moral behaviour over time. The famous doctrine that reason alone is merely the 'slave of the passions' is defended in the *Treatise of Human Nature* (1975). When we contemplate an action or person from a moral point of view – not thinking about

---

9   See, for example: Noddings (2002a) and Noddings & Slote (2002).
10 One can also notice a reverse effect. For example, MacIntyre (1999a) discusses the importance of care in the development of virtue.

our self-interest, but from a general perspective – Hume hypothesises that people will naturally sympathise with those that are affected by somebody's actions. The facts as known must trigger a response by 'sentiments' that inform us whether something is good. The Humean 'sympathy' is not a sentiment itself, but the psychological mechanism that enables people to receive the sentiments of another person. It is what we would call 'empathy' today (Cohon, 2010; Slote, 2010b, p. 126). Depending on the circumstance, empathising with other people can lead one to feel e.g. pride, humility, love or hatred. For example, the feeling of love shows that we morally approve of someone. Both Noddings and Slote draw on this Humean notion of sympathy, although Noddings (1984) calls it 'engrossment' and Slote (2010b) 'empathy'.

Care ethicists never developed a full account of moral development that equals Kohlberg's cognitive development theory. While Gilligan and Noddings provide some clues about what the development of care may look like, the underlying psychological mechanism are not specified, as will be apparent. While the role of empathy in moral development has been investigated by Hoffman (2000), it remains unclear whether empathy and sympathy refer to the same sentiment, and which other cognitive and emotional processes are involved in caring. While care ethicists promised to place less emphasis on caring *acts* and more on the cultivation of a caring *attitude*, it remains a mystery what this attitude does and does not entail, psychologically speaking.

Gilligan's *In a Different Voice* contains a rudimentary developmental model that makes clear that she was still bound to the Kohlbergian paradigm of moral development in the early 1980s (Jorgensen, 2006, p. 186). While interviewing twenty-nine women in her abortion decision study, Gilligan noticed not only that women interpreted the moral domain differently than men, but also that the language these women used suggested a Kohlbergian-style sequence of levels and stages that tracks the understanding of care in human relationships. At the first level, care is primarily directed at the self, in order to ensure survival. Once one discovers responsibilities towards others, however, one also becomes aware that the care for oneself is very selfish. This sense of responsibility becomes more mature when people realise that inequalities also call for moral action. At this stage, being responsible means doing what others are counting on you to do, regardless of what you want for oneself. On the second level, people run the risk of caring too much for others and too little for themselves. This may lead to tensions between the care for others and the care for oneself. This tension disappears on the third level, when care is not understood as something that exhausts and limits the self, but as a self-chosen principle that is "universal in its condemnation of exploitation and hurt" (Gilligan, 1982, p. 74). As one makes moral progress, one will gradually realise that 'self' and 'others' are interconnected and interdependent, and that care enables both the one-caring and the cared-for to flourish.

Noddings' does not present a detailed account of moral development either. However, an attempt will be made here to derive a moral developmental account from her work by interpreting her idea of 'circles of care' developmentally. Is natural caring developmentally prior to ethical caring? In *Caring*, Noddings (1984, p. 114) argues that "when caring must retreat to an inner circle, confine itself, and consciously exclude particular groups, the ideal is diminished, that it is quantitatively reduced." Somebody who approximates the ethical ideal does not longer limit its care to his/her inner circles of family and friends, but extends the care to people that he/she does not know, but who require help. How can this ethical ideal be approximated? In *Starting at Home: Caring and Social Policy*, Noddings (2002b, p. 22) writes that "...we learn first what it means to be cared for. Then, gradually, we learn both to care for and, by extension, to care about others." This is in agreement with Gilligan's idea that initial care for ourselves can be transformed into caring for others. Noddings, however, introduces a distinction between 'caring for' and 'caring about'. We care *for* those near and dear to us, while we merely care *about* people in the wider public realm. After we have been well cared for, and have learned to care for a few intimate others, we can also start to show fellow feelings for others in the wider world, e.g. through charitable gifts, social groups that we support, and our voting.

So it seems that Noddings sees moral development as progress from being cared for as a child, to caring for intimate others, culminating in caring about strangers in need. However, caring-about should not *replace* caring-for. It ideally builds on it and extents care to more and more people. Without its connection to caring-for, caring-about becomes an empty notion (Noddings, 2002b, p. 23). A 'morally educated' person is able to *combine* personal caring for people he/she knows with less personal, humanitarian caring or concern about people he/she only knows about (Slote, 1999). Interestingly, Noddings (2002b, p. 22) calls this caring-about "the foundation of our sense of justice". This remark suggests that the development of care and justice are not two separate tracks, but are continuous with each other. In other words: justice can be understood as a sophisticated outgrowth of care. Noddings blames Kohlberg and other moral psychologists and philosophers for having dismissed care as being too immediate, personal, parochial or emotional. By understanding 'morality' exclusively in deontological terms, they have neglected the extent to which justice depends on care.

While Noddings hardly contributed to an empirically and conceptually sound understanding of the development of 'engrossment' and 'motivational displacement', scarce remarks on the development of care made several things clear. In particular, Noddings enables us to question two dichotomies that are also influential in other approaches to moral education. First, 'care' and 'justice' turned out not to be contradictory. A sense of justice can be seen as an extension of care, but this extension should not replace the 'core' of caring, the more natural care for intimate others. Secondly, a sharp distinction between 'self' and 'other' is difficult to maintain. We can never become morally educated without the care we received from those we depended on during our childhood, and there needs to be some concern for the self before one can care for or about others, too. Care ethics is essentially a *relational* ethics, which regards the task of moral education to help people to care for themselves *as well as* others (Noddings & Slote, 2002, p. 349).

2.4.5 Care Ethics in Schools

As Gilligan formulated a feminine perspective on moral development without paying much attention to moral education, it falls on Noddings to clarify how the care ethical ideal is to be fostered. Noddings (2002, p. 289) views the home as the primary educator and has argued for the re-orientation of social policy to this end. Her goal is not to sideline the role of schools but to recognise what the home, the primary educator, contributes to the development of young people. It means, however, that schools should, as far as possible, use the sort of educational methods that are found in the best homes. This has far-reaching consequences and takes us into the arena of informal moral education. Noddings describes four 'methods' that can be used in schools to contribute to children's moral development: modelling, dialogue, practice and confirmation.

When teachers model care, they show children through their behaviour what it means to care (Noddings, 2010, p. 147). Noddings recognises that actually caring for pupils and colleagues can be an effective way of demonstrating what caring is, but she is hesitant about role modelling as a teaching method. More in particular, she tries to distinguish her strategy from the kind of modelling advocated by Aristotelian virtue ethicists and character educationalists (see §4.2). In her view, character education recommends teachers to embody ideals of full virtue. The risk with this approach, Noddings argues, is that teachers become obsessed with the cultivation of their own virtues, or that pupils focus too much on the teacher, and not on what he/she is supposed to embody. This leads to an overemphasis of the one-caring. Noddings wants teachers to show natural caring and try to sustain the ethical ideal, also in pupils, without too much thinking. If they want to think about how to become a better moral educator, they better reflect about this outside school, when there are no pupils around. Reasoning in the classroom will distract teachers from actual caring. Being a role model "...should not overwhelm their actual caring." (Noddings, 2010, p. 147).

Although care ethics is certainly not the first to use dialogue as a means to morally educate, Noddings has an original interpretation of 'dialogue'. The care ethical dialogue primarily aims at sustaining a caring relation, at helping people to attend to each other. A dialogue will increase the participants' knowledge about what everybody involved in the dialogue is going through, what their needs are, how they see themselves and their relationships. Thus, a dialogue is not primarily *about* something and it should not necessarily result in some kind of solution. It is open-ended (Noddings, 2010, p. 147). Moreover, a genuine dialogue presupposes a reciprocal relationship between the participants that is not that obvious in most educational contexts, in which the roles of the caring-one and the ones cared-for are normally more clearly distinguished.

The third component of a care ethical approach to moral education is 'practice'. Learners should practice care primarily because it will make them better people, and not because their acts will contribute to others' well-being. In schools, teachers can create conditions so that boys and girls are encouraged to have care giving experiences, for example by having them look after smaller children, helping them to cooperate with others, or giving them small housekeeping activities (Noddings, 2002, p. 20). Schools at large can stimulate the practice of care by requiring pupils to participate in community service projects that benefit the community. In such projects, pupils are supervised by people who have an area of expertise and take responsibility for the nurturing of the ethical ideal of the children (Noddings, 1984, p. 188; 1995, p. 191). When pupils serve in a hospital or a nursing home, an experienced professional (a 'master-carer') will show them how to care, inform them about the difficulties and rewards of the work, and demonstrate the importance of caring. He will correct uncaring behaviour and reward pupils' caring behaviours, which is known as 'induction' (Noddings, 2010, pp. 147-148). 'Practicing' is acquiring a caring mentality by immersing oneself in certain experiences under the guidance or authority of a caring person.

The fourth and last strategy to educate pupils from a care ethical perspective is 'confirmation', which means to bring out the best in people (Noddings, 2002, p. 20). When a pupil has done something wrong, teachers will not assume the worst, but keep in mind that, whatever happened, there is much good in the pupil too. In addition, taking the circumstances of the immoral act into account, teachers can think of an explanation for the uncaring behaviour that leaves most of the pupil's good intentions intact. A child is 'confirmed' when the teacher attributes the best possible motive to the cared-for that is still consonant with reality (Noddings, 2008, p. 171). Care ethics hopes that the pupil will realise that it has a 'better self' that does not necessarily coincide with what he has done. So, care ethics presumes that "...there is something admirable, or at least acceptable, struggling to emerge in each person we encounter" (Noddings, 1995, p. 192). When teachers help to remind pupils of their best moments of caring, pupils can start to experience again the natural longing for a caring relationship. Noddings prefers confirmation to 'confession' or 'forgiveness', because in the case of confession, too much emphasis is put on the sin, and forgiving something too easily may not encourage somebody to improve morally. Moreover, both strategies can make it more difficult to have a real dialogue, since they place the teacher, who punishes or absolves, in a higher position.

Noddings (1984, pp. 188-201) is very clear that these four strategies for teachers are only effective if they are used in schools that are changed into caring communities. She does not believe that such communities are easy to establish, and argues that schools as they exist today will need to be 'dismantled'. The problems are diverse. Firstly, the moral climate is dominated by teachers' narrow specialisation. Noddings wants to change this by improving teacher education, teaching future teachers that education is less about the transfer of subject-related knowledge and skills and more about becoming a caring person. Secondly, there are far too many professional administrators, which she refers to as 'the enemy'. Noddings proposes to have administrators replaced by a system in which teachers take care of administrative work in turns every fourth year. Thirdly, with regard to the curriculum, she wants it to be clear how the subjects taught relate to a range of children's experiences, and to the potential application. Noddings also wants caring apprenticeships to have the same status as the regular school subjects. Fourthly, when it comes to didactics, she wants children to learn more from each other instead of from teachers and books. Fifthly, Noddings wants more respect for the multiplicity of children's talents and rejects the uniform application of standards to grade pupils. Sixthly, she endorses school rules, but only in order to have a dialogue and confirm pupils and not in order to enforce them with penalties. Seventhly, and finally, she believes that education can only produce caring people if the relationships between parents, children and teachers are good.

What has become of a care ethical approach to moral education since the early 1980s? Comparing a care ethical approach with character education and cognitive development, Slote (2010b, pp. 1401-411) concludes that "Care ethics (as such) is probably less well represented than either of these other approaches." Nevertheless, he notes that some elements of the approach have disseminated to the field of education. For example, in American schools there is now more training for 'empathy' going on than thirty years ago. Noddings (2010, p. 147) is more optimistic: she calls the care ethical approach 'a relative newcomer' that needs some more time to prove itself in educational theory and practice. Although care ethics seems to have had an effect on the ethics of nursing and healthcare, advocates and practitioners of care ethics working in different school systems seem harder to find.

2.5 Challenges to Character Education

This chapter focused on the ideas that the main proponents of values clarification, cognitive development and care ethics have about the goal of moral education, the psychological conditions that have to be met before these goals can be achieved, and the kind of education that teachers and schools can best use to achieve this goal. These three approaches were discussed to determine in which ways 'moral education' has been conceived of before moving on to a more detailed discussion of a fourth approach, character education. The overview illustrated in greater detail that moral education is a multidimensional domain, to which philosophers, psychologists and educationalists contribute. However, proponents of these approaches have not always paid equal attention to all three sub domains. For example, values clarification was developed by educationalists and was very popular with teachers in the 1970s, despite lacking a thorough psychological and philosophical foundation. Yet, cognitive development theory and an ethics of care were developed by people who had an academic interest in moral education and who later adapted their theories to fit educational practice – and not always successfully. This overview provided some perspective. It showed that the meaning of moral education is controversial and that there is a variety of approaches that all try to articulate something about our experiences about what is at stake in morality and education. This enables us now to determine what character education is and is not about, and which promises it can and cannot fulfil. A full discussion of this fourth approach is included in the next chapters, leaving this chapter to focus on the ways in which the three other approaches have criticised character education. From these critical evaluations, several challenges to virtue ethics will appear. The subsequent chapters on a virtue ethical approach to moral education will make clear whether these criticisms are sound and how virtue ethicists can respond to them.

Before formulating these criticisms and challenges, the main findings of this chapter will be summarised. The findings will be divided into three categories. With regard to the goal of moral education, it was established that values clarification was an anti-authoritarian approach that rejected the traditional inculcation of values and virtues. In the rapidly changing Western societies of the 1970s, pupils were recommended to have clear values – and a 'value' would have to meet seven requirements. The method and goals of values clarification carried with it, at least implicitly, an espousal of a consistent, stable, active and reflective life. Values clarification trusted people's own rational abilities and emphasised pupils' freedom to choose the direction of their own lives. Kohlberg's cognitive developmental approach emerged as a critique of both traditional character education and relativistic values clarification. He distinguished between several levels of moral development and defended, by appealing to both empirical research and philosophical arguments, why a 'morally educated person' has to be understood as someone who can justify moral judgments by referring to universal and prescriptive principles of fairness. Gilligan showed in the early 1980s how the inclusion of women in psychological experiments would change the traditional paradigm in education. Her qualitative research made clear that moral education and development are not fully understood if our emotional involvement in caring for others is not taken into account. Gilligan's work was mainly in psychology, but Noddings worked out an *ethic* of care and a matching approach to moral education. In her view, the goal of moral education is to maintain and enhance caring relationships between the 'cared-for' and the 'one-caring'. Ideally, our care for loved-ones would be extended to include caring about fellow-citizens and strangers.

The second category of findings contains ideas about the developmental process that people go through as they progress towards the goal of moral education. Proponents of values clarification treat moral development as the development from confused to consistent values, but they had disappointingly little to say about the psychology and development of values. We consulted Festinger's theory of cognitive dissonance to explain how teachers can help to make children's beliefs more consistent. To Kohlberg, one develops morally by gaining access to a specific kind of reasons with which one can justify one's choices from an impartial point of view. Inspired by Piaget's research about cognitive development, Kohlberg argued that one would only reach this 'principled' or 'post-conventional' level after passing through an invariant sequence of qualitatively different stages. Care ethics brought about a serious reworking of this notion of moral development. In order to obtain a broader, more realistic picture of moral agency, Gilligan and Noddings assigned a much more marginal role to reason than Piaget or Kohlberg. Inspired by Hume, Nodding elaborated on the importance of being able to sympathise with or be 'engrossed' by others.

Thirdly, the three approaches have different ideas about the strategies that schools can employ best to help pupils become morally educated. Values clarification produced a large number of handbooks, each filled with hundreds of classroom exercises. These are basically variations of the same sequence: teachers ask pupils to pay attention to an everyday, value-related issue with which they have personal experience, they invite pupils to express their opinions by stressing that all contributions are accepted, and encourage pupils to reflect further on the thought, evaluations and actions associated with the values that they disclosed. Cognitive development shares with values clarification that teachers' responses have to be clarifying. However, what has to be clarified is not their values, but their level of *moral reasoning*. Contrary to values clarification, cognitive development focused– at least initially – on group discussions of hypothetical dilemmas. As Kohlberg became involved in the implementation of his approach, he realised that individuals' moral reasoning can only fully develop when some social conditions are met. He recommended to change schools into 'just communities' and identified parts of the curriculum that teachers could seize to bring moral issues to pupils' attention. Finally, Noddings favoured an informal, almost home-like approach to moral education. She advised teachers to use the rather informal methods of modelling caring behaviour, creating opportunities for dialogue,

Chapter 2

helping pupils' to practice caring behaviour, and bringing the best out of pupils through conformation. In order to change schools into caring communities, the current system of thinking about the curriculum, didactics, grading and teacher education would have to be 'dismantled'.

What do values clarification, cognitive development and care ethics have to say about character education? 'Character education' was very influential in American history until the 1930s. In the 1960s, values clarification rapidly became an attractive alternative to the traditional inculcation of virtues and values. It blamed character education for being authoritarian and moralistic, unwarrantedly imposing predetermined values upon individuals. Moreover, proponents of values clarification argued that inculcating values would not be effective, and forcing children to value certain things would only be counterproductive. While values clarification was initially very harsh on character education, this attitude changed when its proponents started to reflect on the values that values clarification presupposed. Kirschenbaum, one of its main advocates, became an active member in the new character education movement in the 1990s. In private conversations during the spring of 2012, he admitted that values clarification had been too critical of character education, since it had actually taken the cultivation of children's character for granted. Another reason why values clarification could not be unambiguously critical towards character education is that the meaning of a 'value' ended up being surprisingly close to what Aristotelians take to be a 'virtue'. When one examines the seven requirements that a value should meet, these 'values' turned out to be a kind of settled dispositions, which entail emotional involvement and deliberation, and which help to make choices that enable someone to lead an meaningful, consistent and integrated life.

While Kohlberg rejected values clarification wholeheartedly, he shared their critical attitude towards character education, albeit for different reasons. His first and most famous criticism of character education is that every teacher can have his/her own 'bag of virtues', which makes it somewhat arbitrary which virtues pupils are being exposed to. Moral education would depend on the character traits that teachers happen to have. With the memories of Nazi indoctrination still in mind, Kohlberg was worried that the character traits that teachers model would not be virtues at all. Secondly, Kohlberg noticed that even if schools manage to identify a number of virtues that all teachers subscribe to, there would still remain much disagreement about the meaning of these virtues. Thirdly, Kohlberg argued that character traits are not stable enough. This can mean two things. As a psychologists, Kohlberg may have had the pessimistic results from the *Character Education Inquiry* in mind. Character traits would be too fickle to base morality on, since they would not lead to consistent moral behaviour in all kinds of different situations. While we may have doubts about the relation between reasoning and moral action, Kohlberg favoured the cultivation of capacities for principled reflection on moral issues. His remark about the instability of character traits can also be motivated by methodological considerations. One important reason why Kohlberg decided to measure children's judgments about hypothetical dilemma's instead of observing virtuous behaviour in real situations was that it is very difficult to measure the influence of teachers' interventions on pupils' virtue development.

Although Kohlberg has become known for the phrase that character education is just a 'bag of virtues', there are also places in his work where he is much more sympathetic towards it. For example, Kohlberg (1981, p. xiii) distinguished between deontological and teleological theories of ethics, and admitted that his own approach is only concerned with deontological issues concerning justice, respect, rights and duties, neglecting moral issues about what ends people pursue. Moreover, he admits that "...moral education as character education for a set of virtues never gets a complete fair hearing in this volume." (Kohlberg, 1981, p. 2). In these passages, Kohlberg acknowledges that his cognitive development theory does not tell the whole story about the goal, development and education of morality. While he remains very critical of the idea that moral education is used as a means to indoctrinate children, he conceives of the possibility that character education can be a critical practice (Kohlberg, 1981, p. 2). He mentions Richard S. Peters, the founding father of the British philosophy of education, as someone who has shown that moral education has to stimulate the development of both virtue and moral reasoning. In Peters' view, moral education is a two-phase process, consisting of the inculcation of a set of virtues and stimulating reflection through free moral discussion. Peters (1966, p. 314) is known for his claim that "the palace of reason has to be entered by the courtyard of habit". While this metaphor makes clear that moral habits are a necessary step in moral development, it continues to emphasise the supremacy of reason. While we may doubt whether this view on the relationship between moral virtues and our rational capacities is strictly Aristotelian, it suggests that Kohlberg believed that it is possible to justify character education in such a way that his relativism objection can be refuted. Chapter 5 examines whether proponents of virtue ethical approaches to moral education can make sense of the idea that virtues have more objective moral worth.

Of the three approaches discussed, care ethics is most sympathetic towards character education. It will become apparent that proponents of a virtue ethical approach to moral education share care ethicists' optimistic view of human nature. They both assume that human beings naturally strive for goodness, and that our moral attitudes are continuous with this longing. Care ethicists and virtue ethicists also emphasise that moral reasoning does not have the central role that cognitive development theory attributes to it. While there are disagreements about whether all or just some emotions are morally relevant, they agree that emotions are the motivating forces that help people to act on their commitments. Noddings even flirted with the idea that care should be understood in a virtue sense, as a quality of agents (Noddings & Slote, 2002, p. 347). In the end, however, she treats caring primarily as a quality of relations, to which both a caring-one and a cared-for have to contribute. Noddings has warned that if we understand care virtue ethically, we run the risk of cultivating our inner life at the expense of caring for others. Although there are ways for virtue ethicists to refute this so-called 'egoism objection' (Hursthouse, 2007), Noddings has a point. Even if virtue ethicists argue that the cultivation of one's own virtues will often contribute to other people's well-being, there is no guarantee that it will. While Kohlberg and (to a lesser extent) Noddings mention the universal moral obligation to care or be just, Aristotelians are more particularistic, since they emphasises the good life of a human being, friends and the community he/she lives in. With regard to the education of virtue in schools, Noddings & Slote (2002) and Slote (2010b) admit that character education is 'back in favour', but worry about the lack of empirical support for the strategies that character education promotes, such as role modelling. In addition, they argue that character education is now more problematic than it was back in the early twentieth century, because the pluralistic nature of society makes it difficult to identify which character traits should be educated in (public) schools.

In short, the three approaches to moral education discussed in this chapter consider character education to be an approach that inculcates certain character traits that are considered to be morally significant by a particular community or society. By looking at the criticism directed at this kind of moral education, a number of major objections stand out. Firstly, there are reservations about the *concept of virtue*. Are virtues really the qualities that help us to *act* virtuously in all kinds of circumstances? Has the *Character Education Inquiry* not showed that people's behaviour cannot typically be explained in terms of virtues? Moreover, what is the relationship between cultivating one's own virtues, and other people's well-being? Are virtues not egoistic? If these worries are to be removed, it will have to be made clear how virtue and virtuous action are related. Most of these issues will be addressed in Chapter 3.

Secondly, even when it is clear what a virtue is and what virtues we have in mind, it remains controversial whether 'being virtuous' is really identical with being 'morally educated'. According to values clarification, character education achieves exactly the opposite of what moral education is about, and according to cognitive development, character education can only be a first phase of a process that has to lead to autonomy. Is educating pupils for virtue moralistic? Does it impose things on children, and if so, is this imposition justified? What is the place of reason in the development of moral virtue? Is or can character education be a critical practice? What it means to 'educate' virtues will be subject of Chapter 4.

A third issue is the question which virtues should be taught, in particular in pluralistic societies in which there would be no consensus about what a good life consists of. Do different people not have different ideas about what counts as a virtue? Can they ever reach an agreement as to the meaning of virtues? It seems that the question of what counts as a virtue can only be answered by depending on the preferences of teachers or the conventions of a community or society. Are virtues then, in the end, not relativistic? These questions make clear that virtue ethicists will have to say something about the sense in which virtues can be seen as objective moral qualities. The moral justification of an education in the virtues is dealt with in Chapter 5.

Finally, the three approaches have some specific empirical concerns about character education. Kohlberg doubts whether character traits are stable dispositions, and whether it is not too difficult to study them psychologically. Moreover, values clarification and care ethics have criticised character education for not being effective. Is there, e.g. any evidence that role modelling stimulates moral development? In this thesis, two sections are explicitly dedicated to issues about which social sciences have something to say too. In §3.3, the consequences of the 'situationism debate' for a virtue ethical approach to moral education will be discussed, and in §4.2, the focus is on how psychologists like Albert Bandura can contribute to a better understanding of role modelling. In the next three chapters, it will become clearer whether Aristotelian virtue ethicist are able to defend a theoretically sound and useful approach to moral education in schools.

Chapter 3
Virtue Psychology and Development

1.1   Introduction

Chapter 2 discussed the three most important twentieth-century approaches to moral education: cognitive development, values clarification and care ethics. Before examining the moral, developmental and educational aspects of a fourth approach – character education – in the next three chapters, a summary of the recent history of moral education will make clear why this Aristotelian approach to moral education emerged in the early 1990s. This enables the reader who is only interested in virtue ethics to skip Chapter 2.

At the end of the 1950s, two publications appeared that were to be a major influence on the development of what is now known as 'character education'. The first publication was Kohlberg's PhD thesis (1958), in which he published the results of his empirical research on the moral development of boys aged 11 to 16. In line with these results, he constructed a normative theory about the goal of moral development, which he conceived of as an autonomous person who can justify moral judgments from an impartial point of view. His 'cognitive development approach' remained very influential until the 1990s, when it had eventually attracted so much criticism that it could not integrate this criticism any more without becoming incoherent. One of the first to systematically criticise Kohlberg's approach was his colleague Gilligan (1982), who blamed him for not having included girls in his experiments. Consequently, Kohlberg allegedly had a very one-sided view of moral development and moral education: he had reduced 'morality' to 'justice', thereby neglecting other aspects of morality, such as 'care'.

The exact relation between 'justice' and 'care' became a much debated topic in the 1980s and 1990s. Whereas some regarded the two to be mutually exclusive, many others believed them to be complementary (Flanagan & Jackson, 1987; Blum, 1988; Hekman, 1995; Rumsey, 1997). This, however, raised the question of *how* care and justice as goals of moral development, and cognitions and emotions as elements of a moral psychology, are to be combined. While character education had completely vanished before, it re-emerged as a prominent approach at the end of the 20th century through the writings of Nucci (1989), Lickona (1992), Ryan & Lickona (1992), Kilpatrick (1993) and others. They went some distance towards offering a solution to the difficult relationship between cognitive developmentalists and care ethicists. Inspired by Aristotle's virtue ethics, they understood 'moral education' as the formation of somebody's character, which accommodates a whole range of virtues and in which cognitions and emotions ideally form a unity. However, the interest of these American character educators was largely practical and their books are filled with countless classroom exercises. In their wake, a large number of commercial character education programmes and websites emerged, especially in the United States.

The theoretical foundation of character education was supplied by a number of philosophers who were inspired by a second influential publication that appeared at the end of the 1950s. In an influential essay, Elizabeth Anscombe (1958, p. 6) argued against ethical theories with 'duty' and 'obligation' as their core concepts, because these notions would only have meaning when one presupposes the existence of a divine law. She argued that in a secular age, the concept of 'obligation' has lost its roots, and that deontology would better be replaced by an ethics based on naturalistic notions of 'character', 'virtue' and 'happiness'. Actions should be regarded morally good because they contribute to somebody's happiness as a human being, and not because they are conducted out of a sense of duty. Anscombe warned that there was still much confusion about the meaning of the main ingredients of a naturalistic ethic. She recommended postponing normative ethics until an adequate philosophy of psychology would have scrutinised these notions.

A large number of philosophers took Anscombe's call to revive Aristotle's moral philosophy seriously. According to Martha Nussbaum (1999), who played an important role in this revival herself, many of these authors found a renewed inspiration in ancient Greek theories of virtue, although there are equally profound disagreements that make 'virtue ethics' a somewhat misleading category. The problem is that the notion of 'virtue' does not only play a role in ancient Greek philosophy, but also in modern theories of ethics, such as deontology and utilitarianism. In this sense, *all* ethical theories are somehow 'virtue ethical'. When referring to the project that Anscombe started, it would therefore be more precise to talk about a 'neo-Aristotelian approach to virtue ethics', instead of using the more general label 'virtue ethics'. However, since this thesis will not expound any neo-Millian or neo-Kantian accounts of virtue, 'virtue ethics' can be used as shorthand for 'neo-Aristotelian virtue ethics'.

The impulses of Kohlberg's ideas about moral psychology and education and Anscombe's reckoning of deontology met in the British philosopher of education David Carr (1991), who was the first in the Anglo-Saxon world to construct an Aristotelian alternative to Kohlberg's cognitive developmental approach.[11] Carr criticised Kohlberg, who was himself a psychologist, for understanding moral education as a vehicle for helping people to develop rational capacities with which they could decide for themselves how they should live. As long as goals are freely and rationally chosen and others' freedom of choice is not infringed upon there could be no good reason to criticise these goals. Carr (1999) accused Kohlberg of not providing people with clues about which kind of life is worth living, and as an antidote to this 'agnostic neutrality', he devoted himself to the project of showing that there are objectively worthwhile goals to be strived after in education, i.e. the Aristotelian virtues.

Before we examine how teachers can contribute to the education of children's virtues in schools (Chapter 4) or why it is desirable to help them to acquire virtues (Chapter 5), this chapter will focus on the question of what it means to become virtuous. In order to answer this question, several sub questions will have to be addressed. In §3.2, the concept of a 'virtue' and a number of virtues will be examined by expounding Aristotle's moral psychology. Although the use of the term 'virtue' may sound odd because we do not often use it in daily life, we talk and think in terms of virtues all the time, e.g. when we say of others that they are friendly, honest or reliable. In §3.3, focus is on the central claim of the so-called 'situationists', a group of philosophers who have drawn on social psychology to show that the Aristotelian notions of virtue and practical wisdom are empirically unsound and should be either adjusted or abandoned. My argument is that these situationists presuppose a very problematic notion of 'psychological realism' and that their critique is, therefore, not as devastating as is often imagined. This is followed by a positive account of how people can acquire virtues in §3.4. In order to understand how people, especially children, can develop morally, several levels of moral development will be distinguished, each involving a specific relationship between desires and practical reason. The question of what this means to the ways in which teachers can stimulate children's moral development is the subject of Chapter 4.

The psychology and development of virtue deserve our attention for several reasons. Firstly, Aristotle's ethics cannot simply be applied to contemporary issues of moral development. As it is not beyond criticism, it is precisely in the attempt to sketch a virtue ethical alternative to other approaches that we *evaluate* the contribution that virtue ethics can make to our understanding of moral development. Since Aristotle's ethical works do not contain a clear-cut moral development model, it is still an open question whether a developmental model can be derived from them that is worth being called 'Aristotelian'. It matters to

---

11   Others would follow, such as Jan Steutel (1997, 1998, with David Carr, 1999; with Ben Spiecker, 2004) and Kristján Kristjánsson (2002, 2006b, 2007, 2010b).

press virtue ethics on this point, because Aristotle believed that ethics, despite being a theoretical enterprise, has a practical aim. An investigation into the nature of virtue is not something we only do for the sake of knowing what good is, but in order to become good; to acquire virtue and actually lead a meaningful life. Now, if helping people to 'become good' is the purpose of moral philosophy, our inquiries would not be complete without an account of what people go through while they try to lead good lives, and what factors can stimulate or hamper this development. Virtue ethics can stand out by providing an account of how children can become the kind of virtuous adults that many contemporary ethical theories take for granted (Annas, 2011, p. 21).

Secondly, a virtue ethical model of moral development can spur psychologists on to do more and better empirical research. Although many psychologists are reluctant to commit themselves explicitly to an evaluative perspective because they believe that they are studying human behaviour objectively, they implicitly promote all kinds of goods anyway, such as autonomy, efficacy or subjective well-being (Fowers, 2012, Kristjánsson, 2011). In the domain in which the psychology of moral development is studied, Kohlberg's impressive empirical research has been the dominant paradigm during the second half of the twentieth century. A virtue ethical perspective could provide psychologists with an alternative and potentially richer, account of morality and its development. It can show how the "...study of moral development might look after it breaks out of its post-Kantian confines" (Campbell & Christopher, 1996, p. 12). While the previously-discussed approaches understand moral development exclusively in terms of moral reasoning (Kohlberg) or moral affects (care ethics), it is not clear how the two are related. Even though some kind of division between the cognitive and affective aspects of moral development is useful for analytical purposes, our daily actions are always a blend of moral thought, feeling and action. Virtue ethics would do a great job if it proposes a more affective account of moral reasoning and a more rational account of our moral affects. Moreover, it would be interesting to see in more detail how the interaction between the two elements changes as someone morally matures.

Thirdly, contemporary character education approaches lack a developmental perspective (Lockwood, 2009, p. 45). While character educationalists provide hundreds of recommendations that can help teachers to implement character education in schools, they do not explain what goes on in children when they develop morally or how the proposed interventions match the developmental stage children are in. Ideally, however, the psychology and education of the virtues would go hand in hand. When we know more about the elements that constitute children's moral minds, the relations between these elements and their potential development, teaching methods can be adjusted to fit the developmental phase that children are in. Even without this knowledge, many teachers will – unconsciously

– do a great job by being good role models to children. However, when teachers also know how adolescents develop and learn, they could become even better models, e.g. by not only acting virtuously, but also by explaining to pupils why they act the way they do (see Chapter 4). In addition, if a moral developmental model makes clear that many people are on the lower stages, this can stimulate educationists to develop new or better pedagogical interventions.

3.2 Aristotle's Moral Psychology

3.2.1 The Human Soul

Before investigating how to become virtuous, the basic question of what a 'virtue' is needs to be addressed. To Aristotle, a virtue is an excellence or perfection of a specific part of the human 'soul'. Therefore, we have to know more about the soul before we can understand virtue. In his famous *De Anima*, Aristotle (1957) understands the soul, its functions and its relation to the body against the background of a general theory of causation and explanation, called 'hylomorphism'. According to this doctrine, which understands sensible things as composites of matter (*hyle*) and form (*morphe*), we need to know four things when we wish to explain why a thing is the way it is. For example, if we want a full explanation of why a bronze statue is the way it is, we need to know 1) what material the statue is made of, 2) what form, structure or shape it has, 3) who is responsible for shaping the matter into its form, and 4) for which purpose the statue was created. These four explanations are also known as the material, formal, efficient and final cause. We can apprehend what these causes have to do with the soul if we understand Aristotle's analogy: the bronze of the statue is related to its shape as the human body is related to its soul. The bronze matter 'realises' a particular shape and it manifests the function of a statue, which is to honour the person being depicted. Likewise, the human body is potentially 'ensouled', but it only fully acquires a soul when it actualises the human form, i.e. when it performs the function of a human soul well.

Now, what is a typical human soul? This can be made clear by distinguishing between different 'faculties' or 'capacities', which are the manifestations of different activities of the soul. The broadest capacity, which is shared by all natural living organisms, is nutrition and growth. On top of that, animals have the ability to perceive and to move. Closely related to this capacity is the capacity of 'appetites' and 'desires', which cannot occur without the perceptual faculty. Finally, among natural organisms only humans have a 'mind', i.e. the capacity to reason. Aristotle argues that these three kinds of souls – nutritive, perceptual-appetitive, and intellectual – form a hierarchy, in which the higher souls include the lower ones. This means that the human soul has a rational element, but also an irrational element which is shared with the animals. The rational element (*logos*) exists partly in a pure form, called 'theoretical reason', and is partly mixed with the desires that arise from the irrational element. The 'mixed' kind of rationality is called 'practical reason'.

How do we get from this outline of the human soul to an account of the Aristotelian virtues? Aristotle's ethics is all about the question of how one can lead a 'good' life, which the ancient Greeks called *eudaimonia*. In English, it is often translated as 'happiness', 'flourishing' or 'well-being'. While the meaning of the concept of *eudaimonia* will be discussed in Chapter 5, it is crucial to notice that *eudaimonia* involves the active exercise of the functions of the human soul just mentioned, in conformity with excellence or virtue. In other words, one can become *eudaimōn* through 'optimal self-realisation', where this 'self' is not understood as an individual self, but as what is characteristically human, i.e. our rationality. As the rational part of the soul has two parts, its excellences or virtues are differentiated accordingly. The excellences of the purely rational part are called the 'intellectual virtues' (or 'virtues of thought'), such as speculative wisdom and practical wisdom. The excellences of the mixed part of the rational part of the soul are called 'virtues of character' (or 'moral virtues'), such as justice, courage, temperance, generosity and friendliness. The function of these latter virtues is to produce actions, emotions and perceptions that have a human mark.

3.2.2 Moral Virtue

When contemporary people, read or hear about *moral* virtue, they immediately place 'virtue' in an existing network of moral meanings that are alien to Aristotle. Furthermore, to read Aristotle's ideas about virtue in light of a modern understanding of morality can easily lead to misinterpreting and undervaluing his ideas about virtue. Two of these potential misunderstandings will be addressed in this section, but more of them will appear in this chapter, e.g. in a discussion of the doctrine of the mean and the relationship between reason and emotion.

To many people, both laymen and philosophers, 'morality' has to do with the ways in which we treat other people. When we praise a child because he did something morally good, this is probably because he helped somebody else, and when a child is blamed for immoral behaviour, it is likely to have something to do with the pain he caused others. If we take this other-regarding concept of morality as a point of departure, the moral virtues just mentioned, such as justice, courage or generosity are likely to be seen as qualities that enable people to contribute to other people's well-being. However, to Aristotle 'morality' is not only about the consequences our actions have on other people. His ethics is primarily concerned with helping people to live their *own lives* in such a way that they can be called good. Aristotle recommends people to arrange their lives so that they suit the rational nature of human beings by acquiring, cultivating and exercising certain excellences, some of which are practical, others more theoretical. By taking a strict distinction between altruism and egoism for granted, it is easy to see why virtue ethics has been criticised for being self-centred. On this account, advising people to cultivate their own humanity will automatically be at the expense of other people's well-being. Admittedly, virtue ethics is more concerned with the good life of one's friends and community than with universal moral duties to all our fellow human beings in virtue of their rationality. Yet realising one's own human potential does not exclude the promotion of other people's well-being. For example, when we acquire the virtue of generosity, this will simultaneously alleviate other people's needs. Also, displaying courage on the battlefield will not only enable a soldier to deal excellently with his emotion of fear, but also increase the chance that his army wins the battle, enabling a country to establish peace (Sherman, 1989, p. 176).

Another possible misunderstanding is the identification of the still formal notion of 'virtue' with a *particular* virtue catalogue, in which modesty, chastity, obedience, decency, patience or humility appear. If we let the association with Christian values or Victorian manners dominate our understanding of the Aristotelian notion of virtue, many people will not find thinking about their lives in terms of virtue very attractive. It should therefore be pointed out that the extension of the original Greek meaning of 'virtue' goes beyond the rather dull list of virtues just mentioned. The Greek word for virtue is *arete*, which can also be translated as 'excellence'. It does not only apply to human beings, but to everything that has a function and can exercise this function well. For example, a knife is 'excellent' if it is the kind of knife that someone would choose who wanted a knife for the purpose of which knives are characteristically wanted, i.e. to cut. In short, we could say that the knife's 'virtue' is its *sharpness*.

Moral virtue refers to the excellent ways in which humans deal with emotions in a number of spheres of human experience. These spheres amount to the cardinal or core humans virtues such as practical wisdom, justice, temperance and courage. Throughout the book, 'moral virtue' and 'virtues of character' are used interchangeably to denote the excellent cultivations of our emotions. Cicero is indirectly responsible for the English concept of 'virtue' (and e.g. the French *vertu* and Spanish *virtud*). In the first century BC, he translated the Greek *arete* as *virtus* in Latin. It had the connotation of valour, courage, worth and (masculine) strength; a meaning that we still recognise in the names of Italian basketball teams, such as *Virtus Roma* or *Virtus Bologna*. Likewise, we also recognise something of these Greek roots when we say that somebody is a 'virtuoso' musician, praising him for his masterly ability, technique or personal style. While we still think of people in terms of virtues or excellences in all kinds of domains, we seem to have limited the use of explicit virtue-language to people with outstanding abilities in the arts, more particularly in music.

Prior to an evaluation of whether situationists are right in claiming that Aristotle's moral psychology is empirically problematic, the Aristotelian concept of virtue calls for more attention. Our exploration in this chapter will be guided by Aristotle's own definition of a virtue. It is a "...settled disposition of the mind determining the choice of actions and emotions, consisting essentially in the observance of the mean relative to us, this being determined by principle, that is, as the prudent man would determine it" (*NE* 1107a15). Four parts of this definition will be discussed subsequently. Firstly, the idea that virtues are settled dispositions; secondly, that these dispositions determine the choice of actions and emotions; thirdly, that good choices consist in the observance of a mean, a mean relative to us; and fourthly, that the mean can be found by someone with practical wisdom.

3.2.3 Character Traits

The question 'What is a virtue?' is somewhat confusing because it can either mean 'Which character traits are virtues?' or 'Which kind of psychological phenomenon is a virtue?'. The first question requires a substantial answer that makes clear how certain virtues are intrinsically related to a good life. For instance, we can imagine people arguing over the question whether 'hope' or 'responsibility' count as virtues, or what the virtue of 'justice' requires in a particular situation. The second question can be answered by giving what Aristotle calls a 'formal' definition of virtue. It means that we describe a virtue as part of a comprehensive theory of human action, and explain how it relates e.g. to knowledge, emotions and actions. The discipline that can be of help in answering this second question is the philosophy of mind and action, which can be complemented, if available, with results from psychological research. The distinction between a formal and substantial definition of a virtue makes clear that our attempt to describe virtues in terms of character traits or dispositions does not yet tell us which virtues are desirable to possess.

Although a virtuous person feels and acts in certain ways, a virtue *is* neither an action nor an emotion. Aristotle calls it a *hexis*, a 'disposition', 'habit', 'or 'character trait' – something in virtue of which we are well or ill disposed in respect of certain emotions and actions. When I become angry because somebody has damaged my good name, this is just an 'occurring' or 'episodic' emotion. However, dealing with the emotion of anger in many instances over a longer period of time can gradually turn me into a certain kind of person. This is the 'dispositional' type of anger. For example, imagine Michael, a headmaster who is not able to reflect well on his achievements. He believes that he has excellent leadership skills and demands that his colleagues treat him with respect, but they consider him to be an arrogant fellow who thinks himself worthy of too much. Michael's lack of self-knowledge makes him increasingly angry with those who correct him when he makes a mistake. When Michael does not adjust his self-concept over time to fit the perceptions that other people have of his achievements, he can become an irascible person, inflamed with rage as soon as his reputation seems to be at stake. However, if Michael comes to know his own strengths and weaknesses, and if he knows whose opinion he should care about and whose not, he could learn to adopt a much milder attitude towards anger. When Michael manages to acquire the virtuous emotional disposition of mildness, he can still be angry when there are situations that call for anger, but as a mild person, he will know what the most appropriate way is to deal with it, taking the circumstances into account. Irascibility and mildness are two different dispositions towards anger, the former being vicious, the latter virtuous. Aristotle also discussed a second vicious disposition towards anger: spiritlessness. The idea that a virtue is a mean between *two* vices, the so-called 'doctrine of the mean', will be discussed later.

While we often say that somebody 'has' a virtue, just as we say that we can 'have' a skill, somebody with a virtue *is* a certain sort of person who has a complex mindset and leads a particular kind of life. A virtue involves feeling certain emotions at certain times, making certain judgments, acting for certain reasons and in a particular manner (Annas, 2011, p. 19). Moreover, it includes having certain perceptions, interests and expectations. This has far-reaching consequences. An honest person, e.g:

> "...chooses, where possible to work with honest people, to have honest friends, to bring up her children to be honest. She disapproves of, dislikes, deplores dishonesty, is not amused by certain tales of chicanery, despises or pities those who succeed by dishonest means rather than thinking they have been clever, is unsurprised, or pleased (as appropriate) when honesty triumphs, is shocked or distressed when those near and dear to her do what is dishonest and so on." (Hursthouse, 2007).

This list makes it clear that when somebody has acquired a virtue such as honesty, it will be well-entrenched in him, or, to put it differently, it is a *deep* feature of the person (Annas, 2011, p. 9).

Psychologists have often operationalised a 'disposition' as a behavioural tendency, and some philosophers too have understood virtues as "long-term stable dispositions to act in distinctive ways" (Harman, 1999, p. 317). The obvious advantage of understanding virtue in this manner is that it enables social psychologists to say something about virtue by studying overt behaviour. For example, they have designed experiments in which situations are manipulated to find out under which conditions people help or hurt others. Although psychologists can contribute to a better understanding of virtue ethics and character education, studying virtue in terms of behaviour is problematic when psychologists conclude that people are not typically virtuous when the majority of the subjects does not show virtuous behaviour in experimental settings. As psychologists often *presuppose* that virtue is identical with virtuous behaviour, it is impossible for them to see that less overt factors also matter when we want to distinguish between more and less virtuous people.

What are these 'less overt factors'? Imagine a girl, who looks like she has just experienced something terrible, begs for money for a bus fare home.[12] Person A is in a bad mood but acts out of principle, person B feels compassion and helps with a warm glow of pleasure, and person C gives because he likes to be seen as a generous person. In this situation, the three people do the 'same' thing, i.e. they give the girl some money. If they were to help across a whole range of situations in which the virtue of kindness or generosity is required, the three would all have a behavioural tendency, or a habit of action – and a virtuous one indeed. However, shifting our attention from the act (giving or not) to what goes on in these agents, some notable differences in terms of their emotions and reasons for acting become clear. Person B feels compassion with the girl, and experiences pleasure when giving because he knows he is doing the right thing. Person B is not 'virtuous' but 'self-controlled', since he had to convince himself that his bad mood was not allowed to interfere with his moral obligations (see also §3.4). True, B can be praised because he managed to control himself, but A is even more praiseworthy as he even managed to give without any preceding internal struggle. Finally, person C knows that giving is virtuous in this situation, but he doesn't give *because* it is the virtuous thing to do. Unlike A, he does not enjoy true virtue itself; he is after social recognition or fame and uses virtue instrumentally. If there were no other people around, he would not give.

Focusing on the agents' emotions and reasons is not only psychologically interesting, in the sense that it helps us understand why A, B and C act the way they do; it also matters from a *moral* point of view, in the sense that they are relevant if we want to evaluate their traits of character. Person A is more virtuous than the self-controlled B, and B is morally more developed than C, who is only instrumentally interested in virtue. This example makes clear that when we want to know whether a person deserves praise or blame not only people's overt action, but also the more 'internal' processes prior to the action need to be taken into account.

3.2.4 Emotions and Actions

It may be clear now that the way in which someone deals over time with frequently experienced emotions such as anger determines whether he becomes mild, irascible or spiritless. In turn, once someone has acquired a certain disposition, he will perform certain actions and feel certain emotions in the relevant circumstances. However, some things are still unclear. If virtues are complex emotional dispositions, we face the question *which* emotions can become virtuous (or vicious) dispositions. Which emotions are morally relevant? We saw that mildness of temper is the virtue that we need in order to deal with the

---

12 The example is adapted from Kristjánsson (2010b), pp. 139-140.

emotion of anger, and that courage is a dispositional version of fear. But what about sadness, surprise, disappointment or disgust? Do they have dispositional version too? And why would they (not)? According to James Urmson (1980), there are no 'morally expendable emotions' to Aristotle. If he is right about this, it means that there are no emotions which ideally, from a moral point of view, can be eradicated (Kristjánsson, 2007, p. 49). This position has prompted criticism that it does not make sense to experience negative emotions. How could anger, fear or shame ever be *good*? Would a life without them not be significantly better?

Kristjánsson (2007) has discussed the concept of 'negative emotions' at length and concludes that especially psychologists use it to refer to *painful* emotions, i.e. emotions that include a painful feeling. But is feeling pain necessarily something negative? For instance, the emotion of emulation (*zelos*), which will be discussed in more detail in §4.2. It involves the feeling of pain when you realise that you lack the moral qualities that somebody else has. While this is surely a 'painful' feeling, it is nevertheless an emotion that people better have than not have, because it contributes to their development towards full virtue. Obviously, being fully virtuous and not having this emotion anymore is the highest achievement, but to people who are not on that level yet, feeling *zelos* makes clear that they are making progress. What Aristotle or contemporary Aristotelians have to do in order to substantiate the claim that *all* emotions are morally relevant is to show for each and every emotion why it is an important component of a human life that is worth being called 'good'. Alternatively, they could try to show that people who eliminate or appease certain emotions lead a less 'happy' life than people who accept these emotions and try to experience them properly, according to the 'doctrine of the mean' (see §3.2.5).

Even when there are no emotions that cannot be shaped into virtuous dispositions, one still needs to answer the question of what an emotion *is*. Otherwise, we still do not know how to distinguish emotions from feelings, desires, cognitions and actions. According to Kristjánsson's broadly Aristotelian theory of emotions, emotions involve *all* of these things: they consist of cognitions and feelings, but include desires and behavioural patterns too. This view excludes several rival emotion theories that focus exclusively on only one or two of these elements, such as Kohlberg's purely cognitive approach, Hume's sentimentalism and Skinner's behaviourism. In Kristjánsson's view, these theories have a grain of truth in them, but none of them captures the complex nature of an emotion completely. One example makes clear how cognitions, feelings, desires and behaviour can be captured in a single concept of an emotion (see Sanderse, 2011).

Imagine, living in an apartment building where new neighbours have recently moved in. They turn out to have the habit of playing very loud music at night. It is such a nuisance that you cannot sleep, and after a couple of days, you ring their door bell to ask them politely whether they can turn down the volume. Your neighbour claims not to know what you are talking about and he complains that it is actually you who causes them nuisance by not respecting their privacy. He slams the door right in your face, and the noise continues, and when you meet the couple in the hallway the day after, they call you names. Imagine how you become angry with them. This implies, first of all, that you have the belief that somebody has belittled you, for instance by saying or doing something humiliating, tormenting or insulting. In addition, you will assume that the person you are angry with is responsible for this belittlement. Secondly, the belief that you have been belittled will lead to the desire to take revenge. Moreover, there is a desire not to be belittled in the first place. Without this antecedent desire, you would not even become angry at the neighbour, since you simply would not care. Thirdly, you will experience a painful feeling, caused by the frustrated desire not to be humiliated. However, you will also feel pleasure at the prospect of taking revenge. Fourthly, you might start to show aggressive behaviour towards the neighbour, e.g. by hammering on the wall when the noise is bad. However, we have to be careful not to identify a typical behavioural pattern that fits anger, because people might just as well remain completely stoic, become sullen, or react with humour.

Aristotle describes a virtue as a 'settled disposition of the mind determining the choice of actions *and* emotion', so it seems that we have to distinguish between two kinds of dispositions: habits of action and habits of emotion. For example, courage would be the virtue to deal with (the emotion of) fear, while the object of generosity is (the act of) giving and receiving money, just as justice has to do with (the act of) distributing limited resources. However, as illustrated above, the concept of an 'emotion' *includes* a behavioural component, any strict distinction between the two corresponding dispositions is not useful. Even though it is not always possible to link virtues to a single emotion, as in the case of the anger-mildness, pleasure-temperance, and fear-courage, the so-called 'habits of action' might involve a compound of emotions.

An interesting case in this regard is the virtue of distributive justice. While it is often understood in a Rawlsian way as a quality of social institutions, it can be understood as a personal and emotional virtue, too (Kristjánsson, 2006b). The Aristotelian notion of *nemesis* disposes one to feel pain at someone's (good or bad) fortune if it is undeserved, and to feel pleasure when this fortune is deserved. For example, a painful feeling at somebody's undeserved good fortune is called 'indignation', while a painful feeling at somebody's undeserved bad fortune is known as 'compassion'. The pleasurable feeling at somebody's deserved good fortune is 'gratulation', and the pleasurable feeling at somebody's deserved bad fortune is 'satisfied indignation' (Kristjánsson, 2006b, p. 100). This account of the emotions underlying the virtue of justice makes clear that justice is a habit of action because it deals with the distribution of limited resources, but it presupposes the experience of all kinds of emotions based on concerns about merit, depending on the exact circumstances. 'Habits of action' turn out to be shorthand for complex 'habits of emotion' in which more emotions are involved.

3.2.5 The Observance of the Mean

So far, we have described virtues as 'settled dispositions that determine the choice of actions and emotions'. However, this definition does not rule out vices such as irascibility, dishonesty and cowardice. The third part of Aristotle's definition of a virtue helps to distinguish between actions and emotions that are morally praiseworthy and those that are not. For the virtuous person, the choice of certain actions and emotion consists in the observance of a mean. In other words, a virtue is an intermediate condition between two vicious states, one involving excess, and the other deficiency. Aristotle does not ground this criterion, but his explanation makes it clear that he understands the 'health of the soul' in analogy with bodily health. Just as strength is destroyed by too much and too little exercise, and health is destroyed by too much and by too little food and drink, the state of a healthy soul lies between extremes of deficiency and excess. Courage can degenerate into cowardice, but also in the opposite vice, rashness. While the coward runs away from every danger and never endures anything, the rash person fears nothing and encounters everything. This model of virtue as a means between two vices does not only apply to courage, but in principle to every moral virtue (see Table 2 below).[13]

Table 2: Aristotelian moral virtues as discussed in the Nicomachean Ethics (Book II)[14]

Virtue	Sphere of human experience	Deficiency	Excess
Courage	Fear of important damages	Cowardice	Rashness
Temperance	Bodily appetites and their pleasures	Insensibility	Intemperance
Generosity	Giving and getting small amounts of money	Prodigality	Wastefulness
Magnificence	Giving and getting large amounts of money	Tastelessness	Vulgarity
Magnanimity	Attitude with respect to honour and one's own worth	Pusillanimity	Vanity
Mildness	Anger towards slights	Spiritlessness	Irascibility
Right ambition	Attitude towards one's aspirations	Under-ambitiousness	Over-ambitiousness
Truthfulness	Truthfulness (about oneself) in speech and behaviour	Self-deprecation	Boastfulness
Wit	Pleasantness in social amusement	Boorishness	Buffoonery
Friendliness	General pleasantness in life	Quarrelsomeness	Obsequiousness
Justice	Distribution of limited resources	Injustice	Injustice

13 For extensive descriptions of individual virtues, see e.g. Curzer (2012), chapters 2 – 13. In this book, Curzer also defends the doctrine of the mean as a plausible and useful organising principle in Aristotle's ethics.
14 Adapted from Nussbaum (1993) and Kristjánsson (2007, p. 16).

Three points have to be emphasised to prevent this so-called 'doctrine of the mean' from being misunderstood. First, the idea that virtues are a 'mean' does not imply that they are an *arithmetic* mean that can be determined in the same way as we calculate that 11 is the mean of 2 and 20. For an athlete, drinking two glasses of water per day will clearly be deficient and twenty glasses might be excessive, but that does not imply that the average of eleven glasses will be the appropriate amount.

This depends on the athlete's age, weight, the sport he practices, the temperature of the place he is in and many other factors. While Aristotle agrees that we should observe a mean that is 'relative to us', it does not follow that virtue and vice are completely arbitrary. What matters to Aristotle is that we cannot find 'the' (absolute) mean in a given situation with the help of a mathematical formula. We will have to know who the 'us' is in the phrase 'relative to us', and we will need full and detailed acquaintance with the circumstances we find ourselves in. The knowledge that we need in order to find the mean is *contextual*, but not relativistic. Second, the idea that a virtue is a 'mean' does not imply that it is 'average' or 'mediocre'. 'Being virtuous' is not a mean between 'being extremely virtuous' and 'not being virtuous', but between two different variations of 'not being virtuous', which is itself the most optimal way to deal with certain spheres of human experience. Note again how our concept of virtue is derived from the Greek concept for excellence (*arete*). Third, dealing virtuously with emotions such as pleasure, anger, fear, jealously or indignation does not imply that we are not allowed to experience them in an extreme way. Experiencing and displaying emotions appropriately is not the same as always experiencing an amount of the emotions that is a quantity between zero and the highest possible level (Kraut, 2010). For example, when you find out that a friend has been spreading lies about you, it may be morally justified to be very angry with him, e.g. if that is the best way to make him realise what he has done. Whether it is appropriate to have very strong feelings completely depends on how serious the situation is.

One could object to virtue ethics that the contextual nature of virtue does not offer agents any advice about *how to act* in the complex and ever-changing circumstances of everyday life. Does the sketchy account of the good not fail to provide exact directive instructions in specific circumstances (Louden, 1984)? This perceived limitation of virtue ethics can be ameliorated by two considerations. Aristotle famously states that a theory must be in accordance with the subject-matter of which it is a theory. As ethics deals with human behaviour, which is very fickle, he concludes that "the whole account of matters of conduct must be given in outline and not precisely" (*NE* 1104a1-5). It is questionable whether what is commonly known as 'ethical theory' can provide us with something like a decision procedure for right action. Besides, it is also *undesirable* to draft a very precise moral theory. If we expect moral theories to 'tell us what to do', this might actually undermine our ability to be free and responsible moral agents. Virtue ethics respects people's freedom to use their own practical judgment about what is best in their lives.

3.2.6 Practical Wisdom

If the mean is relative to who we are the situations we are in, it becomes of the utmost importance to have self-knowledge and perceive circumstances in their *morally salient aspects*. The kind of moral knowledge that people need in order to know how virtues can be applied in the concrete circumstances of everyday life is *phronesis*, which translates as *prudentia* in Latin, and which is commonly translated in English as 'prudence' or 'practical wisdom'. I will use the latter translation because 'prudence' is often associated with a narrow and selfish concern for one's well-being. The 'practical' aspect of this kind of wisdom becomes clear in Book VI of the *Nicomachean Ethics*, in which a crucial distinction is made between the kind of rationality used in purely theoretical forms of enquiry and the rationality involved in more practical (artistic, technical, moral) pursuits (Carr, 1991, p. 57). The 'theoretical' rationality departs from observations about how things are in the world and proceeds to more general conclusions. It expresses necessary and eternal truths, such as mathematical theorems or natural laws. The 'practical' part of our rationality is used to consider things which admit of change, such as the contingencies of everyday life. We generally start to reason from a desire to change something in the world to an action that can realise this desire. The 'truth' in these matters has to do with whether these desires are good or bad. The excellences of the rational part of the human soul are called 'intellectual virtues'. While *episteme* (true knowledge), *sophia* (contemplative wisdom) and *nous* (understanding) are the perfections of the theoretical forms of knowledge, *techne* (craft knowledge) and *phronesis* (practical wisdom) are the excellences of our practical rationality.

Aristotle's view of moral knowledge differs from Plato's, who saw moral reasoning as a kind of theoretical reflection on the world of abstract and unchanging ideas, such as Goodness and Justice. In Aristotle's view, 'knowing' virtue is not a matter of theoretical or scientific discovery but of seeing the particulars in the concrete lives and actions of individuals. We always find ourselves in the midst of practical concerns, and moral reasoning is an attempt to make sense of our emotions, relationships, practices and communities, by reference to our ideas about what is conducive to well-being in such human affairs (Carr, 1991, p. 4). If *phronesis* is, over and against the Socratic identification of virtue with knowledge, a type of knowledge that emerges within a person's desires, then how are reason and desire related? We are in a better position to understand this relationship if we do not employ too strict a division between the rational and the non-rational. In its pure form, reason can be said to *have* a plan or principle (*logos*), but Aristotle argues that desires *share* in reason in the sense that they have the capacity to listen to, follow or obey it. Just as a child can learn to listen to the reason of its parents, desires can learn to listen to the principles of the intellect (*NE* 1102b29-35). In virtue of their reason-responsiveness, desires can interact with the rational part of the soul and become more deliberative.

Wielenberg (2002, p. 292) calls this the 'appropriate emotion task', which should be distinguished from the 'moral knowledge task', which refers to the process that practical reason comes to enjoy deliberating about specific objects, i.e. those things that are morally praiseworthy. Practical wisdom is not a morally neutral kind of knowledge. The person of practical wisdom has already internalised certain values and is concerned about things such as friendship, justice or courage. He has the ability to recognise, acknowledge and select certain salient features in a complex situation, to perceive the situation as an *occasion* for courage, friendship and justice, and respond to it (Nussbaum, 2001a, pp. 305-306). When somebody has acquired this intellectual excellence, he has become a kind of person whose character virtues are disclosed through his actions. His actions have the full weight of their character behind them. Or, to put this differently, he is the 'self in action' (Dunne, 1997, p. 268). The related question of how practical wisdom can cultivate the self by reflecting on and learning from actions performed in the past will be addressed in §4.4. In order to distinguish between the morally formed practical reasoning and a kind of amoral practical reasoning, Aristotle calls the latter *deinotes*, 'cleverness' (*NE* 1144a23–8). In Socratic times, cleverness was associated with the methods of sophists (also called *deinos*), who used *logos* for the wrong purposes and could even make a weak argument look strong (Guthrie, 1971, p. 32). For Aristotle, however, 'cleverness' is not necessarily used to do immoral things; it merely helps people to attain their ends, whatever they are. For the kind of rationality that explicitly aims at immoral ends, Aristotle reserves the term 'knavery'.

What does practical wisdom look like in practice? It involves a chain of reasoning, "…whose first premises concern the human good, whose intermediate steps specify what the virtues require, if the human good is to be achieved, and whose conclusion is the action that it is good and best for us to perform here and now" (MacIntyre, 1999a, pp. 158-159). First of all, an agent has certain desires that provide a necessary context for its reasoning. In the virtuous and practically wise person, these are not just any desires, but already formed desires aimed at the human good. Imagine that one of these desires is to have friends. The second element is the major premise, a general, universal assertion that doing, having or seeking x is good for or needed by an y. One can assert, e.g. that "It is good for friends not to remain indifferent towards each other's mistakes". If this assertion is controversial, e.g. because somebody argues that it is a virtue to accept mistakes that follow from people's weaknesses, one might have to adapt the assertion or explain why the objection is not convincing. The third element is a specific, particular assertion, informed by perception of the concrete circumstances, e.g. that Tim, a good friend of mine, is about to make a huge mistake. The fourth and final element is the conclusion of the practical syllogism. If my practical reason has asserted that friends should not be indifferent towards each other's mistakes, and that Tim is about to make a huge mistake, I can conclude that I should talk to Tim and ask him to reconsider his position. When the major and minor premises are combined, one is forced at once to do it (*NE* 1147a25-30). The conclusion of the practical syllogism is 'epitactic', i.e. it orders and directs us to act. Note that practical reason only has this force when in its full developed form. When people are morally less developed, they might get the major or minor premise wrong, and fail to do what is right. More will be said about such character flaws in §3.4.

3.2.7 Rival Moral Psychologies

A better picture of a neo-Aristotelian account of moral psychology has been presented thus, enabling us to compare it to the developmental accounts advocated by care ethicists and cognitive developmentalist in Chapter 2. Kohlberg was, like Piaget, primarily interested in epistemic operations involved in the development of judgments about the justice of rules. Due to this focus, Kohlberg did not investigate how moral knowledge and reasoning are related to action, or what kind of feelings people have when making a moral judgment. After respondents were presented with the Heinz dilemma, the interviewers' probing questions were meant to clarify respondents' reasoning about the issue of why Heinz should or should not steal the drug to save his wife's life. Kohlberg assumed that people act morally as a simple consequence of being able to articulate convincing moral judgments. Moreover, he presupposed that the moral quality of the feelings involved in moral judgments was determined by their cognitive-structural aspects. Care ethicists corrected what they considered to be the male bias in Kohlberg's work by expanding both his psychological and moral theory. In their view, the concept of a 'morally developed person' included the ability and willingness to care, which they regarded as less a matter of reasoning and more as a matter of sympathy, the ability to feel with another person. Especially Noddings wanted caring to be as natural as possible, and warned teachers about thinking too much about moral education. On the broadly Humean account of moral psychology that care ethicists adopt, people cannot and do not reason themselves through questions of whether others need our care. We care because we are 'engrossed' by them. Reason can only help us to find out what means can best be employed to have our moral actions succeed.

A neo-Aristotelian account of virtue and practical wisdom shares certain important features with both cognitive development and care ethics. It agrees with care ethicists that an account of moral action is incomplete if it does not state something about emotions as forces that motivate people to do good. This implies that cognitive developmentalism does not present the full story about what a morally developed person is like, psychologically. However, virtue ethicists can criticise care ethicists for downplaying the role of moral reasoning. The kind of rationality that we need to do good things and be good people is in a virtue ethical account much more than a morally neutral kind of means-end reasoning. Neo-Aristotelian virtue ethicists such as Carr (1991) have emphasised that they offer a full blown alternative to the kind of rationality that Kohlberg advocated. So in contrast to care ethics, virtue ethics places its bets on the *rational* refinement of our emotions. However, it recognises that humans cannot reason their way to what is valuable in human life autonomously, detached from their practical concerns, relationships, and engagement in social practices. Whether somebody is morally educated or not does not only depend on the structure of one's reasoning about moral values, but also on people having stable character traits that express a commitment to objective moral value.

Despite the marked differences between cognitive development and care ethics, the two have something in common too: they presuppose a split account of what humans are like from a moral psychological point of view. Both theories recognise two rival powers in human nature – reason and desire – and both agree that one of these capacities is morally superior. The only but difficult controversy involves the question of which capacity rules. Kohlberg chooses moral reasoning and disregards the importance of desires in moral life, while Noddings focuses on the sentiments while downplaying the role of moral reasoning. As the proponents of two camps both believe that one of them has to win the fight, they have difficulties understanding how the two can ever be combined in such a way as to strengthen each other. An Aristotelian approach to moral education agrees that a distinction can be made between the more affective and more cognitive aspects of our moral psychology, but refuses to let only one of them play the leading part in our lives. It accepts that neither brute, insensitive reason, nor uneducated desires are reliable guides. They are both *potentially* morally relevant and only become fully directed towards a good life through a proper education that teaches the two how to work in tandem. This process will be described in more detail in §3.4.

To the extent that one clings to the moral philosophies of either Aristotle, Kant or Hume, the controversies between the proponents of different moral psychological accounts are likely to drag on endlessly. The best that philosophers and theoretical psychologists from different schools can do if the domain is to make progress, is to think with one's rivals as far as one's imagination allows, and to appreciate the central points made by others as a challenge to one's own. There does not seem to be a point of view outside these normative frameworks that can help to answer the question of which moral psychology is *best*, as these frameworks have different views about the goal of moral development. In other words, there is no neutral, extra-moral definition of what it means to be 'morally developed'. Recently, the domain has been given a new impetus by philosophers who have turned to empirical research. While this can be applauded, those who make this 'empirical turn' should not be guided by the naive belief that empirical considerations can solve substantive moral issues. It does, however, enable them to scrutinise the tenability of empirical claims (implicit) made by moral philosophers. A case in point is the research on moral development that Kohlberg conducted between the mid 1950s and late 1980s. He conducted a number of experiments to prove that children develop as his normative model predicts, and to adjust his normative model where necessary. However, he deleted the sixth and final stage when none of the subjects reached it. But why did he delete it?

This raises the question of when an account of moral psychology and development is to be revised. When do we conclude that a specification of 'being morally educated' is psychologically too unrealistic? Space and time do not allow us to determine which of the four approaches to moral education is most compatible with the existing empirical data on moral (developmental) psychology. The next section is an evaluation of the consequences the so-called 'situationism debate' has had for a virtue ethical approach to moral psychology.

3.3 The Situationist Challenge to Virtue Ethics

Chapter 2 concluded that the other approaches to moral education had empirical reservations about the existence of stable character traits. In this section, the relationship between moral philosophy and psychology will be explored by addressing the question of how virtue ethicists, and in particular those interested in moral education, can respond to philosophers who claim that robust and consistent character traits do not exist. Instead of rehearsing the situationism debate that has raged through moral philosophy for over a decade, a more recent article by Merritt, Doris and Harman (2010) on the virtue of practical wisdom will be discussed. An evaluation of their critique will reveal certain meta-ethical assumptions about how psychologically realistic moral concepts should be. The plausibility of these assumptions will be discussed by drawing on the work of Owen Flanagan (1991), who defends a principle of minimal psychological realism. It will be argued that the virtue ethical conception of practical wisdom is not too far removed from what psychology has revealed about the human cognitive make-up, and that there is no reason to replace an education in the virtues with the kind of remedial 'situational management' that situationists advocate. The educational approach in this section will make clear that we should be cautious about taking what social psychologists discover about our moral psychology for granted, as if there is no room for improvement.

3.3.1 The Situationism Debate

As seen in Chapter 2, the field of moral education is a multidimensional domain, to which philosophers, psychologists and educationalists contribute. They all deal to a greater or lesser extent with questions concerning the *goal* of moral education, the psychological *conditions* that have to be met before this goal can be achieved, and the *means* that can be used best to achieve the prescribed goal. In today's universities, however, those interested in moral education often work on separate tracks. Educationalists interested in character education programmes hardly benefit from the conceptual analysis conducted by philosophers, while moral philosophers are not that interested in the educational implications of their ideals. In order to illuminate the relationship between pedagogy and philosophy, empirical research into role modelling will be subject of Chapter 4. This section will examine the potential cross-pollination of philosophy and psychology. Many psychologists are reserved about investigating moral (educational) issues because they have difficulties conceptualising terms like 'moral' and 'virtue' or are afraid that normative conclusions will be drawn from their research (Kristjánsson, 2011). Meanwhile, moral philosophers believe that their discipline is an autonomous field and cannot be influenced by results from psychological research. Psychology is hardly interesting, they think, because empirical research can only inform us about how people morally develop, which is not of help if we want to know what kind of character is *desirable* to have.

One of the aims of this section will be to examine whether psychology and philosophy can have a more fruitful relationship. This is done by examining whether a particular empirical assumption that educationalists and philosophers make about the notion of 'character' is affected by what has become known as 'situationism', a philosophical movement that has been advocated by John Doris (1998, 2002) and Gilbert Harman (1999, 2000). The assumption under attack is disturbingly simple but very fundamental, i.e. the idea that people's actions can be explained in terms of character traits. For example, in everyday conversations, people explain and predict people's actions on the basis of character traits. Character education programmes confidently claim that "students' actions are determined by their characters", and that a "character consists of stable qualities that determine one's responses regardless of the circumstances".[15] And Aristotle and many of his contemporary heirs assume that moral virtues, qua stable dispositions, are conducive to human flourishing. Section 3.2 of this chapter is a point in case.

In *Lack of Character*, Doris (2002, pp. 22-23) concluded on the basis of experimental psychological research that empirical evidence in favour of a certain kind of character traits – the 'robust' or 'global' ones – is very limited. Character traits would typically fail to be *consistent* and *evaluatively integrated*. This means that character traits are not manifested in behaviour across a diversity of situations,

---

15 Both claims are aired in the introductory film by the character education program Character First. Retrieved from www.youtube.com/watch?v=VqEHDlGK3V4&feature=related, March 31, 2011.

and that character traits do not exhibit evaluative affinities with other character traits. Doris does, however, allow for the existence of *stable* traits – or what he calls 'local traits' – which are dispositions to behave in certain ways in very narrowly-specified kinds of situations. For example, one can be a very honest person in 'husband-situations' and a ruthless businessman at work. As people lack character in a global sense, Doris recommends to revise theories and practices that involve reference to such robust character traits. He also suggests that moral education would aim better at teaching children to reflect on psychological research in order to judge, feel and act better in ethically challenging circumstances than at cultivating robust character traits (Doris, 2002, p. 109). For example, children could learn to avoid certain situations (situational selection), or create and sustain certain social contexts that help them to do the right thing (situational modification), instead of always following Aristotle's advice cognitively to change emotions into stable dispositions (See also: Gross, 2010, p. 500; Peterson & Seligman, 2004, p. 502).

The situationism debate has gained so much attention over the last decade, that there are hardly a self-respecting virtue ethicist or moral philosopher left who has not added something to the literature on this topic (e.g. Miller, 2003; Kamtekar, 2004; Webber, 2006; Wielenberg, 2006; Appiah, 2008; Kristjánsson, 2008; Kupperman, 2009; Upton, 2009). Doris's and Harman's publications have even yielded so many (mainly critical) reactions that the literature has reached a saturation point (Kristjánsson, 2010b, p. 129). However, I believe that there are three good reasons to scrutinise Doris's work once more. Firstly, Doris recently edited *The Moral Psychology Handbook* (2010) to which he, together with Merritt and Harman, contributed an article on 'character'. It examines the virtue of practical wisdom, which was, strangely enough, left out of *Lack of Character*. Secondly, there is hardly any literature which takes an educational perspective on situationism, and it is therefore valuable to spell out these implications in more detail.[16] Thirdly, Doris's work is not only interesting because of his appeal to empirical research, but also because of the meta-ethical assumptions he makes about the relationship between empirical facts and moral (educational) ideals. An examination of Doris' work can be illuminating if we want to find out how psychologically realistic moral concepts should be.

3.3.2 Practical Wisdom under Siege

Before looking at meta-ethical assumptions and educational consequences, a critical examination of the argument made by Merritt, Doris and Harman (2010) is essential. Although their article is called 'Character', the authors focus almost exclusively on the consequences of psychological research on practical wisdom, previously not scrutinised by situationists. However, Merritt et al. begin by rehearsing situationists' critique of robust character traits: systematic observation of behaviour has not revealed pervasive behavioural consistency, and since

---

16 For an exception, see Pamental (2010).

robust traits could be expected to reveal such behavioural patterns, behaviour is not typically controlled by such traits. Merritt et al. admit that the existence of character traits cannot only be affirmed or falsified by observing overt behaviour. An agent's 'emotional and rational propensities' have to be taken into account too. However, these 'inner states' cannot explain why character traits are robust, because "cognitive functioning has itself been shown to be highly susceptible to situational variation" (Merritt et al., 2010, p. 359) While they admit that practical wisdom could 'save' robust character traits, they also argue that practical wisdom is influenced by the situation an agent is in and can, therefore, not help us act consistently across a diversity of situations.

In order to show why the notion of rationality operative in a virtue ethical understanding of character is empirically problematic, Milgram's (1974) obedience studies are taken as point of departure. What these experiments illustrate, the authors claim, is 'moral dissociation', i.e. the phenomenon that people do not always act according to their norms, e.g. when there is a countervailing consideration. In the Milgram experiments, we would expect most subjects to endorse a moral prohibition against harming innocent agents against their will, but 65 percent obeyed the experimenter and continued to administer severe shocks to the (fictitious) test subject. The subjects' behaviour shows that practical reasoning is unable to determine what should be done in the particular circumstances of the experiment and, more generally, that people rarely act on (what they take to be) reasons. Merritt et al. (2010, p. 366) suggest that many of the processes implicated in moral functioning are largely unaffected by individuals' reflection and are beyond rational control. Jonathan Haidt (2001) argues that moral judgments are typically the result of quick, automatic evaluations, called 'intuitions', which can be cued by morally arbitrary situational factors. In Haidt's framework, practical reason is a means to make up a story about the moral significance of an act *after* its execution. It provides people with a so-called 'post-hoc rationalisation'. When we are asked to explain why we act the way we do, we make up a (meaningful) story that really does not capture the intuitions that caused us to do the things we did. As a consequence, the function that virtue ethicists commonly attribute to practical wisdom – putting our character into action through deliberation and choice – would very rarely be exhibited in everyday life. Situationists do not prove that practical wisdom is impossible or non-existent, but they show that it has an altogether different function to what many virtue ethicists think.

How problematic is this? The authors admit that these results do not have to be taken for granted. Firstly, there are also cognitively less demanding situations that make it possible for people to arrive at the right action through conscious reflection. Haidt (2001, p. 829) argues that "...a person could, in principle, reason her way to a judgment that contradicts her initial intuition". Secondly, there are 'remedial measures' that can compensate for people's limited cognitive resources. For example, people can explicitly formulate the goals that they want to achieve in advance, and try to identify the situational factors that might hamper the achievement of these goals beforehand. Thereby, the influence of automatic, countervailing tendencies, such as obedience to the experimenter, could be diminished. When people's judgments and choices are determined by the situation, instead of by their characters, the best way to make the world a better place is by putting people in environments that influence behavioural outcomes. We could try to avoid ethically dangerous circumstances that are "near occasions for sin" (Doris, 2002, pp. 146–147). A substantive education of the virtues could be replaced with a programme of 'situational management' (Wielenberg, 2006, p. 488).

At this junction, several points are worth discussing. One is Merritt et al.'s description of the notion of practical wisdom. They attribute all kinds of claims to virtue ethicists, but from what we wrote about practical wisdom in §3.2.5 it is to be seen whether these claims are correct. Another critical issue is the psychological 'evidence' cited. Do Merritt, Doris and Harman's interpretations of Milgram's obedience experiments make sense? For example, are the experiments not so far removed from everyday moral reasoning that we should be very cautious with generalising the results? If the situationists' reasoning is watertight, the question is whether virtue ethicists and educationalists who recommend teachers and pupils to cultivate practical wisdom (e.g. Dunne, 1993, 2011; Kristjánsson, 2007; Higgins, 2011) should stop claiming that practical wisdom is necessary in order to make moral decisions. Had we, except for some remedial measures, better stop educating children's practical reason?

3.3.3 The Solution: Virtues as Ideals?

One way to deal with the situationists' critique is to 'bite the bullet': virtue ethicists can stick to their central claims *and* agree that practical wisdom provides rationalisations after a moral judgment was passed on other grounds. In particular narrativists could possibly pursue this line of defence. In *After Virtue* (2003), MacIntyre explains that somebody's life can be envisaged as a unity if we consider him to be a storyteller who tells a narrative about how the virtues he needs in different practices are integrated into a whole human life. He calls the kind of knowledge one needs in order to arrange the virtues in a narrative 'integrity' or 'constancy', which is analogous to the Aristotelian notion of *phronesis* (MacIntyre, 2003, pp. 183, 203). However, the disadvantage of describing practical wisdom exclusively as an intellectual virtue that is needed to write a coherent story about one's life, is that we lose sight of its function to arrive at a good action through reflection on the moral goal to be achieved, the circumstances, and one's own strengths and weaknesses. Another way to take the edge off situationism is to focus on the assumptions made about the realism of moral concepts. I submit that if empirical research has demonstrated that moral reasoning rarely leads to moral judgments, character education programmes such as *Character Counts* should stop claiming that "students' actions are determined by their characters", or that a "character consists of stable qualities which determine one's responses regardless of the circumstances". To the extent that these claims purport to say something about all or most children's virtues and characters, they are plainly false. But what if we interpret the *Character Counts* slogans as saying that pupils' actions *will be* determined by their character if they follow the program?

The question now is: does this programme make reasonable promises? Does it make sense for people to strive for robust notions of the moral and intellectual virtues? Doris (2002) argues that if psychological research shows that most people do not possess robust, global character traits, they are not very likely to have the underlying capacities needed to develop these traits. On the basis of this likelihood argument, he concludes that it is not realistic to ask of them to develop such traits. His reasoning is tricky here because ideas about what we 'cannot' are a general extrapolation from what we 'have not' and 'do not'. Doris does not *prove* that the underlying capacities needed to develop robust character traits are non-existent. He just deduces this from observed behaviour. Doris (2002, p. 112) seems aware of this relatively weak spot in his argument, as he admits that he has given "…no reason for thinking that the realisation of virtue is strictly impossible". He adds that virtue ethicists who take his work seriously can still propagate ideals of virtue – even if nobody or hardly anybody will actually live up to these ideals. Such ideals, embodied in a couple of moral saints, could inspire people to behave better even if full virtue is unattainable. Being completely virtuous is impossible, *striving for* virtue is not, as Doris (2002, p. 112) puts it. Doris seems after all quite sympathetic towards virtue ethics.

There are, however, two problems with his solution. The first is that virtue ethicists who embrace this 'idealists' position would lose an advantage that they supposedly had over deontology and utilitarianism, i.e. that it is compatible with psychological and neuroscientific evidence (Merritt, 2000, p. 368; Casebeer, 2003). To conceive of different ethical theories as rivals and acknowledge that the rivalry between these theories cannot be decided purely on normative grounds, the theory with an empirically sound moral psychology is preferable. However, should ethical theories be regarded as offering rival answers to the same basic question? This seems a misrepresentation of what ethical theories are about. While deontology and utilitarianism offer a theory in which the central question is how we ought to *act*, virtue ethics is only interested in acts in a derivative way, that is, as following from virtuous character traits, which are part of leading a good *life*. Since deontology and utilitarianism are, in turn, only interested in character traits in a derivate way, i.e. as a means to produce moral behaviour, one cannot really blame them for not having developed the kind of moral psychology that

Aristotelians have. This means that the first problem is not really a problem at all.

The second, genuine problem with transforming virtues into ideals is that virtue ethics would become much less practical. Aristotle did not want moral philosophy to answer the question what 'good' is in a purely theoretical fashion; he wanted theoretical insights to enable people to actually lead good lives and be(come) good people. If ethics is not to be 'merely theoretical', this means that it must attend to the question of how these virtues can come to bear in people's lives (Appiah, 2008, p. 23). When virtue ethicists interpret psychological experiments as showing that most people are defective practical reasoners and that being virtuous is, indeed, a very difficult achievement, this is somehow at odds with the practical character of virtue ethics. Naturally, virtue ethics does not have to claim that *everybody* can easily acquire all the virtues, but the fact that only a mere *handful* of people can become virtuous undermines virtue ethics' practical import.

In the extreme case that everybody is virtuous, a normative model of practical wisdom loses its critical potential, but if nobody or hardly anyone is virtuous, the gap between the normative model of practical wisdom and the model emerging from psychological research becomes so big that this 'unrealistic' ideal will not move people to change. Formulating these two extremes shows that we expect a moral theory to be normative and critical on the one hand, and motivating and action-guiding on the other (Tiberius & Plakias, 2010, p. 401). The question is: when are the concepts of moral philosophy and the results from the social sciences *too far* removed from each other? According to Merritt et al. (2010, p. 362), the moral philosophical ideal of practical wisdom should not be "radically unlike" what science has revealed to us about the facts. But how 'unlike' can a theory of moral education be before it fails to motivate people? When should virtue ethics, and more in particular a virtue ethical approach of moral education, take results from psychological research seriously?[17] The question is essential, because those who have a very minimal notion of psychological realism will not be very impressed by the work of Doris, Harman and Merritt, while those who care much about the practical feasibility of moral concepts will take their work much more seriously. Formulating the issue at stake in these terms means that the debate between virtue ethicists and psychologists on the virtue of practical wisdom moves from issues of empirical psychology to the realm of meta-ethics.

3.3.4 Minimal Psychological Realism

In order to answer the question of how psychologically realistic the concept of practical wisdom should be, we turn to the pioneering work of philosopher Owen Flanagan (1991 p. 34), who formulated a 'principle of minimal psychological realism' (PMPR) that reads: "Make sure when constructing a moral theory or projecting a moral ideal, that the character, decision processing, and behaviour prescribed are possible, or are perceived to be possible for creatures like us." This

---

17 For those interested in psychological realism from a utilitarian point of view, see Rietti (2009).

principle is both descriptive and evaluative: it tries to describe the aspiration of most moral theories and also offers a criterion to evaluate theories in terms of this aspiration. Two of its features deserve a closer look.

The first is the distinction between 'possibility' and 'perceived possibility'. The *possibility* is an objective criterion, referring to certain facts about 'creatures like us'. By including the *perceived* possibility, Flanagan emphasises that such facts are not the only things that matter to psychological realism. Even though some things may not be possible, like setting yourself the goal of running 100 meters in 9 seconds (when the current world record is 9.58 sec.), your *perception* that this is possible can nevertheless motivate you to improve your time significantly. The problem with the perception is, however, that one can overestimate (or underestimate) one's 'real' possibilities to such an extent that it eventually leads to frustration. Still, the perception matters, because the point of Flanagan's principle is to make sure that people are motivated to strive for the ideal character. If they do not *recognise* a virtuous life as a possibility, it does not matter if it *is*.

The second interesting feature about Flanagan's principle is the concept of 'creatures like us'. In a footnote, Flanagan (1991, p. 340) explains that this phrase refers to all members of the *Homo sapiens*. This means that the question 'can we become practically wise?' can be reformulated as 'can human beings become practically wise?'. In order to answer that question we need to know whether practical reason is part of human nature. Flanagan makes a helpful distinction between 'natural' (or biological) traits, on the one hand, and 'narrow' (or social) traits, on the other, although he recognises that any such distinction cannot be substantial, since natural traits are the raw material on which the social traits are constructed. Natural traits are "...features which turn up in some recognizable form regardless of cultural context and historical time, and therefore are taken to lie closer to our basic biological and cognitive architecture than certain other traits" (Flanagan, 1991, p. 41). He mentions six basic emotions (anger, fear, disgust, happiness, sadness and surprise), the perceptual input system, propositional attitudes, biological sex, sexual desire, hunger, thirst, linguistic capacity, and the capacity to learn (to be classically and operantly conditioned), to reason, and to remember. These emotions, attitudes, desires and capacities are shared by all normal members of the species *Homo sapiens*.

Flanagan's principle of minimal psychological realism is a version of 'ought implies can': if you are morally obliged to perform a certain action or develop certain traits, you must also be able (biologically, psychologically) to perform it. While not *all* moral psychologies are possible, Flanagan's principle allows for an enormous range of variations, each specifying this shared human nature somewhat differently. Flanagan sets the bar for moral theories to be psychologically realistic low: he acknowledges that a great variety of moral traditions can meet the criterion of psychological realism (Flanagan, Sarkissian & Wong, 2008, p. 52). However, he believes that the bar is high enough to rule out some kinds of utilitarianism, Kantian deontology and forms of virtue ethics that include strong claims about the unity of the virtues. For example, in the case of act-utilitarianism, the hedonistic calculations required are too demanding and involve impossible levels of constant attention.

Moreover, once we have become members of a culture, socially constructed traits constrain our ability to realise particular psychologies in the future too. For example, in Tibet, polyandrous marriages are allowed. A group of brothers can marry a single female and all have intercourse with her. Flanagan (1991, p. 43) finds this practice unappealing, but admits that this might have been different had he been raised as a Tibetan. The fact that somebody is disgusted by the idea of having sex with a woman whom his brothers are also sleeping with can be explained by reference to Flanagan's personal narrow psychological traits. Some deep-seated, socially specific traits *have become* extremely difficult or even impossible for him (and more generally, us) to achieve, given the particular moral psychology we have developed as members of a particular (sub) culture. Like natural traits, narrow traits limit our possibilities somehow, but the advantage of the latter is that they can always be adjusted through education, albeit over generations, whereas the former cannot. Flanagan warns against being too conservative about the possibility of moral development: "We could seek to change the practices and the attitudes of subsequent generations, even if it were very difficult to purify completely our own entrenched attitudes and dispositions." (Flanagan, 1991, p. 43). Moral theories are only too demanding if they are no 'real option', i.e. people can no longer live 'inside their actual historical circumstances', cannot 'retain their hold on reality' and 'engage in extensive self-deception' (Flanagan, 1991, p. 46 cites Bernard Williams, 1985, p. 160). Flanagan's principle shows that psychology provides a general picture of how human beings are put together, delimiting our ideals about which kind of intellectual and character virtues human beings should acquire.

This puts us in a better position to evaluate the claim that experimental psychology has shown how virtue of practical wisdom is something different than assumed. Although practical wisdom may be difficult to achieve for many individuals, especially for those who already have deeply entrenched dispositions, the answer to the question whether the Aristotelian virtue of practical wisdom is psychologically unrealistic is clearly negative. Haidt (2001) and Merritt et al. (2010, p. 397) do not rule out that in daily situations, when people experience less stress than in psychological experiments, they might be able to arrive at the right moral judgments through conscious reflection. Even during the Milgram experiments, about 35 percent of the subjects refused to obey the experimenter at one stage or another. Situationists' claims about practical wisdom would be much stronger if they did not only show that people do not *act* according to virtue – simply assuming that they do not have the underlying capacities that are needed to develop these traits – but if they could show that the *underlying capacities* required to develop the desirable character traits are non-existent. It seems that for the last twenty years, social psychologists have revolted against personality psychologists by focusing on social features of behaviour to such an extent that such 'inner' personality constructs have been neglected. It seems time that the debate about the psychological realism of virtues moves on to the meaning of mental categories, such as 'capacities' and 'dispositions'.

3.3.5 Prospective Practical Wisdom at Last

This last section criticises situationism further by showing that situationism *presupposes* the kind of practical wisdom it rejects. The starting point is a telling example. "Imagine that a colleague with whom you have had a long flirtation invites you for dinner, offering enticement of sumptuous food and fine wine, with the excuse that you are temporarily orphaned while your spouse is out of town." (Doris, 1998, pp. 516-517) You may think that there is no cause for concern, because you are a morally upright person and you consider yourself to be a very faithful and loyal person who would never cheat on his wife. Doris warns, however, that your virtues will probably not be predictive of your behaviour, and you would better avoid the dinner. To him, this is not a sign of weakness; we have to be honest with ourselves and recognise that some situational influences are overwhelming. Why wait for situations to arise in which we will need to show our courage, temperance or kindness? Doris recommends us to think in advance about the probability of such situations arising. By doing this, we can consider not to engage in certain situations in the first place.

Now, what kind of reasoning do you need to decide whether or not to accept the invitation? The most important thing to know would be *that* there is something at stake, morally. Deontologists, (rule) utilitarians and virtue ethicists would probably agree, albeit for different reasons, that cheating on your wife is not a good thing to do. If you did not know this, you would not even consider the invitation to be a morally challenging situation, and it would not have crossed your mind to consider what to do. Secondly, once you recognise that your fidelity is at stake here, you would have to think about your own strengths and weaknesses. Even if you know that being faithful to your wife is the best attitude towards your marriage, this does not mean that you are *capable* of being faithful in the situation. Have you accepted similar invitations in the past? Do you often have more or less romantic dinners with female friends? In honesty, can you resist your colleague? Thirdly, you would also need to know a lot about the colleague and other circumstances in order to make a good decision. Does she have a history of sleeping around with guys? Does she really fancy you? What was her body language like when she invited you?

Suppose you consider this carefully and decide to refuse the invitation. This illustrates that – if you follow Doris' advice and think about avoiding certain situations – you need *much* practical wisdom in order to make the right choice. You will need to know that fidelity is a virtue and that this particular situation calls for this trait. Moreover, you will also need to possess self-knowledge, and knowledge about other relevant aspects of the situation. Finally, you will have to think about what this all means for the question whether you should accept the invitation or not. So, one would need precisely what Merritt et al (2010, p. 397) claim to be very rare and difficult, i.e. to "arrive at the right action through conscious reflection". Admittedly, the moral reasoning could be less demanding if you decide to refuse the invitation purely on the basis of an unarticulated intuition that the situation is morally charged. In that case, you do not have to think much at all; you just avoid as many potentially overwhelming situations as possible. The downside of this option is that – since almost every situation is somehow morally charged – you would not be able to leave your house anymore if you were afraid to make moral mistakes. What this shows is that situationists can only reasonably advice people to avoid a particular *kind* of moral situations, i.e. those that are cognitively extremely demanding and very stressful, such as the Milgram experiment. Moral reasoning may indeed be very difficult in such circumstance. It is therefore slightly ironic that situationists recommend us to do much of this reasoning *in advance*. Whether this prospective use of practical wisdom contributes to moral development is another issue; courage, for example, requires certain opportunities for endurance of great danger, in order to develop (Sherman, 1989, p. 192).

We scrutinised the notion of practical wisdom, because Merritt et al. (2010) argued that the existence of robust character traits cannot be derived from observed behaviour only. Being virtuous, they admitted, also involves feeling certain emotions and acting for particular reasons. Leaving the issue of the emotions aside (a problem in itself!), the problem with our moral reasoning would be that psychological experiments have shown that practical rationality often does not help us to do what we should do. Because practical wisdom is itself susceptible to situational influences, situationists argue that it cannot account for the robustness of character traits. Instead of going deeper into the empirical evidence or the concept of practical wisdom that situationists use, we examined what it means for certain virtue concepts to be 'psychologically realistic'. It turned out that the kind of practical wisdom that virtue ethicists and character educationalist promote, is – in light of the psychological evidence – not impossible to human beings to possess or acquire. The 'remedial measures' that Merritt et al (2010) advocate presuppose that educational methods that stimulate the development of intellectual virtues and stable, consistent character traits, are not going to be effective. However, if my critique of situational management makes sense, we can be hopeful that, despite the picture of human cognition emerging from the social and cognitive sciences, people can become practically wise. Still, this educational perspective on moral psychological issues matters, because it prevents us from concluding too soon that it is impossible to change certain dispositions on the basis of empirical research, especially in the long run. We can be hopeful in not having to stick to facts of human nature and the way that human life goes (Hursthouse, 1999, pp. 220-222). Admittedly, to most living things it holds that they *cannot* do something if they *do* not do it, but to humans beings things are different, precisely in virtue of their practical rationality. This capacity enables us to assess what we do, which makes room for ideas of what we may be able to do and also to live better.

3.4 A Neo-Aristotelian Model of Moral Development

Is it not too easy to express the hope that people can become practically wise? Should not we make clear in more detail how practical reason can become an intellectual virtue and how in this process, the emotions are simultaneously moralised into virtues of character? In this last section, a neo-Aristotelian model of moral development will be presented that does precisely that. The model is *neo*-Aristotelian, because Aristotle's own ethical works do not contain a clear-cut developmental model.

3.4.1 Categories or Stages?

In Book VII of the *Nicomachean Ethics*, Aristotle describes several groups of people who are more or less morally developed. For example, he distinguishes between *hoi polloi* (the many), *akrates* (the weak-willed), *enkrates* (the self-controlled) and *phronimos* (the practically wise).[18] Even though Aristotle is interested in moral education, he does not present these categories as *stages*, nor does he explain why or how people in one category could move on to another. Only rarely does Aristotle admit that un-self-controlled people can learn to control their passions, or that self-controlled people lose their self-control. In addition, truly virtuous people seem not to have any shortcomings and do not morally decline, while wicked people persist in their irrational passions and never show remorse.

The moral progress or decay of morality is probably not at the centre of Aristotle's attention because his main goal is to relate to Socrates' ideas on (the lack of) self-control. Socrates, who assumed that nobody knowingly does wrong, formulated the difficult question of how it is possible that someone can fail in self-control when he believes correctly that what he does is wrong (*NE* 1145b21-27). If

---

18 These categories are notoriously difficult to translate. Some leave *akrasia* and *enkrateia* untranslated, others translate *akrasia* with 'weak-will', 'incontinence' or 'lack of self-control' and *enkrateia* with 'self-control' or 'continence'. The ancient Greeks did not have our concept of will, and because (in)continence has the association of excretory functions, the translation of '(lack of) self-control' will be adopted in this section. Following Broadie & Rowe's translation (Aristotle, 2002), people who have or lack self-control will be called 'self-controlled' and 'un-self-controlled', respectively.

people do bad things, Socrates argued that it must be because people are ignorant about the good. Aristotle sees it as his task to investigate what, if Socrates is right, the nature of this 'ignorance' is. Compared to Socrates and Plato, Aristotle takes seriously those people who, in a sense, 'know' what is good, but still act differently under the influence of certain passions. He stays within the Socratic paradigm that moral knowledge proceeds moral action, but does not agree with Socrates that moral knowledge cannot be trumped by countervailing passions (Kraut, 2010). He shows that Socrates has a too simplistic understanding of the concept of 'moral knowledge' by distinguishing between *having* moral knowledge and *using* it. For example, when we look at the practical syllogism (§3.2.5), it becomes clear that someone can know the universal major premise, but either lack the time or wisdom to perceive the specific situation well, thus, getting the minor premise wrong.

Despite this, the Aristotelian categories of *akrates* and *enkrates* can be interpreted as successive stages or levels in a comprehensive developmental model. The categories can be read diachronically instead of synchronically, i.e. simply as rankings of worse to better states of character. There are two reasons for this. Firstly, it is in line with Aristotle's general view of human nature and development. In his view, a child is potentially human and acquires, while morally developing, the definite 'form' of humanity. Ascribing to Aristotle the thought that a child is potentially virtuous is, however, not completely uncontroversial, because Aristotle contrasts human children and animals with morally mature adults. This seems to make virtue a matter of all or nothing (Kristjánsson, 2007, p. 22; Sherman, 1989, p. 161). Yet, insisting that there is a gap between children and adults in terms of morality and rationality is not incompatible with the idea that children can learn to bridge the gap. Moreover, there are passages in which Aristotle states that children have deliberative capacities from a very young age, albeit still in an underdeveloped form (*Politics* 1260a32-33). We can, therefore, defend a neo-Aristotelian model of moral development in which children are viewed as "in progress toward full humanity" (Sherman, 1989, p. 162). Secondly, interpreting the categories developmentally has the advantage of illuminating Aristotle's claim that no substantial separation can be made between practical wisdom and moral virtue (Bowditch, 2008; May, 2010). We saw in §3.2.5 that practical reason interacts with the desires, but we can only understand that and how these two are interdependent if a story is told about how reason and desires *became* interdependent.

While several stages in the development of virtue will be identified, we should keep in mind that we do not necessarily have to share Kohlberg's conception of a 'stage'. Kohlberg conceived of stages as parts in an invariant and universal sequence that every individual can pass through, regardless of culture or religion. Moreover, he assumed that people are only at one stage at a time, do not skip stages or relapse into lower ones. From an Aristotelian perspective, there are no reasons why some children might not start out at the second level (e.g. because of the natural virtue they are endowed with from birth) or conquer their lack of self-control in such a way that they become virtuous at once, skipping the self-controlled stage (Kristjánsson, 2007, p. 22). In addition, people seem to be able to exemplify combinations of self-control and lack of self-control (Curzer, 1998). Furthermore, a virtue ethical account of moral development is not unsympathetic to the idea that the meaning of the final stage depends to a large extent on what particular communities take this to be, while Kohlberg's model hinges on a strict separation between conventional and post-conventional (or principled) levels of moral development.

During the last twenty-five years, several neo-Aristotelians have identified a number of developmental stages in Aristotle's works, ranging from three to six. For example, Sherman (1989) and Tobin (1989) distinguish between three stages, the 'novice' or 'initial' stage, an 'intermediate' stage and finally the stage of 'full virtue and rationality'. Garrett (1993) argues that Aristotle's ladder has five steps: the 'fully wretched', 'most other people', the 'incontinent', the 'continent' and the 'virtuous'. Like Garrett, Curzer (1998, 2002) distinguishes between the 'incontinent', 'continent' and the 'virtuous', but he treats the 'fully wretched' and 'most other people' as one category ('the many'), while he introduces a new category (the 'generous-minded') that fits between 'the many' and the 'incontinent'.[19] Kristjánsson (2007, 2010b) also follows the distinction between 'the many', 'incontinent', 'continent' and 'virtuous', but he leaves, like Curzer, some space between 'the many' and the 'incontinent'. Inserting the levels of the 'soft' (or 'self-indulgent') and the 'resistant', his account of virtue development counts six stages. While Sherman's and Tobin's three-level accounts is clear and convenient, they are also overly simplistic and not very Aristotelian since hardly any reference is made to the categories mentioned in Book VII of the *Nicomachean Ethics*. Since the other three authors are in concord about four levels that are also explicitly mentioned by Aristotle, they will be used as a point of departure. It should be noted that Aristotle also discusses two stages that are either below or beyond the 'human' ones. Below the level of 'the many', one finds the 'beasts', and beyond the level of complete virtue, there is a kind of god-like virtue. These two categories underline Aristotle's central idea that humans are, as rational and social animals, an intermediate species between needy animals and self-sufficient gods.

The main disagreements between the three authors who recognise these four stages concern the details of the first two stages. The first issue is: who is included in the first group of 'the many'? It is not a phrase that names a group of people of similar ages (Curzer, 2002, p. 156). Instead, it includes – at least in our society

---

19 Only at the time of press did I read Curzer's *Aristotle and the Virtues* (2012), in which he also distinguishes between people who are naturally and properly virtuous, and in which he adds four categories of 'Aristotelian losers', i.e. the vicious, the brutish, natural slaves and tragic heroes.

– the majority of people (Garrett, 1993, p. 173). Since there are different ways in which one can be uncommitted to a virtuous life, this is a very heterogeneous group. For example, it includes completely vicious people, children who have the potential for virtue but are still on a pre-moral level, and a morally childish multitude that believes that happiness consists in money, fame or pleasure instead of virtue. Since we are primarily concerned with the moral education of children in schools, we leave the questions of how thoroughly wicked or morally indifferent adults can become virtuous for another time, and focus on the issue of how children, whose potential to become virtuous has not completely been wasted, can acquire the virtues.[20] To avoid confusion, the children who are on the level of the many will be referred to as 'the uncommitted'.

The second disagreement is over the question of whether there is a group between 'the many' and the '*un-self-controlled*'. Curzer inserts the category of the 'generous-minded' (*eleutherios*) here, while the others do not, possibly because it does not appear in Aristotle's standard list of character types.[21] In practice, it is difficult to distinguish the generous-minded from the *un-self-controlled*, but a separate category may matter because of a small but significant difference: generous-minded people are far removed from 'the many' because they are eager to become virtuous, while 'the many' are not (Curzer, 2002, p. 157). The *un-self-controlled* and generous-minded share a commitment to virtue, but unlike the *un-self-controlled*, the generous-minded are still unable to identify virtuous acts. Since we are especially interested in the moral development of children, Curzer's distinction between people who do not have the desire to become virtuous and those who do, but are not able to recognise virtuous actions since they lack the necessary practical wisdom, seems useful. In the developmental model described below, it will be treated as a sub-level of those who lack self-control.

It is more doubtful whether Kristjánsson's (2007, p. 21) distinction between 'the soft' and 'the resistant' can also be justified. Admittedly, the two categories occur in Aristotle's writings: 'softness' and 'resistance' (or 'endurance') are two attitudes towards feelings related to the *pain* of touch and taste, while 'self-control' and 'lack of self-control' are attitudes towards feelings of *pleasure* (*NE* 1150a10-15). However, if it is true that 'softness' and 'resistance' are two developmental stages, children would not enjoy any bodily pleasures until they have reached the stage of the un-self-controlled. As this is plainly nonsense, the only explanation possible is that Kristjánsson has restricted the categories of 'the soft' and 'the resistant' to pleasures of *virtuous* activity. In his view, virtue is painful to 'the many', and people will only start to enjoy *virtue* on the level of the un-self-controlled. However, Aristotle makes clear that these categories are not attitudes towards the pleasure of virtue, but towards pleasure, in general. 'Softness' should be understood as the specific attitude of the un-self-controlled person towards pain, while 'endurance' is

---

20 This means that vice never gets a fair hearing. See, for example. G. Taylor's (2006) book on the seven deadly vices (or sins), and C. McKinnon's (1999) accounts of cruelty, hypocrisy, envy and selfishness. Gilead (2011) discusses ways in which character education can counter the vices.
21 Although it appears elsewhere. See *NE* 1079b7-13.

the specific attitude the self-controlled person has towards pain. In sum, softness and lack of self-control are simply two sides of the same coin, just as endurance and self-control are. Softness and endurance are not developmentally prior to the stage of lack of self-control.

Below, the four main stages of moral development will be discussed in more detail. Each stage will describe (1) whether people are committed to virtue, (2) whether people act virtuous or not, (3) whether they virtuously act with pleasure or pain, and (4) which desires and (5) reasons they have. As virtue will be considered in a general way, the account would ideally be complemented with more precise accounts of the development of separate virtues.

3.4.2 Stage 1: Morally Uncommitted

'The many', the lowest step on the ladder of moral development, includes vicious people, adults who are committed to a life of money and fame, and uncommitted children who have not made a real choice for or against virtue. The following mainly focuses on this last group. What all people on the level of 'the many' have in common, however, and what distinguishes them from the other categories, is that they have a particular understanding of happiness. They believe that it consists of things such as bodily pleasure, honour or money (NE 1195a22-23). They are especially concerned with money as it can be used as a means to any end. There is no place for the idea that virtuous action or philosophy could play a role in their flourishing, since they have not had a taste of what Aristotle considers to be truly fine and pleasant. They are at the beginning of the moral developmental path, lacking the ability to determine which acts are virtuous and why, and certainly not having developed stable dispositions of action and emotion (Curzer, 2002, p. 155).

When Aristotle reviews the ideas that different people have about happiness before constructing his own account, he does not take 'the many' seriously. He notices that they talk randomly about almost everything and change their mind frequently about the content of happiness. For example, when someone becomes ill, he will come to believe that health is the most important thing, but when he loses his job he will suddenly think that money matters more. The life of 'the many' is unstable and chaotic because they live by their whimsical passions and because these passions are impenetrable to the voice of reason (Garrett, 1993, p. 174). They nevertheless use a kind of immature cleverness (*deinotes*) with which they can reason from means to end (Sherman, 1989, p. 174). At the very least, this enables them to distinguish between the immediate gratification of their desires and what is beneficial to their satisfaction in the long run. Interestingly, the kind of reasoning needed to delay immediate gratification for a greater gain in the future has been empirically investigated by Mischel et al. (1989) and others.[22] They investigated the psychological mechanism underlying children's ability to

---

22 For poignant footage of these experiments, see e.g. www.youtube.com/watch?v=6EjJsPylEOY.

resist a treat and found that those who lacked self-control as children were more likely to struggle in stressful situations when they were older, had also trouble paying attention, and found it difficult to maintain friendships. This makes clear how important control over one's desires is, both for one's personal and moral functioning.

Young people differ in a number of ways from the others in the category of 'the many'. According to Aristotle, the young live by their desires, expect great things in life, are spirited, hot-tempered, ambitious, witty and hopeful. They are trusting and therefore easily deceived, but when such failures are accompanied by disappointment, they can learn to be less confident in their own abilities and others' good will (*Rhetoric* ch. II, 12-13). The origins of the violent desires of the young have to do with certain biological changes in adolescence and with the rather uncultivated state of their habits. In many cases, these desires are educable and habituation can help the young to develop virtuous habits of feeling and action (Garrett, 1993, p. 187; Kristjánsson, 2007, p. 20). Older people have much weaker desires, lack energy, and do less than they ought. They are inclined to fear everything, they are small-minded and slaves to their own gain. Moreover, the chance that their already well-entrenched habits will change through habituation or teaching is very small. Their lives have been such that it has become extremely difficult for them to change (Garrett, 1993, p. 188).

What is going on in children at the level of 'the many'? Suppose that John, who is 16-year old, enters a store to buy a T-shirt, but spots a sweater instead, the possession of which would contribute to his status in his peer group.[23] John does not have enough money to buy the sweater, so he is tempted to shoplift. However, when he notices a store clerk who is suspiciously looking his way, his fear of being caught and punished takes over. When he decides to leave the shop without the sweater, it is not because he knows it is bad to steal, but because he could be arrested and face penalties. This example illustrates that when 'the many' obey laws, it is not because they see its purpose, but because they are afraid that bad consequences will follow. Moral educators would be well-advised to take into account that people who are on this level can come to abstain from vicious deeds through external pleasures and pains, and the association of virtue with reward (Sherman, 1989, p. 190).

The dominant emotion in such a situation is fear, and not shame, which is experienced when somebody does something that is disgraceful and unworthy of himself (Garrett, 1993, p. 184). Shame would have been an indication of moral seriousness and the implicit acknowledgment that John did not live up to his moral standards. However, as John does not have such standards, the emotion of shame does not function as a warning signal (Kristjánsson, 2002, p. 112). The absence of shame also indicates that John has not really acquired a moral identity yet. Had John felt shame when the store clerk spotted him, this emotion would

---

23 The example is adapted from Garrett (1993), p. 183

have told him that what he was about to *do* was not in line with who he really *is*, i.e. with his moral standards and deepest commitments. The feeling of shame indicates that a person does not coincide with his (bad) actions.

People who do not have a stable (virtuous) character and are mostly interested in money and pleasure will have great difficulties in forming or maintaining what Aristotle calls 'character friendships'. Naturally, young people will have many friends, in the general sense that they mutually recognise each other as bearing goodwill and wishing well to each other (*Ethics*, VIII.2). Aristotle notes, however, that there are different kinds of friendships, some better, more encompassing and longer lasting than others. He distinguishes between friendships based on utility, pleasure and virtue – the last of which is called 'character friendships'. If we look at our description of 'the many', it is clear that the kind of ideal character friendship, which presupposes that both friends are virtuous and appreciate each other because of their virtue, is not within the reach of most children (yet). Children are more likely to have friends for the sake of sharing fun experiences and finding the other person's company pleasurable (Garrett, 1993, p. 187). Once a child has character friends, however, these friends will further stimulate the child's moral development, e.g. because the child can become inspired to develop when he/she sees the admirable qualities in those he identifies with (Sherman, 1989, pp. 138-144). This presupposes that people have already acquired the ability to recognise somebody else as a virtuous model.

3.4.3 Stage 2: Lack of Self-Control

The major difference between 'the many' and the 'un-self-controlled' is that the latter has chosen to lead a virtuous life, instead of a life guided by the desire for wealth or fame. Although the label 'lack of self-control' may not sound very promising, they have made a giant leap on the path to moral virtue: they have correct opinions about what is morally right, they desire to do virtuous things for their own sake and act virtuously on a regular basis (Kristjánsson, 2007, p. 21). Yet how can the gap between the many and the 'un-self-controlled' been bridged? This question can be answered if we look at Curzer's category of the 'generous-minded', a sublevel on which people are, like the 'un-self-controlled', already committed to virtue, but who do, unlike them, neither have habits of virtuous action or feeling, nor the knowledge to determine which acts are virtuous (Curzer, 1998). In the previous section, we saw that 'the many' sometimes do not engage in immoral behaviour because they fear the pain associated with punishment. But when children internalise the punishments they receive from their parents or other educators, they will eventually learn to refrain from doing bad things, even when there are no educators around. They learn, in other words, to punish themselves. Although the generous-minded are not able to reliably identify virtuous acts yet, they have started to acquire a sense of *shame*.

Stressing the importance of shame in moral development implies that, at least on the lower stages of the developmental process, moral progress is achieved through pain rather than pleasure. According to Curzer (2002, p. 158-159) pain is not just a side effect of a minor contributor to moral development, but the catalyst behind the whole process. He disagrees with Burnyeat (1980), who maintained that children are first told which acts are virtuous, and then internalise these lessons by repeatedly performing and enjoying these activities. Curzer suggests that people become able to recognise virtuous acts by internalising punishments through the painful emotion of *aidōs*, the encompassing Greek concept for 'shame', 'guilt' and 'remorse'. For example, Jane, an adolescent with a sense of shame, might hear the voice of her parents in her head when she wakes up with a hangover after a night of heavy drinking. Whether or not her 'conscience' works, depends at least partly on whether her parents have already criticised her harshly and angrily before for her excessive drinking (Curzer, 2002, p. 159). While Jane would be more virtuous if she did not drink too much in the first place, experiencing shame after doing something bad is better than not feeling it, i.e. being shameless. It is a mistake to think that shame tells Jane that the act is wrong. She does not discover that excessive drinking is bad until she has experienced shame. Experiencing shame *presupposes* that Jane already believes that an attitude of temperance is the best way to deal with the pleasure of drinking. The emotion emphasises the belief that something she did was vicious, and helps to internalise this judgment even more. Curzer (2002, p. 160) also mentions two other functions of shame. While shame indicates that something bad was done, this does not imply that it is immediately clear what was so vicious about a certain action. Shame can motivate people to explicate the tacit knowledge further, and help them think about how the disgraceful acts could have been prevented. Finally, this kind of retrospective thinking can have a prospective function when it makes people think about new situations. When a child is about to do something bad, e.g. to go shoplifting with friends, he can be revolted by the very thought in advance. In this case, shame "says no to acts before the learner performs them" (Curzer, 2002, p. 161). In addition, one can also feel shame, just as pride, vicariously, e.g. when Jane feels ashamed when a friend becomes completely drunk at a party the following weekend. Our reactions to other people's moral mistakes reveal a lot about ourselves.

The generous-minded can move on to the level of the 'un-self-controlled' when they have, through shame, acquired the rational capacity to discriminate between virtuous and vicious acts. This means that they have to become practically wiser, which includes discerning the particulars of the situation, reading a situation in their moral salient aspects, and hitting the mean in their emotional responses. Despite their ability to identify what is virtuous, the 'un-self-controlled' are easily overcome by desires that point in other directions. When they are distracted, the full grasp of what should be done in a situation comes too late (Kraut, 2010).

During the decision-making process, people who lack self-control do not have any internal conflicts. It is only after they have acted and recognised the error made that they start to deliberate. Reasoning plays a different role in two kinds of *akrasia*: impetuosity (*propeteia*) and weakness (*astheneia*). The weak person deliberates about what should be done but makes a choice that is influenced more by a passion than by reason. For example, a weak person can become excessively angered at an insult, even though he judged correctly that he has reason to be angry (Stohr, 2002, p. 359). Impetuous people do not deliberate and do not make a reasoned choice (*prohairesis*) at all; they just do what their passion tells them to do.

There are several ways to deal with lack of self-control. Imagine that I succumb to my desire to eat fatty foods as I pass by a fast food chain, even though I value my health and know that fries are not healthy. When friends confront me with the inconsistency between my self-declared healthy lifestyle and buying junk food, there are several ways to deal with the cognitive dissonance (see also §2.2.3). For example, I can change my desire for the fries and buy a salad instead, I can deny that fries are bad for my health, or I can continue buying fries, and continue feeling sorry about it. Aristotle explains that this feeling of regret or remorse distinguishes the 'un-self-controlled' from vicious people. While children and morally childish adults do not think much about what is good, vicious people have used their reason and deliberately chose to live an unhealthy life (*NE* 1150a18-21). They do not regret anything, and are, according to Aristotle, 'incurable'. Or, we might say, uneducable.

Aristotle writes that the 'un-self-controlled' *have* the right moral knowledge in theory, but do not use it, and to explain this distinction he compares the 'un-self-controlled' with actors: the former 'know' virtue in the same way as the latter know their text (*NE* 1147a24). When actors perform a part in a play, they have to find their own way of becoming the character they are impersonating. However, some actors might just recite the text that they have learned by rote, without relating to it or really understanding what the texts is about. They know the text in an impersonal way and have not made the character *their own*. Likewise, people who lack self-control often say things that one expects from virtuous people. They are virtuous in disguise. They imitate or parrot others in what they say and do, but this kind of knowledge has not been assimilated, has not become part of their character – which, as Aristotle notes, takes time. Whatever virtuous things somebody who lacks self-control does, they are not done out of character, i.e. on the basis of stable emotional dispositions. For the difference between imitating someone else and acquiring a virtue yourself, see §4.2.

The description of the 'un-self-controlled' enables us to see something important about the situationists' claims discussed in §3.3. While Merritt et al (2010) argued that the virtue of practical wisdom is psychologically unrealistic because 65 percent of the subjects in the Milgram experiment obeyed the experimenter while they knew that hurting people is wrong, we now know (1) that many subjects lacked self-control, (2) that this is a developmental stage, and (3) that there are ways to educate them, especially when they are still young, to become self-controlled. With regard to the Milgram experiments, Badhwar (2009, p. 261) notices that "[e]ven as the experiments challenge globalism, they support the hypothesis that the vast majority of people are disposed to be *akratic* or weak-willed, and remarkably so, in certain domains of their lives." True, the experiments show that the lack of self-control is even more easily invoked than Aristotle envisaged. For example, people are not only under the sway of their own desires, but they are also inclined to shirk their critical judgment to a group (Asch, 1951), or to somebody with authority. Should we conclude from this that people are confronted with so many temptations in their daily lives that the stage of full virtue should be abandoned altogether? My argument is that social psychological research does a great job in identifying the circumstances that tempt the 'un-self-controlled' to refrain from acting virtuously, but that it leaves virtue as the goal of moral development intact.

3.4.4 Stage 3: Self-control

Aristotle is not directly concerned with *enkrateia* (self-control) as a state of character. For reasons mentioned earlier, he starts Book VII by discussing *akrasia* and mentions *enkrateia* as its counterpart. Due to this connection, his definition of self-control is restricted to a particular domain, i.e. the mastery of one's desires for bodily appetites, the same sphere to which the virtue of 'temperance' applies (see §3.2.5). So strictly speaking, not the broad category of 'virtue' succeeds 'self-control' as the final stage of moral development, but the virtue of *temperance*. When we apply self-control to other domains than bodily appetites, we have to add a qualification, such as, 'with regard to x', where x can be e.g. anger.

Acquiring self-control is, according to Aristotle, certainly praiseworthy but not the final stage of moral development. How do the self-controlled person and the virtuous person differ? Imagine that Bob and Marley are watching their favourite television programme, and a friend calls for help with a broken car.[24] Both Bob, who is virtuous, and Marley, who is self-controlled, have a commitment to virtue, and reason enables both of them to specify what good is at stake in the situation: they know that helping a friend in need is the best thing to do. Moreover, they will both go out and help, and – at the time of the action – they will also have the same desire. However, the self-controlled and the virtuous person differ with regard to their desires *prior to* the act (Gould, 1994, p. 179). Marley also wants to stay at home and watch television, and he is frustrated that his friend calls for help at this hour. So even though he 'knows' that helping a friend is more important than watching the programme, he feels pain at the loss of something that he recognises as relatively unimportant. So he is insufficiently moved by something that he recognises as very important. Gould (1994) distinguishes the self-controlled from

---

24 The example is adapted from Stohr (2002, p. 362)

someone who *endures* his passions. The person of endurance (*karterikos*) manages to act virtuously but only with fierce difficulties, since they want to do otherwise all of the time. In this reading, people who 'endure' their base passions still have these passions *while* acting, while the self-controlled persons have mastered their desires *before* they act. So, if Marley remained annoyed all of the time, complaining to the friend that he really hated to be distracted from the programme, he would not qualify as self controlled, but rather as somebody who merely endures his unruly passion.

In any case, whether Marley 'endures' or 'masters' his desires, there is still a kind of discrepancy between knowledge and feelings that are absent in virtuous people. The difference between self-control and temperance has to do with the way that the agent's reasons and feelings are connected: "If the agent's feelings and inclinations reflect her correct judgments of value, then she is virtuous. If they do not, then she is merely continent." (Stohr, 2002, p. 362). We can also try to understand the difference between self-control and virtue in terms of the pleasure and pain involved in deliberation. People who endure or control their passions go through psychological conflict before acting virtuously, and so it is often assumed that virtue will not be completely *pleasurable* to them. The self-controlled person would be someone who performs virtuous actions, but who struggles with contrary inclinations and finds virtue difficult and unpleasant. In contrast, the fully virtuous person is supposed to act with ease and pleasure, not having the need to overcome competing inclinations (Stohr, 2002, p. 340). The assumption that Aristotle made, and which we probably still make, is that internal conflict, stress and frustration are signs that something is wrong, and that it is better not to have these conflicts, and to prefer a kind of harmony between feeling, reason and action. Annas (1993, p. 53) even emphasises that:

> "[i]t is important to respect in ethical theory the everyday contrast between someone who does the right thing, but has to battle with his feelings to do so, and thus acts reluctantly and with a sense of pain and loss, and the person who does the right thing and whose feelings endorse the action, and who thus acts gladly and with pleasure."

However, can we really make a sharp distinction between the conflicted self-controlled person and the virtuous person who acts 'gladly and with pleasure'? Can the distinction between self-control and virtue be based on the presence or absence of pleasure? Curzer (2002) has not only argued that the path to virtue is painful for learners, but he maintains that virtuous acts are not *overall* pleasant for the fully virtuous either. For example, the virtue of 'good temper' deals with the emotion of anger, which is a painful feeling. As the good-tempered person is someone who deals with this emotion appropriately, he will still feel the pain that accompanies the emotion of anger. In addition, two people who have a character friendship will sympathise with each other in such a way that if one suffers a misfortune, the other will be pained by it, too. There are many more examples that illustrate that it is not especially plausible to maintain that it is a failure to find virtuous action painful (Stohr, 2002, p. 352). One option to accommodate these examples is to say that virtuous actions sometimes involve some pain, but that the pleasure involved is always greater, and that virtuous acts will be overall pleasant to the virtuous person. According to Curzer (2002, p. 152), this option is problematic too. Imagine coming home from work, and encountering two thieves stealing your computer. If you decide to fight the robbers because you consider it the courageous thing to do considering the circumstances, roughly two outcomes are possible. If you succeed in overpowering them or chasing them away, retaining your computer, the pleasures may outweigh your fear and the leg wound you suffered. However, if you lose and the robbers leave you behind with a wounded leg and no computer, the pain will dominate, even though you will experience some pleasure in knowing that you did the courageous thing. Is virtuous action overall pleasant? Assuming that fighting the thieves was virtuous[25], it partly depends on the outcome of the action. Courage does not necessarily lead to success or victory, and being virtuous never guarantees a successful outcome. Due to unforeseen circumstances, virtuous actions can have painful outcomes (but they will not be admired less for it, see Annas, 2011, p. 111). We may have a strong belief that virtuous action is overall pleasant to virtuous people, that it pays off in the end in terms of pleasure, but this belief cannot be attributed to Aristotle (Curzer, 2002, p. 152).

Virtue and pleasure are, however, not completely unrelated. Firstly, people will enjoy the satisfaction of their well-formed desires, such as eating a nutritious dinner, just like immoderate people will enjoy tasting junk-food. Secondly, people who act virtuously will find pleasure in the belief that they do the best thing. This is a kind of attitudinal pleasure, to be distinguished from sensory pleasure. A virtuous person will not always take sensory pleasure in his virtuous actions, but he can be pleased that he has done what he should (Stohr, 2002, p. 353). Thirdly, we should make a distinction between virtuous acts and a virtuous life. While virtuous acts may be painful when a certain goal is not achieved or when it is achieved with severe drawbacks, a virtuous *life* can be called overall pleasant, since it does not have an 'external goal' that we can fail to achieve. Virtuous people will find virtuous action very painful, precisely because their life is *eudaimōn*. As they find it worthwhile to be alive, they know better than anybody what is at stake in virtuous – and often risky – behaviour, since they might be deprived from great goods. The pain that comes with virtuous action presupposes the recognition of the value of the goods that one is potentially sacrificing (Stohr, 2002, p. 355).

---

25 The second scenario raises the question whether fighting the thieves was courageous in the first place. If you are weak and the thieves appear to be strong, is it not reckless to start a fight? Is remembering their faces and calling the police not much wiser?

3.4.5 Stage 4: Full Virtue

The last stage in the Aristotelian model of moral development is full virtue. From sections 3.2 and 3.3, it can be inferred that virtuous people are 'happy' in the sense that they perform the distinctive activity of being human, i.e. rationality, well. Their life is not more pleasurable than the life of those on the other stages, but they will derive joy from doing virtuous things and also from knowing that they do this. Virtuous people have a stable and firm commitment to the good over a lifetime, are practically wise and hit the mean with regard to actions and emotions in all kinds of circumstances. They also perform these action for certain reasons. Moreover, they will be admired for their character, and be an inspiring ideal to others.

After discussing all kinds of all-too-human emotions involved in moral development, such as fear, disappointment, prospective shame and remorse, it is doubtful whether complete virtue can ever be exemplified by anyone. Being virtuous, i.e. having reached the last stage of moral development, would mean that one has ceased to experience these emotions. As it is difficult to imagine that this is possible for a human being, would it be better to remove this stage of the Aristotelian developmental model? Does the Aristotelian model suffer the same problem as Kohlberg's, when the last stage was deleted because he discovered that there were no respondents who justified their judgments by appealing to universal principles of justice (§2.3.3)? Another solution would be to think of the 'last' stage of moral development as an indeterminate and open-ended level. What does this mean?

A metaphor can be illuminating in this context. Reaching the highest stage should *not* be compared to a racing cyclist who has made it to the finishing line, steps off his bike and has time to relax. Virtue is more like a finish that *moves with* the cyclist as he approaches the finishing line, and that will spur him on to do even better. Likewise, we can say that the goal of moral development is not something fixed that can be given in advance, already grasped by learners, as if they only have to work out *how* to achieve it (Annas, 2011, p. 123). Even for the virtuous person there is room for improvement. Firstly, when a virtuous person encounters new situations and deliberates about what and how to feel and act, there are several ways in which they can and sometimes do act wrongly (Curzer, 2005). Secondly, the virtuous person's grasp of the good life can be refined. Moral development is on this level not only about improving habits of emotion and action, but also about an increased *understanding* of virtue. Attempts to arrive at a more or less comprehensive conceptualisation and systematisation of a practical way of life is not typical of an Aristotelian approach, but is recognisable throughout ancient philosophy (Hadot, 1995).

At first sight, a more theoretical understanding of virtue seems discontinuous with the kind of practical wisdom necessary for appropriate desire and action.

However, a theoretical exploration of virtue is in line with the practical *know-how* to act and feel well. Moral development does not start with learning about the ultimate principles of virtue. Aristotle writes: "...arguments seem to have enough influence to stimulate and encourage the civilised ones among the young people, and perhaps too make virtue take possession of a well-born character that truly loves what is fine, but they seem unable to turn the many toward being fine and good." (*NE* 1179b5-11). People first acquire a taste for and commitment to the good life through habituation, and can later be taught to understand why this commitment is worthwhile. Questions about the 'why' of virtue are not the questions of a moral sceptic, but of already morally formed people who have an interest in living well, like the young men who followed Aristotle's courses (Sherman, 1989, p. 196).[26] In the hypothetical situation that Aristotle would have to reply to Thrasymachus' unabashed defence of injustice in Plato's *Republic*, Aristotle would probably admit that whatever he is going to say to this rhetorician will not be convincing because he lacks a proper moral education. In the Aristotelian model, even the most critical inquirers are believed to depart from (and return to) practical questions about how they are to live.

The distinction between the 'that' (or 'how') and the 'why' (or 'because') of virtue is useful to make clearer what moral reasoning is like on the level of virtue. Somebody who knows the 'that' knows how to act in particular circumstances of life. Someone who, in addition, knows the 'why' has a more reflective understanding of the values embodied in his practical decisions. He can "justify his decision by reference to those general goods which are achievable by human action" (Tobin, 1989, p. 196). This has several advantages. Firstly, the explication of the normative dimension of human action is needed when one is held responsible for one's actions. Secondly, it is useful when there is an (apparent) conflict between different goals or virtues (Annas, 2011, p. 19). Thirdly, it has an educational function for others, e.g. when one has to give reasons to children, enabling them to go ahead in different situations and contexts. Fourthly, arguments can have a therapeutic function for oneself. The attempt to justify one's life theoretically and to conduct dialogues with others about this attempt can contribute to a change of one's self (Hadot, 1995). For example, in antiquity, Epicurists and Stoics recommended their followers to meditate and write about the central doctrines in order to become in the mood to live as a Epicurean or Stoic.

Note that 'justifying' does not mean that the practically wise person can completely detach himself from his life, and assess it from an external point. The question how to live your life is always asked by people who already have a life (Annas, 2011, p. 150). This means that the justification of one's choices is much more of an *articulation* of the often implicit ways in which we pursue the goal we considers to constitute human flourishing. In contrast to linear thinking, this can

---

26 The *Nicomachean Ethics* is considered not to be a unitary treatise, but a collection of different lecture notes that were put together later.

be called structured or 'teleological' reflection.[27] In daily life, we usually think of actions following each other as parts of a causal chain until our life ends. We can, however, also ask why we are doing the actions that we do. Pursuing this question for some time will make clearer what we are aiming for in our life; for the sake of which we are doing things. We answer this question not by reporting causes, but by giving *reasons*, which can, in turn, motivate us to act in certain ways in the future.

3.4.5 Towards a Virtue Ethical Alternative to Kohlberg

Many important things mentioned in this section were not original. The points that (1) the relation between reason and desire can only be understood well if we approach virtue developmentally, (2) that the Aristotelian categories can be turned into stages and (3) that the emotion of shame works as a catalyst for moral development have all been made before. However, no one has integrated these ideas into a more elaborate account of virtue psychology and development, taking debates about the correct interpretation of Aristotle's *Ethics* seriously and keeping contemporary moral education in mind, too. Section 3.4 distinguished between four main stages of moral development:

> Level 1: being uncommitted to virtue
> Level 2: being committed to virtue, but lacking self-control
> Level 3: being committed to virtue, and having self-control
> Level 4: being fully virtuous

A number of features about this model are worth emphasising. Firstly, focus was on the pre-moral and still pre-rational children who are part of 'the many', neglecting the 'fully wretched' and morally indifferent adults. Secondly, the 'generous-minded' were treated as a sublevel of the 'un-self-controlled', still being very close to the uncommitted. Thirdly, a distinction was made between two kinds of lack of self-control, one being impetuosity, the other weakness. Fourthly, 'softness' and 'endurance' were presented not as separate stages, but as attitudes towards pain of the un-self-controlled and the self-controlled. Fifthly, pain was considered to be involved on all of these levels. Sixthly, the idea that a more theoretical understanding of virtue is continuous with practical wisdom at the lower levels was discussed.

Drafting this account matters from both a practical and theoretical point of view. Theoretically, this neo-Aristotelian account of moral development is of interest because it challenges Aristotelians to fulfil the promise that it does not provide abstract knowledge about what is good, but helps people to lead good lives. An account of how people can get to the level where they consider virtue to be an essential part of their flourishing seems to be part of this. Moreover, this account

---

27 The division between two kinds of thinking is derived from Annas (2011), p. 121. The label 'teleological reflection' is mine.

can help us to go beyond Kohlberg's still dominant cognitive developmental paradigm. As most recent handbooks on developmental psychology (see e.g. Miller, 2011; Shaffer & Kipp, 2010; Kail & Cavanaugh, 2010) only discuss Piaget's and Kohlberg's ideas on moral development, much needs to be done to correct assumptions that psychologists make about which capacities and powers are involved in moral development. Finally, by giving a more comprehensive account of virtue development, virtue ethics has something to offer that educationalists who conceive of moral education in terms of e.g. 'values education' or 'moral reasoning'. It can show how a commitment to moral value can be developed into rationally endorsed habits of feeling and action, and how reasoning and desire are related on different levels. A virtue ethical approach to moral education is much more convincing when it has a story to tell about what happens to children in terms of their reasons, desires and actions as they are morally educated.

What would have to be done to make this virtue ethical approach to moral development also an evidence-based alternative to Kohlberg's model? Firstly, philosophers would have to study Aristotle's writings much more carefully, offering better and more nuanced descriptions of the levels. Secondly, philosophers and psychologists would have to cooperate to conceptualise the Aristotelian moral psychology in such a way that it is still 'Aristotelian', but fits the terminology of the social sciences. This means that moral emotions (such as shame), the core concepts in a virtue ethical moral psychology (such as 'desire', 'reason', 'disposition', 'virtue' and 'character') and the relationships between these elements should be scrutinised by (as Anscombe proposed) a philosophical psychology, and by learning from what empirical research about these concepts, e.g. self-control, has yielded. Thirdly, psychologists would have to think carefully about how to measure these stages empirically. For example, there are ways to measure children's ideal and real moral self-concepts (Higgins, 1987). Although people's self-concepts are not necessarily identical with their character (see §4.2.4), psychologists could improve these methods to capture subjects 'character' better, and compare the emotions, reasons and actions that children and adolescents have in morally demanding situations over longer periods of time.

3.5 Conclusion

After discussing three other approaches to moral education, this was the first out of three chapters to make clear what a fourth, a neo-Aristotelian virtue ethical approach, entails. First, the role of emotions, virtues and practical wisdom as elements in an Aristotelian theory of action were described. Second, the critique of situationists on some central virtue ethical notions was examined and evaluated. Philosophers such as Doris and Harman argued that the concept of a global character trait is empirically problematic because social psychological experiments show that many people do not exhibit such traits. This challenge to virtue ethics was addressed by specifying a neo-Aristotelian account of moral development that made clear how people who are yet uncommitted to virtue can make progress. The question remains in which ways the Aristotelian account of moral psychology and development that was defended in this chapter enable us to understand moral education better.

Teachers often take virtues to be simply 'desirable character traits' or 'moral qualities', so this chapter made clear that moral qualities or character traits have to meet certain formal criteria in order to count as an Aristotelian virtue. If these and other formal criteria are taken seriously, teachers will be able to notice certain things about their pupils that they would otherwise have overlooked. For example, if teachers experience anger, or see that pupils are angry with each other, a virtue ethical perspective enables them to see that there are morally better and worse ways to deal with this emotion. Also, if teachers judge someone to be irascible, quarrelsome or boorish, they will now know that these are vicious cultivations of emotions that have a virtuous counterpart.

Another advantage of the formal definition of virtue expounded in this chapter is that it can be applied to more modern moral qualities that are often referred to as virtues, such as 'respect', 'authenticity', 'integrity' or 'responsibility'. For instance, Lickona's (1992) influential book *Educating for Character* is all about teaching two virtues: respect and responsibility. However, it is by no means clear that these two moral qualities are virtues in the Aristotelian sense. The formal definition of virtue enables us to adopt a critical attitude towards the seemingly endless and arbitrary lists of virtues produced by (American) character educationalists. The virtues on such lists would be better treated as 'candidate virtues' that need to be put to the test. This 'test' can include questions like: 'Which emotions are the candidate virtue a cultivation of?', 'Are there two extreme, vicious ways to shape this emotion?', and 'How is the candidate virtue related to a good life?'.

Even if the candidate virtues do not pass the Aristotelian test, looking at them through a virtue ethical lens can uncover certain things that would otherwise have been ignored. For example, it is obvious that calling someone 'irresponsible' involves a negative evaluation of his character. If responsibility, however, is an Aristotelian virtue, it would have to be possible to identify a second vice. So virtue ethics enable us to see that 'over-responsibility' can be a vice, too (De Ruyter, 2002). If responsibility is described as a basic "readiness to respond to normative demands" (Williams, 2008), responsibility could pass the test if we managed to show that it also makes sense to say that we can be *too* ready to respond to normative demands, e.g. when we neglect important non-normative demands.

The more fundamental issue at stake is whether we should *care* whether such moral qualities pass the Aristotelian test. Why would moral qualities have to meet certain Aristotelian criteria in the first place? The first option is to be very lenient, e.g. abandon the doctrine of the mean and assimilate all kinds of 'virtues' in a comprehensive kind of character education that is not recognisably Aristotelian. The second option is to be very strict and reject all candidate virtues that do not pass the Aristotelian test, even when they are very popular in character education programmes or society as a whole. As a consequence, 'accountability', 'cleanliness', 'creativity', 'eloquence' and other commendable qualities would have to be removed from popular virtue lists.[28]

My own position is somewhere in between: while I do see the merits of an Aristotelian approach to virtue and moral education, I do not think that moral education should necessarily be restricted to the education of Aristotelian virtues. Why can Aristotelian, quasi-Aristotelian and other kinds of moral qualities not exist alongside each other in practice? We can *try* to see whether Aristotle's definition of virtue works for modern moral qualities like 'responsibility' or 'respect, but we do not have to be disappointed in either Aristotle or our modern moral vocabulary if it does not. Maybe, a contemporary approach to moral education will always be something of a 'mixed bag', an assortment of moral concepts some of which can be clarified by ancient Greek philosophy and some that cannot. I understand virtue ethics as a way of thinking that enriches the study of morality, psychology and education, without claiming that everything that falls outside its scope is worthless.

When we focus on the developmental aspects of Aristotle's moral psychology, this chapter made clear that – in contrast to cognitive development and care ethics – a virtue ethical approach goes beyond an easy dualism of desire and reason. Virtue ethics affirms a strong intuition that the other two approaches have difficulties apprehending, i.e. that moral development is essentially a matter of both heart and mind. However, it would be a mistake to think that desire and reason are interdependent from the start. It is more adequate to say that they are receptive to one another, and start to interact as people make moral progress. The developmental model made clear how reason and desire can ultimately be united in a virtuous person. We also examined some emotions that accompany moral learners at different stages of their development, such as the fear of punishment (on the level of the uncommitted), shame, which presupposes that someone knows that he has done something unworthy of himself (on the level of the uncommitted), and the frustrations or irritations when one does what is virtuous but is insufficiently moved by it (on the level of the self-controlled). Moreover, we saw that the acts of the virtuous person are not necessarily pleasurable. A virtuous person maybe pleased that he has done what he should, but there is no guarantee that virtue will pay off in the end.

These elements are a welcome alternative to Kohlberg's rigid model, which completely ignored the complex interplay between moral emotion, reason and

---

28 Such as the lists on www.virtuescience.com/virtuelist.html or www.virtuesproject.com/virtueslist.html.

action. Admittedly, the conceptual work on developmental psychology would ideally be supplemented with an empirical part, but there are practical reasons why there has not been as much longitudinal research as virtue ethicists would want. In a time when psychologists, like all other researchers, are under pressure to obtain quick results, longitudinal studies about character development are at a great disadvantage (Kupperman, 1991, p. 163). While the virtue ethical model of moral development is still sketchy and lacks empirical validity, it offers teachers a conceptual framework that can help them to look at children's development differently. However, the model does not explain how teaching methods can be adjusted to fit the developmental phase that children are in. For example, it was not specified which pedagogical interventions can be used best to help pupils become committed to virtue, to acquire self-control or acquire practical wisdom. As a philosopher, I try to contribute to a better understanding of three ways in which virtue can be education in schools (role modelling, the use of arts and Socratic dialogues) in Chapter 4, but I leave it up to teachers and educationalists to determine how these and other strategies can be linked best to the developmental stages described in this chapter.

When discussing the viability of an Aristotelian approach to moral education, one final point of emphasis is the relationship between Aristotle's philosophical psychology and the kind of experimental psychology to which situationists like Doris and Harman refer. Note that situationists' central message that people's actions cannot be explained in terms of character trait is not new. Chapter 2 showed that the results from the massive *Character Education Inquiry*, carried out in the 1920s, were interpreted as proof that there are no unified traits of character. Mainstream psychology and pedagogy lost interest in notions like 'virtue' and 'character' for about sixty years. The situationism debate in the early twenty-first century can be seen as the introduction of such empirical concerns in the field of moral philosophy, in which virtue ethics has gradually become the third dominant approach to ethics. Do virtue ethicists have to take experimental psychology seriously? Yes and no. In this chapter, it was argued that even though character traits often fail to be consistent and evaluatively integrated, full virtue does not have to be dropped as an ideal, and character education can be more than teaching children to identify and avoid ethically challenging situations. When adopting Flanagan's criterion to determine whether moral or intellectual virtues are psychologically realistic or not, we found no reason why it would be impossible for human beings to acquire virtues.

In general, the developmental perspective on the situationism debate made clear that the results from social psychological research do not mean that this constitution is fixed once and for all. There is almost always room for improvement, even if this progress will often be difficult and sometimes have to be established over generations. At the same time, the situationism debate created a perfect opportunity for a large number of (virtue) ethicists to debate the status and nature of the virtues. Moreover, the second half of the twentieth century yielded a score of psychological experiments that made clear that the majority of people lack self-control in certain domains of their lives. The experiments showed that the lack of self-control appears to be even more easily invoked than Aristotle envisaged. When there are countervailing considerations, people are easily temped to forget their moral norms. Social psychological research has done a great job of identifying the circumstances that prevent many people from acting virtuously.

Chapter 4
The Education of Virtue in Schools

4.1 Introduction

The previous chapter was an attempt to improve teachers' understanding of what it means to cultivate pupils' moral virtues by presenting a neo-Aristotelian approach to the psychology and development of virtue. This yielded a number of formal criteria that character traits have to meet before they deserve the label 'virtue'. It also provided a detailed account of what happens in terms of feelings, reasons and actions when children make progress towards full virtue and practical wisdom. However, the question that was hardly touched upon is what teachers can do in schools to stimulate children's development, given the limits of what is humanely possible. What does character education in schools look like from an explicit Aristotelian point of view? Chapter 3 showed that the other three approaches were rather sceptical about character education, because it would stimulate pupils to acquire mindless habits, which would be detrimental to critical thinking. Moreover, there was no evidence that character education 'worked'. Addressing these challenges implies that we will not only describe and evaluate some important character educational strategies, but also address the questions whether character education can stimulate children's moral reasoning, and whether results from social scientific research can affirm its effectiveness. These questions will be returned to in the conclusion.

Besides rebutting the criticism aired by rival approaches to moral education, there is also a positive thesis to be defended in this chapter. Three distinct 'methods' will be included to illustrate that character education is *continuous with* everyday teaching, and not an extra task that is essentially unrelated to the transfer of subject-related knowledge and skills. Therefore, character education is presented as a more deliberate and systematic approach to a dimension of teaching that normally remains implicit, even though teachers engage in it all of the time. The dimension in question refers to the communication of moral qualities in the daily interactions between teachers and pupils. Teachers are more or less honest, patient, responsible, wise, caring, just, reliable people, and these character traits have a *moral* dimension, in the sense that to possess these virtues enables people to lead more or less meaningful lives as human beings – also in the capacity as a teacher. Whether teachers have 'character' does not only become clear through what they say, but especially through their actions. Their character is not expressed through what they teach, but has to do with *how* they teach it. When schools take the moral dimension of teaching very seriously, 'character education' can become an encompassing theme included in the curriculum, staff meetings and teacher training and thus embedded in a school's culture. However, even when there is no support for a broad approach, individual teachers can still put character education into practice.

In this chapter, three 'methods' are described in which teachers can cultivate pupils' virtues in school. Note that these 'methods' have less to do with the didactics of teaching morality, but much more with being a moral teacher. Also, note that the more general 'virtue' is used instead of 'moral virtue', because the third method to be discussed is a means to practise one of teachers' *intellectual* virtues. So, in the title of this chapter, the education of *virtue* in schools refers to both moral and intellectual virtue. The previous chapters highlighted how the two are related in a person who is fully virtuous and practically wise. When we understand character education as a sophisticated attempt by teachers to contribute their share to the development of pupils' virtues, an obvious first 'method' is the use of role models. Therefore, the subject of section §4.2 will be the meaning of role modelling in character education. While people who exemplify morally desirable character traits can be found in stories, movies and the media, too, the first question is what it means for *teachers* to be role models. We will investigate what teachers should be a model of, what modelling involves, and whether it is effective.

In §4.3, the moral educational use of the arts will be discussed. Especially those involved in teaching languages and arts will choose novels or poems to be analysed in class or will tell enthusiastically about books they have recently read. However, at some point, all teachers will somehow become involved in the (narrative) arts: e.g. they will start the class with a 'thought for the day', in which moral lessons are drawn from (biblical) stories, select a movie as part of a project or supervise pupils when performing a classical play. This section looks at the questions of *which* arts are to contribute to pupils' moral development, and how exactly the arts are supposed to be morally educative. How can, e.g. reading books or listening to music make one a better person?

Finally, §4.4 will be dedicated to the question of how dialogue between teachers and pupils, but also among teachers themselves, can contribute to the character formation of pupils. While all teachers have conversations with pupils, and while some of these conversations are about moral issues, it is worth investigating *which kind of* conversation would be best suited from a moral educational point of view. In this section, we will examine whether the moral enquiries demonstrated in the 5th century BC by Socrates, and formalised by Leonard Nelson in the 19th century, can be an instrument to practice the Aristotelian virtue of practical wisdom.

4.2 Role Modelling[29]

Character education considers teachers to be role models, but it is unclear what this means in practice. Do teachers model admirable character traits? And do they do so effectively? In this section the relevant pedagogical and psychological literature is reviewed in order to shed light on these questions. First, the use of role modelling as a teaching method in secondary education is assessed. Second, adolescents' role models and their moral qualities are identified. Third, the psychology of moral learners is critically examined, using Bandura's social learning theory as a point of departure. It turns out that role modelling is rarely used as an explicit teaching method and that only a very small percentage of adolescents recognises teachers as role models. If role modelling is to contribute to children's moral education, teachers are recommended to explain why the modelled traits are morally significant and how pupils can acquire these qualities for themselves.

4.2.1 Introduction

Of the four most influential twentieth century approaches to moral education (values clarification, cognitive development, care ethics and character education) values clarification and cognitive development have been reluctant to recommend teachers to model morally desirable attitudes and behaviour. According to values clarification, teachers' only moral educational responsibility is to clarify pupils' values, refraining as much as possible from the inculcation of values and virtues. Kohlberg's cognitive developmental approach mainly wants teachers to be Socratic dialogue mentors who illuminate children's moral reasoning structures, so they can eventually justify their values from a universal and impartial point of view.

Kohlberg's influential theory attracted more and more criticism in the 1980s and early 1990s, when feminists, virtue ethicists and others increasingly blamed him for having a limited understanding of morality and the psychological mechanisms underlying its development. For example, Carr (1991, 1999) accused Kohlberg of only developing children's rational capacities with which they could decide for themselves how to live, not providing them with any clues about what kind of life is worth living. As an antidote to teachers' 'agnostic neutrality' with regard to substantial moral issues, Carr tried to show that there are objective moral

---

29 Section 4.2 has been accepted for publication and will appear as 'The meaning of role modelling in moral and character education' in the *Journal of Moral Education*. The article can be retrieved from http://dx.doi.org/10.1080/03057240.2012.690727.

goals that teachers can encourage in children, such as the virtues of courage, temperance, justice, honesty and compassion. In this view, the moral dimension of teaching has less to do with explicit moral didactics, but with morality in a basic sense: moral education does not equal 'teaching morality', but being a 'moral teacher', which means extending everyday morality into the nuances of teaching.

Noddings (2010), the most important representative of a care ethical approach to moral education, treats modelling (besides 'dialogue', 'practice' and 'confirmation') as an important means to nurture ethical caring in schools. Besides care ethics, the approach to moral education that has relied most on role modelling is character education. Several character education-based handbooks and websites offer a repertoire of teaching materials on role modelling (e.g. Lickona, 1991, pp. 308-311). The idea that teachers can only cultivate children's character if they display it themselves is even considered to be "the most important moral lesson in the character curriculum." (Lickona, 2004, p. 118). Moreover, several virtue theorists interested in the philosophical underpinnings of this educational practice, such as Carr (1991, pp. 258-259), Kristjánsson (2002, p. 190; 2006a; 2007, ch. 7; 2010b, p. 237) and Steutel and Spiecker (2000, p. 329; 2004, p. 544-546) have discussed role modelling. At the same time, social learning theory (Bandura, 1963, 1986) contributed greatly to a better understanding of the psychological mechanisms underlying this educational practice. Bandura found that a considerable amount of learning takes place through a process in which children learn behaviours, attitudes, values, and beliefs by observing others and the consequences of others' actions.

Although it may be uncontroversial among care and virtue ethicists that teachers cannot easily separate their professional role and personal character traits, modelling becomes more problematic – and more interesting – when we realise two things: teachers' character traits do not necessarily have to be admirable, and even when teachers do model admirable character traits, this may not be done effectively. Unfortunately, teachers' function as role models has been taken for granted to such an extent that it has prevented people in both educational theory and practice from enquiring whether modelling can be improved. Firstly, there is no reason to assume that all teachers model virtuous behaviour. Teachers may also be weak, spiteful, vain and greedy, thereby qualifying as bad teachers (Carr, 1991, p. 258). This implies that we should distinguish between good and bad role models, where good teachers model praiseworthy character traits and bad teachers blameworthy ones. In order to substantiate this distinction, certain traits should be identified as morally desirable. An Aristotelian approach could justify such traits as virtues by explaining why certain character traits are necessary for flourishing as human beings. This approach has been advocated by a number of virtue ethicists, such as Nussbaum, MacIntyre and many others (see: Chapter 3, and for an overview, Crisp & Slote, 2007). Secondly, even if all teachers model desirable character traits, it does not follow that their modelling is effective as an educational method. Therefore, it is worth examining how modelling can best contribute to children's moral development.

In the remainder of the section, social scientific literature will be reviewed in order to find out whether and how moral educational theory can benefit from empirical research and vice versa. Although the psychological processes and mechanisms involved in role modelling are discussed, emphasis is put on the ways in which teachers and pupils conceive of role model education in secondary education. In §4.2.2, it will be examined how teachers use modelling in education and whether adolescents recognise teachers' efforts. §4.2.3 offers a closer look at the virtues that adolescents value in role models, and at the virtues that teachers consider to be important. In §4.2.4, focus is on the psychological state children have to be in before they can be considered to have a role model. Is simply admiring and imitating a teacher enough, or should they also know why the teacher's qualities are worth having? In §4.2.5, the relevant pedagogical literature is consulted to provide teachers with tips on how their modelling can be improved. The conclusion, will answer the question of how philosophy and the pedagogical sciences can benefit from each other in the field of moral education.

4.2.2 The Use of Modelling

The first issue is whether teachers use role modelling as a means to morally educate, and if they do, in which way. Despite attempts to use modelling on a large scale as part of mentoring programmes in Dutch vocational education (Meijers, 2008), there is consensus in the pedagogical literature that the moral aspects of teaching receive attention in mostly unintended and unconscious ways (Hansen, 2001, p. 852). Moreover, the literature on teacher education suggests that preparing future teachers for moral education is often implicit and unplanned (Willemse et al., 2005; 2008). From interviews with 54 teacher educators, Willemse et al. (2008) concluded that moral education is highly dependent on the personalities of individual teachers, and that they hardly morally educate by inculcating values or virtues. Instead, they try to infuse the classroom somehow with their manners, style and judgment. Klaassen (2002, p. 155) makes the same observations: teachers shy away from talking about norms and values explicitly, and try to serve as models in a predominantly non-verbal manner. If most of the modelling in (teacher) education is implicit, it can hardly be called a teaching *method*.

If these observations are right, and most of the role modelling in education remains implicit, not many pupils would be expected to mention teachers as role models. In this section, four large surveys will be reviewed that can help answer this question. First, there is the survey by Bucher (1998) among 1150 Austrian and German pupils aged 10 to 18 years. Data was collected using a questionnaire, which included the open-ended question 'what persons are your personal models, and why?' Multiple responses were possible. Spontaneously, parents (45%) and

Chapter 4

other family members (31%) were mentioned most often. These results were confirmed when pupils had to rate forty persons on a scale from 1 ('no model whatever') to 4 ('a very important model for me'). Teachers were only mentioned as role models in another part of the survey, when pupils were asked to recall *former* models. Again, parents and other relatives were highest on the list, but 10% of the participating pupils mentioned teachers as former role models this time. Second, there are two surveys on the relation between having a role model and health-risk behaviour (Yancy, Siegel & McDaniel, 2002; Yancy et al., 2011). In both studies, adolescents aged 12 to 17 were asked about the persons they 'admire or look up to' or 'want to be like'. Parents and relatives were chosen most often, while teachers were mentioned by about 3% of the respondents. In total, 4759 adolescents participated in these surveys. Finally, there is a survey by Bricheno & Thornton (2007) among 379 British pupils aged 10 to 16 years. This study differs from the other three as its explicit purpose was to explore whether children see their teachers as role models. Data was collected using a questionnaire in which pupils were asked about their 'most important' or 'best' role model. Overall, a third of the pupils chose one or both parents as their most important role model and 1.9% mentioned teachers as their most important model.

When we examine these studies, it is worth noting that between 28 and 44 percent of the adolescents did not mention a role model at all. From this, we should not conclude that their lives are not influenced by parents, siblings, peers or others, but for one reason or another, they simply are not able to *recognise* this influence. Secondly, all surveys found that relatives, and in particular parents, are important role models to adolescents (on average, about one-third mentions them). Thirdly, when children are asked about their current models, teachers turn out to be very low on the list, typically about 3%. In addition, when asked about their most important model, the figures are even lower. However, if adolescents are asked about their *former* models, one in ten recognises a teacher as a role model. Moreover, in a study by Timmerman (2009), thirteen teacher educators (between 32 and 60 years old), who had taught in secondary education for several years and eventually became teacher educators, were asked about which teacher models impressed them. Interestingly, all but one respondent "had vivid memories of their teachers, particularly in secondary education" (Timmerman, 2009, p. 230).

What this suggests, is that parents, friends or teachers do have a certain formative influence on our (moral) development, but that we only realise their contribution to our development in retrospect. Only when we have acquired certain character traits ourselves can we identify educators who had similar traits and tell a story about how they contributed to who we have become. Although such a narrative process would explain why adults have a better memory of their role models than children, it does not offer an explanation as to why teachers are only mentioned by a minority of pupils. There may be other factors that can explain why teachers are not mentioned often (e.g. the fact that kids spend more time with parents, siblings and peers than with teachers), but despite this, it seems reasonable to assume that if schools pay more serious attention to modelling, figures could be higher. Of course, this raises the question of why it is important for teachers to be role models, and what they should be models of.

4.2.3 Teachers as Moral Exemplars

The question of what teachers should be models of can be answered in several ways. To know what character traits are morally desirable, the writings of moral philosophers can be consulted. However, another potential source is ordinary people's intuitions. Provided that this kind of research is valid and reliable (Bogdan & Biklen, 2003), teachers can be asked which virtues they want to be a model of and pupils what character traits they value in teachers. Obviously, philosophers may show that the intuitions of teachers and pupils are inconsistent, but people's ideas about virtues are at least a good starting point for philosophical reflection.

The first question that must be confronted, however, is whether we can think of role models *in terms of character traits*. The concepts of 'moral development' and 'moral maturity' were understood predominantly along Kohlbergian lines in the twentieth century.[30] In line with the results from his empirical research, Kohlberg constructed a normative theory about the goal of moral development, which he conceived of as an autonomous person who could justify moral judgments from an impartial point of view. It was only in the early 1990s that psychologists started to correct his philosophical conception by investigating how ordinary people understand 'moral excellence'. Especially Colby & Damon's (1992) study of twenty-three recognised moral exemplars helped to alter the landscape of moral development and education. It showed that moral exemplary people are not distinguished by their level of moral reasoning, as one would expect if one follows Kohlberg, but by their moral personality or 'self' (Power, 2007, p. 92). Subsequent studies (Hart & Fegley, 1995; Walker et al., 1995; Matsuba & Walker, 2004, 2005) confirmed that character traits play an important role in distinguishing moral exemplars from ordinary people. Hart & Fegley (1995) discovered that young moral exemplars referred more often to moral and caring character traits than a group of comparison adolescents. In addition, Matsuba & Walker (2004) found that exemplars describe themselves e.g. as more trusting, modest and caring than comparison peers do. According to virtue ethicist and character educationalists, a 'character' (or 'personality', which is arguably its modern psychological equivalent) is an integrated set of virtues, which are essentially dispositional emotions (see Chapter 3). These virtues are intrinsically related to a flourishing human life, which philosophers have traditionally referred to using the Greek notion of *eudaimonia* (see Chapter 5).

---

30 Although neo-Kohlbergian models of development are still being supported. See Rest et al. (2000).

Chapter 4

If a role model can be characterised as having a moral character or being a kind a person, the next question is which character traits are appreciated in teachers. Although there are a number of studies that have investigated the personality factors that people associate with the abstract *concept* of 'moral exemplar' (Walker, 1999; Walker & Hennig, 2004), there are only a few studies that look at the character traits that people attribute to their own role models, teachers included. Research by Bricheno & Thornton (2007, p. 388) shows that pupils admire people who are honest, help other people (to learn), are hard working and successful in his/her career, have a sense of humour, and are respected by others. Each of these attributes was mentioned by at least one third of the respondents. However, we cannot conclude that pupils specifically wanted *their teachers* to have these attributes; pupils use these attributes to describe all of their role models – whether they are teachers or not.

The only empirical study which goes some way in answering the question of what pupils admire in teachers is a study conducted by Timmerman (2009), who interviewed 13 teacher educators about their former role models in high school. One reason why we have to be cautious in using these results, however, is that she asked these teachers to recall specific *teaching* (and not: moral) qualities. They are, nevertheless, interesting, because the respondents' descriptions of their former models contain moral concepts. Timmerman classified the qualities mentioned in three categories. The 'storyteller' can tell fascinating stories that pupils never forget; the 'personal teacher' type is admired because of his human interest in the pupils and the way in which he shows his 'self' by teaching a subject in his own typical way; and the 'playful' teacher is admired, because he uses all kinds of experimental ways to motivate pupils to engage in the learning process, and because he manages the class in a light, natural way. What this means is that respondents were impressed by teachers who were not just experts, but who were also interested, engaged and playful, who fascinated and inspired them, and who dared to show their personality and their identity as human beings. Although it is not immediately clear why being 'interested', 'engaged' or 'playful' would be *moral* qualities (or virtues), Timmerman's study emphasises that children appreciate teachers who show through their behaviour what kind of person they are. As teachers place a heavy emphasis on setting a good example themselves (Klaassen, 2002, p. 155) and parents endorse teachers modelling values (Veugelers & De Kat, 2003, p. 84), there seems to be ample room for teachers to model virtuous conduct.

It is now clear what pupils appreciate in teachers. But which virtues do teachers (want to) model? There are only two studies available that can indirectly help to answer this question. Van Oudenhoven et al. (2007) asked 83 Dutch teachers to mention what they take, in general, to be positive character traits or virtues. These teachers worked at both public and religious (e.g. Protestant, Catholic,

Islamic) schools. The 195 virtues that the teachers mentioned were categorised by the researchers in 15 categories. 'Respect' was the most often mentioned (cluster) virtue, followed by 'justice', 'wisdom' and 'joy'. When teachers were asked to rate the virtues on a scale from 1 (least important) to 5 (most important), 'respect' was again rated highest (4.5). 'Love' came second (4.2) and 'justice' and 'reliability' third (both 4). One reason why 'love' was not among the virtues mentioned most often while it did receive high ratings has something to do with the religious nature of some of the schools: it turned out that especially teachers with a Muslim background held the virtue of 'love' in high esteem. When the teachers were asked how virtues can be paid attention to, they considered role modelling to be by far the most important method. It is tempting to interpret this study as saying that character education is very much alive in Dutch schools, because teachers can articulate which virtues they consider to be important and because they have an idea about how to educate them. However, the fact that 'respect' is valued most, suggests that things are more complicated.

In education, the meaning of 'respect' often seems to be close to what R.S. Peters (1966, p. 59) described as the "awareness one has that each man has his own aspirations, his own viewpoint on the world; that each man takes pride in his achievements, however idiosyncratic they may be." Ideally, this would imply that pupils are taught to listen to what others have to say, to accept personal differences, to be considerate, and not to ignore others' needs. In liberal societies, respecting others often comes down to treating people's moral values and virtues as a matter of personal choice. As long as teachers' and pupils' conduct does not violate certain minimal standards, their morality remains a private business (Klaassen, 2002, p. 155). In this case, 'respect' is nothing but a formal meta-virtue that teachers agree upon precisely because they do not agree on anything substantial. Understood in this way, the importance teachers attach to (the virtue of) respect is a mixed blessing. While Van Oudenhoven's study makes clear that in denominational schools, teachers are still committed to teaching something like the traditional religious virtues, such as love, faith and hope, the popularity of 'respect' suggests that the moral content, i.e. the virtues that enable a pupil to flourish as a human being, is still a controversial subject, especially in state schools.

Van Oudenhoven et al. (2007) inform us about the virtues that teachers *profess* to value, but they do not show which virtues teachers actually model in the classroom. Fallona (2000) empirically studied how three teachers, who taught a reading course at an American middle school, exhibited moral virtues. She concluded that these teachers exhibit Aristotelian virtues all of the time, but that not all virtues that were identified beforehand turned out to be immediately visible. Most observable were friendliness, wit, bravery, honour, mildness, generosity and magnificence. Virtues that were less visible and needed higher degrees of interpretation were magnanimity, temperance, truthfulness and justice (Fallona,

2000, pp. 689-690). For example, justice, which was understood as fairness in the application of both rules and norms to individual children, turned out not to be readily observable – not because it was absent, but because it pervaded all aspects of classroom life. If a teacher's attention is seen as a scarce good, then distributing it amongst a group of pupils is already a matter of fairness. Fallona's research is important because it makes us realise that we should not conclude too soon that virtues are not modelled if they cannot be seen.

4.2.4 Habituation as Imitation and Emulation

When reviewing the pedagogical studies on role model education, the notion of 'role model' was operationalised in several ways. For example, adolescents were asked whether they 'admire', 'identify with', 'look up to' or 'want to be like' certain people they know. The way these questions are framed presupposes that teachers are only role models to children when these children have a certain attitude towards teachers. This raises the question of (1) what effect teachers' modelling brings about in learners, and (2) what effect we think modelling *should* bring about. Are we content when adolescents adore their teachers and imitate them, or is there something worrying about this? What effect modelling has on children depends on how 'modelling' is conceived of. In this section, two kinds of modelling will be distinguished. In both cases, modelling is understood as a kind of Aristotelian *habituation*, which is learning by doing virtuous things frequently and consistently under the guidance or authority of a virtuous tutor (Steutel & Spiecker, 2004, p. 536).

Firstly, we can understand habituation as a kind of instrumental conditioning. The educators' character traits are inculcated as they connect to the child's behaviour with different reinforcing and punishing stimuli (Miller & Dollard, 1941). It is suggested that this kind of conditioning works particularly well if there is a mutual loving and trustful relationship between child and tutor. In that case, the child will experience pleasure when the tutor praises him and experience pain when he is blamed or punished. As no effort is made to make children understand moral concepts, children may not know *why* they are praised or blamed. Research by Bandura (1963) affirmed that modelling is a powerful process that can account for diverse forms of learning, but his research revealed that modelling can also occur in the absence of reinforcement stimuli to observers. Children can learn new patterns of behaviour vicariously, i.e. without actually performing actions or receiving rewards. Moreover, Bandura regarded modelling as a much more cognitive process. To him, "...modelling was not simply response mimicry" (Craighead & Nemerhoff, 2001, p. 171).

Following this second interpretation of modelling, the child does not only want to resemble the actions and emotional reactions of the model, but also recognises the educator as representing a virtuous ideal, knowing what is virtuous about him or her. This kind of habituation will only be effective if educators explain to children why they act the way they do. According to Bandura (1997, p. 93), this more cognitive kind of modelling works particularly well in situations in which it is difficult for pupils to learn by observation only, e.g. in cases where teachers' thoughts are not adequately reflected in their actions. When models verbalise their goals and strategies as they deal with moral quandaries, children's cognitive skills are stimulated too.

Although Bandura rightfully emphasised the cognitive nature of modelling over and against Miller & Dollard's behaviouristic approach, his social cognitive theory can only be of limited help to understand modelling *moral* behaviour. It takes individuals to be rational actors and downplays the experience of moral emotions, while these play a major role in moral development from an Aristotelian perspective. If we want to know what goes on in children's minds when they are habituated, Kristjánsson's (2006a) article on the emotion of emulation is helpful. His point of departure is Aristotle's treatment of emulation (*zelos*), which we still recognise in the English 'zeal', enthusiastic devotion to a cause, ideal, or goal and tireless diligence in its furtherance. In the *Rhetoric*, Aristotle (1991, p. 161) describes it as "a kind of distress at the apparent presence among others like him by nature, of things honoured and possible for a person to acquire." One might be tempted to call this kind of distress 'envy', but envy differs from emulation in that envious people try to prevent others from having certain qualities or goods, while an emulative person tries to attain similar goods for himself (Kristjánsson, 2006a, p. 42).

A neo-Aristotelian approach to emotions enables us to distinguish between affective, conative, cognitive and behavioural aspects of emotions (Kristjánsson, 2006a, p. 45). The affective element of role model education consists in the kind of pain that the learner experiences for not having a desired quality that is possessed (to a greater degree) by the role model. The conative element is the learner's motivation to acquire this quality, without taking it away from the model. The cognitive element consists of two parts. First, there is the learner's understanding of why the quality that is possessed by the model is worthy of being valued. Secondly, the learner will need to think about the ways in which he can alter himself in order to acquire the quality. The behavioural aspect of emulation is that the learner takes action in order to acquire the desirable quality.

Combining Steutel & Spiecker's ideas on habituation with Kristjánsson's ideas about the moral psychology of the learner, we can conclude that there are roughly two ways to model moral actions and emotions, thereby guiding pupils' moral development. First, teachers can *condition* pupils, which results in pupils *imitating* their role models. In this case, pupils will feel the pain of not being able to act or emotionally react in the way that the virtuous model does, this feeling will motivate them to acquire this quality, and they will take action in order to behave like the model does. Second, teachers can *educate* pupils, which results in pupils *emulating* their role models. Pupils will not only feel pain, be motivated to change and take the appropriate action, but they will also understand that teachers are not the measure of moral virtue and vice. They merely embody them. Although virtues are morally justifiable independent of the role model, there is pedagogically no other way to become virtuous than by emulating role models (Kristjánsson, 2006a, p. 47).

Once pupils recognise that a distinction can be made between 'becoming like the teacher' and 'becoming like what the teacher exemplifies', the question beckons what it means to the pupil to have this quality himself. This will involve deliberation about what kind of person one currently is, and how one can alter one's character to become a paragon of virtue in one's own way. When modelling is used in the educational sense, it will make pupils ask: 'what does it mean *for me* to be virtuous?'. In her recent book *Intelligent Virtue*, Annas stresses a point that was also made by Kristjánsson (2006a): understanding is paramount to moral development because it enables pupils to acquire for themselves the virtue that teachers embody. This means that the reasons that educators give are a kind of explanation that puts children in a position to go ahead in their own situations and contexts (Annas, 2011, p. 19). They should not follow the teacher, but understand what to follow in the role model, so they can use this knowledge when the teacher is not there. Although Bandura talks about 'rules' instead of virtues, his basic view is in accord with Kristjánsson and Annas: modelling is not productive if people follow scripts, i.e. if they simply enact fixed action sequences. In his view, children would ideally develop a "generative guide for constructing actions to fit changeable circumstances", so that they can move beyond what they have seen the teacher do or heard the teacher say (Bandura, 1997, p. 90). The three authors agree that 'emulation' enables children to go their own way – which really is what moral education is all about.

However, this is not to say that children who have had excellent role models in high school can do without role models in the future. Probably because the foundations of the moral self are laid early in development (Narvaez & Lapsley, 2009, p. 441), there is hardly any research on the use of modelling as a strategy to cultivate a *virtuous character* in post-adolescent life. However, there is abundant evidence that role modelling remains an important strategy to construct people's *self-concept* in professional contexts (Javidan et al., 1995; Ibarra, 1999; Gibson, 2003). The difference between someone's self, as a subset of someone's character, and his self-concept is that a self-concept is a set of beliefs *about* his or her real self. Although the self-concept does not merely describe the self, but also influences it, some character traits are rather resistant and very hard to change (Kristjánsson, 2010b, p. 31).

Interestingly, Ibarra's research on the styles and management techniques that junior consultants and investment bankers adopt from colleagues in order to experiment with their professional self-image reveals that they also emulate many moral virtues, such as trustworthiness, integrity, honesty and humour. Moreover, Gibson (2003) has pointed out that the tendency to observe role models does not change throughout people's career, although professionals in the middle or late-stage of their career are more likely to see their role models as sources of specific rather than global attributes. Especially people with only a couple of years work experience "spoke of role models as providing a range of attributes in 'one package', including personal traits" (Gibson, 2003, p. 598). If Gibson's results also apply to educational contexts, experienced teachers will probably still have role models. As people grow older, their models are more often 'negative' (e.g. colleagues demonstrate how *not* to act), but teachers may equally be inspired by pupils who are eager to learn. This shows that in the field of moral education, the traditional division of roles between 'teachers' and 'pupils' may also be reversed.

4.2.5 Improving Role Modelling

If teachers want pupils to emulate them, they will have to explain to pupils how their actions and emotional reactions are related to an ideal of the virtuous life. However, teacher educators often lack the knowledge and skills needed to make their own teaching explicit (Lunenberg et al. 2007, p. 597). They know that they should 'teach as they preach' and 'walk their talk', but they do not connect their moral ideals to their actual behaviour in the classroom. If teachers want to be good, effective models, they need to become "reflective in their own work, working at a meta-cognitive level in their own teaching by explaining their actions in words in relation to why and how they teach as they do." (Smith, 2001, p. 11).

The pedagogical literature offers a number of recommendations that can help teachers to think – individually and as teams – about questions, such as: Which virtues do I/we want to be a model of? Why do I/we want to model these character traits? How can I/we model these virtues best? First, modelling could be made more productive by giving so-called 'meta-comments', verbalising feelings and explaining to pupils which choices they make and why (Wood & Geddis, 1999). Second, teachers can learn from their experiences in the classroom by keeping a 'professional ethics' journal, in which they clarify their pedagogical choices. In this journal, they can describe (1) the moral situations they were in, (2) their thoughts, feelings and actions, and the way pupils or colleagues reacted, (3) their self-image, what they consider to be their virtues and vices, and (4) what the best reaction would be, and which virtues need to be developed further in order to bring this about. Third, teachers can teach together (co-teaching). Thereby, they can observe each others' teaching and discuss how colleagues put virtues into practice. Useful for this purpose is the Leadership Virtues Questionnaire (LVQ), developed by Riggio et al. (2010). Fourth, teachers can benefit from reading and discussing literature on moral education, because theories can offer a moral language that enables them to recognise and talk about the moral aspect of their work (Swennen et al, 2008; Willemse et al, 2008). Finally, it is recommended to target current as well as future teachers. As teacher training programmes barely prepare teachers for the moral educational aspects of their work (Willemse et al., 2005), it seems that paying serious attention to moral education in teacher training colleges could help future teachers to develop the virtues, skills and techniques to become morally better and pedagogically more effective role models. Therefore, Koster et al. (2005) recommend colleges to extend competence profiles to include teachers' attitudes, motives and personal characteristics, so that they are made aware of their existing attitudes and are, if necessary, encouraged to develop new ones.

4.2.6 The Cross-fertilisation of Philosophy and Social Science

Many teachers want to be a model to pupils, parents endorse this and pupils like teachers who show their personality, but the inconvenient truth is that modelling has been taken for granted to such an extent, that the question of whether teachers are morally good and effective role models has hardly received any serious attention (Javidan et al., 1995, p. 1272). Colleges for teacher training hardly prepare new teachers for this role, and most modelling in schools is unintended and unplanned. For philosophers working in the domain of moral education it is, therefore, not enough to repeat the old message *that* teachers have to be role models. What teachers do not realise yet, is *what* this really means, *why* it is important, and *how* it can best be achieved. This section made these things clearer by distinguishing between two kinds of modelling and by explaining why we need emulation if modelling is to contribute to children becoming more morally mature. Moreover, we examined the body of didactical literature suggesting ways in which teachers can improve their role modelling, e.g. by keeping a professional ethics journal.

By conceptualising and justifying role modelling well, philosophers can also contribute to better (and more) social scientific research into the effectiveness of role modelling as a teaching method. In most of the studies mentioned, children are simply asked who they admire/identify with/look up to/want to be like. Leaving aside the question whether these are really the same (e.g. why could a child not choose a role model that they *cannot* identify with yet?), the more pressing issue is whether having a personal role model includes more than such motivational aspects. Drawing on Aristotle, both Kristjánsson and Annas have argued that children should learn to *understand* what in the role model is worth following. If social scientists want to take role modelling seriously, questionnaires should be designed to measure this cognitive aspect of modelling too, including questions about what respondents take the (moral) qualities of their role models to be and how they attempt to acquire these qualities for themselves.

Finally, it was apparent in the field of moral education that philosophy can also benefit from social scientific research in various ways. Firstly, several studies showed that role modelling is even more problematic than we thought: only very small percentages of pupils mention teachers as role models, and many teachers consider 'respect' to be the most important virtue. Secondly, psychological research confirms the virtue ethical insight that moral exemplars can be distinguished from 'ordinary' people in terms of their character and virtuous behaviour. Thirdly, psychological research made clear which virtues teachers value, and which qualities pupils value in teachers. This research could be extended, e.g. to find out whether teachers need some virtues more than others. A starting point for this research would be to find out that what emotions teachers experience in morally critical situations (e.g. Maas, 2010, p. 144). If virtues are understood as dispositional emotions, empirical research about frequently experienced emotions can inform philosophers about how to determine which corresponding virtues are worth exploring.

4.3 The Moral Educational Use of the Arts

4.3.1 Introduction

While teachers are, qua human beings, an inevitable role model to pupils, role modelling can be very demanding. Teachers are saddled with the 'burden of exemplification', as Carr (2006c, p. 108) calls it. To make this task more bearable, teachers can deploy other means to morally educate pupils, such as literature, poetry, film or even music. Neo-Aristotelians generally agree that the arts can be used to sensitise pupils to ethical questions, help emotions become virtuous dispositions and promote critical thinking (Kristjánsson, 2007, p. 80; Lickona, 1991, 2004). But is the use of the arts compatible with Aristotle's own writings? In Chapter 3, we saw that Aristotle's educational aim is to help people acquire reason (*logos*), which consists of a purely theoretical part which aims at truth, and a practical part which is mixed with the desires to produce good actions. As part of the education of both kinds of rationality, Aristotle recommends young people to study mechanical (manual) and liberal arts from the age of fourteen (Verbeke, 1990, p. 19). However, he also warns that citizens should not focus *too much* on the acquisition of manual skills, since this kind of labour is to be performed by slaves. For the upper class, the free citizens, it is more fitting to practice the liberal arts, such as grammar, music and design. Aristotle does not even recommend these liberal arts unconditionally: they should not be studied as a goal in itself, but as a means to a further end, i.e. the education of one's character.

Recall that someone's character is composed of a set of virtues, which are dispositional emotions. Because music and other arts are believed to have the power to influence people's emotions, Aristotle believed that they can also be used to change such emotions for the better. For example, music can purify the soul of excessive emotions and passions (Verbeke, 1990, p. 20). If the arts can shape people's emotions, they will matter primarily at the preliminary stages of moral development, because a *complete* Aristotelian education includes the cultivation of all the intellectual virtues, most importantly *sophia* (see §3.2.5). And this is not the task of art, but of philosophy. Since the subject of this thesis is the cultivation of moral virtue and character, the training of the intellect is restricted to the intellectual virtue of practical wisdom.

Aristotle recommended the arts to be used for moral educational purposes, but the connection between art and morality, or between 'the good' and 'the beautiful' is today far from self-evident. Core subjects such as mathematics and the acquisition of languages receive most attention in secondary schools. When pupils read novels and poems, attend a play, watch a movie, listen to music or admire statues in a museum on a school trip, these activities are rarely justified from an moral educational point of view. There is a "curious silence" about the moral educational value of stories, both in educational practice and in the academic fields that study the use of arts, such as psychology, philosophy, education and literature (Hilder, 2005). However, because teachers use arts all of the time, they could be used for moral educational purposes, provided that teachers were more aware of the possibilities. Aristotle's distance from us makes him, and contemporary Aristotelians who share his assumptions, valuable sources. He may be able to make something clear about the relationship between art and morality which is difficult for us to see, not sharing Aristotle's pre-modern paradigm. In this section, the yet unclear relationship between morality and art will be explored by looking at three issues. In §4.3.2 and §4.3.3, we will examine four reasons why works of arts can be used to educate children morally. In §4.3.4, an assumption will be analysed that has to be made if aesthetic experiences are to be valuable to people's moral lives at all, i.e. the idea that arts and our lives are both narratively structured. Finally, we turn to the question of what virtue ethicisists consider to be the best narrative structures, and which virtues are needed to make one's life a narrative unity.

4.3.2 Learning a Moral Lesson

When reviewing virtue ethical on the relationship between arts and moral education, four arguments are frequently mentioned for a positive relationship between art and moral education.[31] In this paragraph, the first three arguments will be examined. Firstly, the arts can help us postpone our moral judgments; secondly, they can contain specific moral insights about virtues; and thirdly, they can pass on a moral heritage from one generation to the next. In section 4.3.3, a fourth reason will be discussed.

According to the first argument, "...the contemplation, appreciation, or plain enjoyment of music and other arts may yet provide considerably morally

---

31 Several objections against the moral value of art are discussed and refuted by Carr (2012).

therapeutic respite – albeit temporarily..." from the constant necessity to make important and difficult decisions in our daily lives (Carr, 2006c, p. 115). Carr refers to the experience of forgetting pressing practical affairs for a moment while admiring a painting in a museum, being moved by a piece of music on the radio or dancing to favourite music, e.g. tango. This possibility to detach oneself for a moment from daily concerns about work, family or children can be very helpful when having to make important moral decisions. If we look at art in this way, it is precisely not concerned with passing direct moral judgments. Many musicians, dancers or painters are not trying to convince people of one view or the other, but they enable us to postpone our decisions a little while. In this way, they make room for thought. Moreover, because "human beings are also in key part what they imagine themselves to be", our lives would be seriously diminished if literature and other arts would not show us what our lives can be like (MacIntyre, 2006). Aesthetic experiences can also provide *new perspectives* that make us question our moral assumptions and re-evaluate our established emotional responses (Carr, 2005, p. 148).

While all kinds of arts, such as dance, music or visual arts can train our imagination, narrative arts often contain more specific moral lessons, or are at least often interpreted as containing them. These 'lessons' can in principle be as diverse as the moral domain. For example, morally relevant issues that are raised in novels include the corrupting effect of ambition (Shakespeare's *Macbeth*), human nature (Golding's *Lord of the Flies*), justice and duties to one's kin (Sophocles' *Antigone*), love, marriage and honesty (Tolstoy's *Anna Karenina*), racism (Harriet Beecher Stowe's *Uncle Tom's Cabin*), guilt and conventional morality (Dostoyevsky's *Crime and Punishment*).[32] Several virtue ethicists have suggested themes that can be found in literature and are worth discussing as part of character education programmes in schools. Firstly, one can think of the ways in which novels and movies make clear how certain desires (e.g. for love or power) or character flaws (lack of self-control) may lead to bad ends, and how practical wisdom is needed in order to ascertain the best moral outcome (Carr, 2005, p. 148). Secondly, the characters in books and movies can help us to become acquainted with the difficulties that people with a morally upright character have to go through in order to become virtuous. Stories can offer useful insights into the internal struggles that have to be controlled and external pressures that have to be resisted in order to remain virtuous. Thirdly, virtue ethicists have stressed that many literary works, and especially the ancient Greek tragedies, demonstrate a kind of uncertainty, ambivalence and conflict that comes with many moral decisions. The genre of the tragedy reminds us of the fact that our decisions are rarely a complete success. Even if we make the best decision considering the circumstances, our actions will often involve a loss. By referring to stories such as Aeschylus' *Agamemnon*, who is forced to choose between losing his daughter and

---

32 For more examples of ethical themes in the great works of literature, see Pojman & Vaugh (2010) and Singer & Singer (2005).

never reaching Troy with his fleet, Nussbaum (2001) has illustrated that making a rational decision does not rule out the experience of emotions such as shame or regret.

While the difficulties involved in moral development and the rewards of virtuous action are typically Aristotelian, the theme of 'the tragic' seems to fit an Aristotelian framework less well. The idea that happiness depends to a large extent on blind fate, and that humans are largely unable to understand their (mis)fortunes are not central to Aristotle's worldview (Verbeke, 1990, p. 15). Although Aristotle makes clear that one must not only possess virtue, but some external goods, such as friends, wealth, power, good birth, children and beauty in order to be happy, he insists that the highest good does not come to us by chance. If taking the formation of one's character into one's own hands is an important part of Aristotle's message, why would contemporary virtue ethicists advice us to read plays in which people's fate is determined by other forces? Neo-Aristotelians who are interested in moral education, such as Carr and Nussbaum, seem to believe that *Antigone*, *Oedipus* and other tragedies can gain insight into a dimension of our lives that is insufficiently touched upon by Aristotle.[33] Recommending pupils to read tragedies as part of a virtue ethical approach to moral education is a corrective to the idea that our goodness and happiness ultimately depend on factors that are all within our reach (Verbeke, 1990, p. 16).

The question of *why* certain books or plays should or should not be used as part of educating the virtues in schools has been approached differently by two influential neo-Aristotelians. Throughout his oeuvre, Carr approvingly cites the nineteenth century British poet and cultural critic Matthew Arnold (1994, p. 5), who argued that being (morally) educated involves being acquainted with the "the best that has been thought and said in the world", in order to turn "a steam of fresh and free thought upon our stock notions and habits". In Arnold's view, there is a corpus of classic masterpieces one should be acquainted with if one wants to become critical of the conventions of the society one lives in. Carr takes from Arnold the idea that knowledge from books can only have real educational significance when these books explore universal moral themes that can in principle be recognised cross-culturally. Works of art that only deal with parochial issues cannot be of interest from an *educational* point of view, because they do not help us to become critical of our conventional morality. Carr (2005, p. 147) emphasises that "…there is clearly a legitimate and urgent educational job to be done to assist the young to appreciate great works of arts and literature, regardless of their particular cultural origins." Carr presupposes a distinction between 'socialisation' and 'education': the former is a kind of initiation into conventional morality of a particular tradition, while the latter must be answerable to objective rational criteria. In his view, books like *Don Quixote* or *Hamlet* do not appeal to us because we share Cervantes' or Shakespeare's conventional moralities, but because these

---

33 However, the analysis of tragedy constitutes the core of the discussion of dramatic and literary theory in Aristotle's *Poetics*.

writers have touched upon normative insights that we still share in virtue of our common humanity. The same applies to the use of Greek tragedies as part of an Aristotelian approach to moral education. If *Oedipus* and *Antigone* are to be read or performed by pupils, it is because Sophocles articulated an important part of our moral experience, which Aristotle turned a blind eye to.

MacIntyre, by contrast, recommends the reading of a common body of texts for different reasons: it creates an 'educated community', a specific body of individuals who participate in active rational debate, who recognise one another as members of this public and who take their debates to have practical import for the shared social life of a particular community (MacIntyre, 1987, p. 19). For MacIntyre, the widespread reading of canonical texts and the discussion of moral issues touched upon in these texts can reinforce the moral beliefs and improve the practical quality of life of the members of specific moral communities. This makes clear that to Macintyre (1998, p. 1) "moral concepts are embodied in and are partially constitutive of forms of social life". He would disagree with Carr that texts only have genuine moral or educational value when they are appreciated outside a community's conventional morality, and he would argue that the kind of tradition-independent 'objective rational criteria' that Carr has in mind do not exist (see §5.5). However, MacIntyre would admit that the moral educational value of texts would certainly be *greater* when a text that is produced by a community is also appreciated by the members of other cultures.

MacIntyre's final goal is not the education of individual human beings – whatever community they are a member of – but to maintain educated communities that survive these individuals and which can provide an education for future generations, too. Adults who have come to appreciate the moral value of arts would ideally feel responsible for making the same cultural and moral heritage accessible to the children in their care. However, MacIntyre (1987) is pessimistic about teachers' abilities to use arts for moral educational purposes. He is afraid that many teachers do not know which specific traditions they are a member of, nor which literary sources they have at their disposal to articulate this heritage.

4.3.3 Cultivating Compassion

While some books and movies provide clear-cut moral insights, there is also another sense in which in particularly the narrative arts are morally educative: the very activity of reading contributes to children's moral development. When one reads a book or watches a movie, children can become involved and sympathise with the story if they relate to the characters, and have the stories resonate with their own lives. Such effects can be brought about if the audience does not only look at art as an opportunity for enjoyment, but if they see the lives of the main characters "with more than a casual tourist's interest" (Nussbaum, 1997, p. 88).

Making readers personally relate to the story is relatively easy if the characters are very much like the readers, but more imagination may be needed when stories are written in the eighth century before Christ (Homer) or in the sixteenth century after (Shakespeare). Virtue ethicists have argued that the kind of literary sympathy needed to understand the fictitious lives of characters is conducive to the moral ability to put ourselves in the shoes of *real* people. But how does this work?

A moral quality that can grow out of literary imagination is a virtue known as 'compassion' (Nussbaum, 1997) or *misericordia* (MacIntyre, 1999a). They have regarded moral imagination as the virtue that one needs in order to deal with the vulnerability of human life. Or, more specifically, it has been described as the attitude that one needs in order to deal with people who have suffered significant undeserved pains or misfortunes. It involves a recognition that other people are different, but in some ways similar to oneself. Similarly, in the sense that the same misfortunes, such as illness and death, can or will befall oneself at one point or another. "Without that sense of commonness, Aristotle claims, I will react with sublime indifference." (Nussbaum, 2001b, p. 317). Simply knowing that one has certain things in common with fellow human beings is, however, not necessarily sufficient to *motivate* people to be compassionate. One will also have to feel bad about another person's undeserved fortune (MacIntyre, 1999a; Kristjánsson, 2006b). This specific feeling of pain matters, since the experience of pleasure towards another person's undeserved bad fortune would be much more problematic. It is known as *Schadenfreude*, or malicious delight. In the virtue of compassion, the bad feeling and the more cognitive recognition go hand in hand: one feels sorrow over someone else's distress *insofar* as one understands the other's distress as one's own (MacIntyre, 1999a, p. 125).

As mentioned before, Nussbaum corrected Aristotle by drawing on ancient tragedies to emphasise the role of luck in life. Something similar seems to happen with the virtue of compassion: despite being an Aristotelian, MacIntyre (1999a, p. 127) is very critical of Aristotle when writing about compassion. He corrects his ideas about *megalopsychos*, the Aristotelian crown of the virtues, by drawing on Thomas Aquinas, because Aristotle would have underestimated the vulnerability of human life and the extent to which we depend on others for our well-being. Nussbaum and MacIntyre also adapt Aristotelian virtue ethics in another way. They recommend to expand compassion to people outside their own particular community. They argue that virtue should not only be exercised towards people in one's intimate inner circle of relationships, but towards *all* fellow human beings (MacIntyre, 1999a, p. 126; Nussbaum, 2001b, p. 92). These neo-Aristotelians recognise the need to make virtue ethics less particularistic – only being concerned with the well-being of those living in one's vicinity – and more impartial and universal in a world in which we are constantly confronted with people's suffering, knowing too that we are partly responsible for this.

It is now clear what it means for virtue ethicists to claim that the very activity of reading contributes to children's moral development. This brings us to the question: does imagination really works like this? For example, it does not seem too difficult to imagine people who are deeply moved by movies or novels, but who remain dishonest, unfaithful and unreliable in their daily life. Useful in this regard is the work of the Flemish philosopher Patricia de Martelaere (1997), who has criticised the moral educational use of art by making a distinction between identification with people on the basis of fictional emotions and identification on the basis of real emotions. One example will make this distinction clearer. For example, when a friend tells you a story about his sister, and you are harrowed by it, you may be embarrassed when the friend tells you that he invented the story. You are embarrassed because you were taken in, and maybe you are also a bit ashamed of your friend because he made you believe that somebody really suffered (Radford, 1975, p. 68). If your friend tells you *in advance* that he is going to tell you a fictional story, you may still be harrowed by the fate of the fictional sister, but this feeling is different. Using this distinction, Schaubroeck (2005, p. 439) concludes that Nussbaum ignores or neglects the distinction between our attachments to fictional and real people and that this can endanger the whole project of turning to literature for ethical purposes. Because Schaubroeck is sceptical of the idea that we can *truly* be moved by the fate of a fictitious character, she warns not to replace real moral experiences with fictional ones. Although novels, plays and movies may actually be part of a moral educational programme for children, these objections remind us of the possibility and desirability to help children acquire the virtue of compassion by habitually doing compassionate things to others under the supervision of a virtuous person.

4.3.4 Life as a Narrative Unity

The idea that literature can be used to educate people morally, and the idea that the virtue of compassion can be acquired by relating to characters in books presupposes that texts and people's lives have something in common: a narrative structure. This section examines what it means for a life to have a narrative structure and what virtue ethics and narrativism have to do with each other.

There are two more extreme narrative views about the relation between texts and lives. One option is to argue that narratives are the key means with which people give meaning to their lives. For example, Hardy (1968, p. 5) writes "We dream in narrative, daydream in narrative, remember, anticipate, hope, despair, plan, revise, criticise, gossip, learn, hate and love by narrative". In Hardy's view, narratives are so important to life that it is not far off the mark to say that when we tell a story about our lives, we verbalise an existing narrative structure. Life itself would be an untold story that is waiting to be told. The idea that stories describe the self according to some correspondence theory of meaning is problematic because it does not leave much room for interpretation. Another option is to argue that life is not yet narratively structured when it is experienced; it only becomes a story when these experiences are articulated (Mink, 1970). The problem with this view is that making up stories about ourselves can be self-deceiving. While both Hardy's and Mink's views are problematic, there is also something of value in each of them. Firstly, a story adds something to an experience that was not there when it was experienced. Secondly, a story can only be told about one's experience if the story somehow 'fits' the experience. Ricoeur (1983) has combined the strength of the two views by arguing that life has a *pre*-narrative structure, which does not have the exact same order as a story, but which does nevertheless contain a structure that can be interpreted further. The story *specifies* the pre-narrative structure of life, which can, in turn, influence somebody's experiences. Ricoeur's solution creates room for a variety of interpretations of our experiences while it also enables us to talk about narratives in terms of truth.

The relationship between acts and interpretation can be illustrated with an example derived from MacIntyre (2003, p. 206). Imagine seeing Jack, your neighbour, with a shovel in his garden, and you ask yourself what he is doing. Is he just digging a hole, gardening, exercising, preparing the garden for winter or pleasing his wife? And how do we determine which of these (combinations of) interpretations is the right one? According to Macintyre, this depends on the neighbour's intentions. Simply *watching* Jack using a shovel will not get us beyond a description such as 'he is using the shovel in the garden'. If the description is to be a little more meaningful, Jack's intentions matter. If you know your neighbour well, you may be able to guess his intentions, otherwise you will have to initiate a conversation to find out. If Jack's primary intention is to prepare the garden for winter, then the gardening is an episode in an annual cycle of domestic activity. However, if he explains that he is pleasing his wife by exercising, the digging becomes part of a history of marriage. While the two stories may be equally convincing, there are also some answers that would probably not make a lot of sense. For example, if Jack referred to his 'wife' without being married, or if he told you that he is exercising while he is not a sportive type at all, you would certainly raise an eyebrow, and probably conclude that Jack is joking. There may even be a point when you start to realise that Jack is a downright liar. MacIntyre uses the example to show that human behaviour should not be understood as 'facts' that can only be given a mechanical explanation. While Macintyre admits that people's already existing character traits and relationships to others somehow limit the stories that they can and cannot persuasively tell about their lives, people's behaviour leaves room for multiple interpretations.

According to MacIntyre and Carr, a narrative approach does not only make clear that life has a narrative structure, but it also has something to say about which kind of structure is best: a 'good' narrative is conceived of as a narrative that enables us to make our life a *unity* (Carr, 2003b, 2006a, 2006c; MacIntyre, 2003, ch. 15). In *After Virtue*, MacIntyre argued that virtues are needed on the level of practices, individual life narratives and traditions.[34] On the level of practices, people will need all kinds of virtues, depending on the practices they participate in. For instance, let us assume that boxers need more courage than patience, while teachers need more patience than courage. However, teachers who like boxing or professional boxers who teach pupils how to box will need courage and patience to the same degree. This illustrates a more general point: as most people participate in several practices, they will benefit from knowledge of how to relate the virtues in different practices.

MacIntyre (2003, p. 204) assumes that there is a kind of knowledge that integrates all practice-dependent virtues on a second level, the level of one's life as a whole. When people tell a story about what kind of life they pursue, the unrelated virtues and activities on the level of practices acquire a single purpose. MacIntyre contrasts a harmonious collection of virtues that are coherently displayed through action in several practices with an atomistic or Sartrian conception of a self, which separates the 'self' from its *roles*, and maintains that the 'self' is nothing, which makes us free to choose our identity. Chapter 3 described that MacIntyre's view is also at odds with the situationists claim that virtues are not manifested in behaviour across a diversity of situations, and that character traits do not typically exhibit evaluative affinities with other character traits.

Why would we prefer an Aristotelian self to its Sartrian and situationists rivals? An all-persuasive argument in favour of Aristotle's ideas about the self will not be presented here, since it is difficult to convince people of the virtue ethical point of view if they do not already have an interest in an unified or integrated life. Instead, it will be highlighted how an Aristotelian approach can answer a question that most people ask themselves every once in a while, i.e. 'what is good *for me?*'. The appeal to people's existing desire means that the Aristotelian answer is only conditionally valid: it only has meaning to people who already want to be able to answer this question. For example, imagine your daughter comes home with a man she introduces as the one she is going to marry.[35] You, her father, discover that he is a ruthless businessman with a reputation of doing whatever is necessary to destroy his competitors. This may cause you to doubt whether this man will be a caring and loving husband. When you share your worries with him, he is very surprised. Why can he not be a caring, attentive husband and an insincere businessman at the same time? If you, as the fiancé does, divide your life into separate domains that are only weakly connected, the question whether care and ruthlessness can be combined will simply not arise. Only when you start to care about being the same kind of person in several domains, like the father, will the Aristotelian task to make your life a unity through narratives become an attractive ideal.

---

34 MacIntyre's account of virtue will be discussed more fully in Chapter 5.
35 Adopted from Musschenga (2001, p. 225).

4.3.5 Integrity and the Speed of Moral Development

The virtue that one needs to transform the practice-dependent virtues into a united human life is called 'integrity' (MacIntyre, 2003, p. 203). This virtue does not appear explicitly in the Aristotelian list of virtues, but Aristotle, nevertheless, acknowledges the importance of a unified and integrated life. For example, in Book VI of the *Nicomachean Ethics* he argues for the 'unity of the virtues', the claim that moral virtues cannot exist independently, because each and every virtue presupposes the possession of practical wisdom. This Aristotelian understanding of the 'unity of the virtues' should be distinguished from a stronger, Socratic, thesis, according to which virtues are one because the different virtues – such as courage, temperance and justice – refer to different aspects of a single property. On the Socratic account, the virtues have their own definition, but the essence of each virtue is wisdom or knowledge.

To Aristotle, the virtues concern different spheres of activity, and the knowledge required for facing dangers (courage) differs from the knowledge needed to spend money well (generosity). At the same time, one only knows how important it is to face a danger or to spend money if one also knows the relative importance of these values in a single life (Wolf, 2007, p. 150). A courageous person does not just risk his life (this would be rash), but knows when the stakes are worth it. While this knowledge of what is important in life is also required for the full possession of the virtue of generosity, this does not mean that courageous people are also generous or possess any of the other virtues, because they may still lack the necessary *experience* in the field of giving and receiving money. In this domain, people may still have to learn to give the right amounts to the right people for the right reasons in the right way.

While the 'unity of the virtues' thesis is conceptually and empirically controversial[36], it hints at the idea that a virtuous person has not mastered several distinct and separated excellences, each in its own domain, but leads a life of virtue that is coherent (Cottingham, 2010, p. 3). Somebody who leads an integrated life can still experience emotional and moral conflicts, but she will be able to work out her priorities, because she has "an understanding of the significance of all her various goals and desires, and the true place of each in her overall life-plan – how they fit in with her sense of who she really is." (Cottingham, 2010, p. 8). For the virtuous person, integrity is not a moral virtue, but a second-order, meta or master virtue, more akin to practical wisdom, which helps him to put in order the various virtues and goods of different types of activities in different domains or practices, and enables him to explain to significant others who he is and which motivations he has (Dudzinski, 2004, pp. 304-305).

There is, however, another dimension to integrity that is often overlooked. People may be able to tell a coherent story about why they are committed to the lives they are living *now*, but that does not mean that their lives will remain in good

---

36   See e.g. Flanagan (1991), ch. 13; Doris (2002), p. 22; Hursthouse (1999), pp. 153-157; Annas (2011), ch. 6.

order *over time*. When your life undergoes a significant change, e.g. because you start a new relationship or quit your job, this requires certain adaptations. When you have close and critical friends, you can expect them to ask whether these choices will make you happy and whether they do justice to the other goals and other commitments you have in life. In a diachronic sense, integrity guarantees the unity of the self, which "resides in the unity of a narrative which links birth to life to death as narrative beginning to middle to end." (MacIntyre, 2003, p. 205). In the diachronic sense, integrity is the virtue that one needs in order to deal with self-change (Cox, La Caze & Levine, 2008). It is the virtue to accompany moral development *par excellence*. People who master this virtue will be able to bring into harmony and acknowledge the experiences and influences from the past that have led up to their present character (Cottingham, 2010, p. 7). However, this does not mean that one merely takes on the habits of parents or other educators, without trying to understand what their basis is, or thinking these habits through for oneself. That is what the 'ethically lazy person' would do (Annas, 2011, p. 24). People who do not understand why certain character traits are virtues, and have never asked what it means for them to acquire these virtues will be ill-suited to cope with circumstances that differ from the ones that their parents had to cope with. People who have acquired diachronic integrity will save the best from the past *and* have a desire to learn and a drive to aspire.

It was concluded that integrity is not a (complex) dispositional emotion like courage, temperance, mildness or justice, so it can be doubted whether integrity meets the Aristotelian criteria of a moral virtue (see §3.2.2). The doctrine of the mean can nevertheless illuminate something about diachronic integrity: it helps us to recognise two familiar but not very virtuous ways to deal with development. One extreme way dealing with self-change is to understand oneself as being something completely fixed and steady, which makes development impossible. For example, some people believe that their character is given at birth, while others believe that their characters are completely determined by the education they received as children. Either way, they believe that they are who they are, that there is no room for character development, and that moral education is essentially useless. The second extreme way to deal with self-change is to understand one's 'self' as completely changeable and variable. People will just 'go with the flow', embracing change without ever becoming emotional. For example, when you move to the other side of the country, nobody will be surprised that you will have some mixed emotions: you will be excited about the new place, but you will probably also be a bit melancholic when you realise what you leave behind.

These two vicious types can be compared by saying that the first has an 'unchangeable self', while the other engages in 'selfless change'. What these two vicious extremes have in common is that such people never ask themselves whether such changes are good *for them*. Formulating the two extremes in this way enables us to see that diachronic integrity is a means between the vices of rigidity or dogmatism, on the one hand, and capriciousness or self-deception, on the other. With integrity, one can steer a course between the Scylla of a fixed, complete self and the Charybdis of a fragmented, divided self. Integrity helps one to stick to certain goods and cherish the virtues that help one to attain these goods, but combine this with the flexibility, practical wisdom and courage to change when the time is right.

4.3.6 Narrative Strategies in the Classroom

Returning to the topic of this section, the moral educational use of the arts, the question is in which ways moral education can be enriched by our discussion of a narrative understanding of moral character. Three strategies will be recommended that go beyond the use of existing works of art and look at teachers' and pupils' *own* stories and creativity (Burns & Rathbone, 2010).

Firstly, the previous sections on narrativism made clear that narratives are not only 'out there' in works of art, but that pupils also understand and construct *themselves* through a process of imagining and telling stories about their lives. This means that teachers will have to be prepared to listen to and engage with these stories, which presupposes, in turn, that teachers need to spend much time with them. If this time is not available, the narrative strategy could be limited to situations in which pupils engage in immoral conduct. Instead of emphasising the consequences of bullying his fellow classmates, a teacher can ask a bully to explain what he has done, how he came to do it, and what kind of person bullying makes him. Secondly, a narrative approach makes something clear about role modelling (see §5.2). If pupils are to have a good picture of what a moral life is like, teachers who have the virtue of integrity do not necessarily have to be morally perfect. Instead, teachers can show that they have strong value commitments and that they are also willing and capable of learning and changing. They are "imperfect, but progressing" moral agents (Burns & Rathbone, 2010). This presupposes that teachers are willing to share their own life narratives, their various moral successes and failures, with pupils.

Thirdly, teachers can ask pupils to write about their moral experiences. This is an interesting suggestion, as we have interpreted the use of the arts so far primarily as exposing pupils to already existing stories. The skills and virtues that pupils use while *writing* a story can also help them to become the 'moral author' of their life (Bouchard, 2002, p. 408). However, teachers should keep in mind that there is a difference between 'telling a story' and 'being an author': a storyteller lists events that happened, while an author takes events as a starting point to discover things, also about himself. He *creates* something that, when he reads it, can change him. While people often want to know whether a novel contains autobiographical elements, this conceals that creative works of art should not be traced to their authors, but the other way round (Mulisch, 1974, pp. 80-82). Just as Shakespeare has been created by Hamlet, and Beethoven has been composed by his symphonies, pupils can create themselves by writing, making music, sculpting etc.

4.4 Socratic Dialogue

4.4.1 Introduction

The approaches discussed in Chapter 2 criticised character education for being authoritarian and moralistic, imposing predetermined values on children. However, in Chapter 3, it became apparent that moral action is guided by reason, and that the development of practical wisdom is implied in the cultivation of one's emotions. Moreover, the section on role modelling made clear that habituation does not have to be interpreted as a mindless process that conditions children to feel or act in certain ways. It would be better understood as a critical practice that also encourages children to deliberate about which character traits teachers are a model of, and how they can acquire these virtues for themselves. Teachers can enhance pupils' critical thinking by giving reasons for their actions and emotional reactions. By doing so, they articulate the (often implicit) ways in which they pursue the goals they considers to be part of human flourishing. However, is this all that virtue ethics has in store to educate children's moral reasoning capacities? Is there no place for a more systematic *exchange* of reasons between pupils and teachers? What place does dialogue have in the cultivation of pupils' virtues? This question will be examined in this section by focussing on three issues. First, it will be made clear what a 'dialogue' is by looking at its Socratic roots, and by describing a modern reformulation of this method that can be used in today's schools. Second, it will be investigated what contribution the 'Socratic method' makes to an education in the Aristotelian virtues. More specifically, it will be discussed how Socratic dialogues contribute to the improvement of practical wisdom. Third, we will also look at whether the Socratic method can make something clear about the meaning of practical wisdom.

4.4.2 Plato and the Socratic Dialogues

The genesis of dialogue can be related to the democratic nature of Athenian culture in the fifth century BC (Goldhill, 2009, p. 2). In the assembly, the key political institution, different views were laid open to public scrutiny in order to reach the best decision about which course of action to follow. Being able to give speeches and evaluate speeches by others were basic skills in these forums. They were also useful in court, where equal parties (for the law) had to articulate their positions before a jury of citizens. While many teachers were well-paid

Chapter 4

for teaching young men to become successful in the Athenian democracy by persuading and convincing others, Socrates (470-399 BC) was something of an odd figure. He was not primarily interested in what entertained, impressed or persuaded an audience (rhetoric), but adopted a method that is known as 'dialectic'. The purpose of the dialectical method is not to *win* an argument, but to find out what is *true*. In Socrates' view, a dialogue is not a battle of one against the other, but a shared enquiry by persistently asking each other questions that stimulate critical thinking and illuminate and justify the meaning of ideas. Socrates approached a conversation by showing that his interlocutor's hypothesis about e.g. the nature of friendship, piety, courage or justice led to a contradiction, thereby forcing the person to withdraw the hypothesis as a candidate for truth. The cross-examination was not a silly game about the meaning of words, but a serious and personal business, because Socrates was ultimately after the improvement of the interlocutors' soul, freeing them from knowledge that he *supposed* to be true, fuelling their desire for the truth.

What kind of truth did he have in mind? In Plato's later dialogues, the character called 'Socrates' became more of a literary spokesman for Plato's metaphysical project. For example, in *Meno*, Plato compared Socrates' method to midwifery (*maieutics*), because his intelligent questions would help to 'give birth' to ideas that were latent in the mind of human beings. In this dialogue, Socrates makes a slave boy realise that the area of a large square is twice the area of the smaller one by asking him questions only. Plato intends to show that, as nobody told the slave what the answer was, he can only have reached it by recollecting what he already knew – but had forgotten. Although Plato's metaphor of the midwife illustrates that Socrates was not a conventional teacher who transferred (moral) knowledge to pupils, Plato used the metaphor as part of an argument to prove that the soul is immortal. He saw Socrates as a midwife who aids the birth of knowledge of Ideas that have been in the interlocutor's soul from eternity. In Plato's view, human beings are, like everything else in nature, composed of two parts: one the one hand, there is the body, perceptible and composed of parts, and on the other hand, there is the soul, which is intelligible and exempt from dissolution and destruction. Plato argued that the soul participates in the world of Ideas, an "eternal self-existent world transcending everything in ours, exempt from the vagaries and vicissitudes which afflict all creatures in the world of time" (Vlastos, 1991, p. 76). Socrates' own belief in an afterlife of the soul was, however, just like mainstream fifth century Greek culture, weak and unclear (Claus, 1981, p. 68). Socrates assumed that an unexamined life was not the kind of life that suits human beings (Plato, *Apology* 38a) and that freeing people from knowledge that they supposed to be true would improve their moral character and contribute to their happiness as a human being. He had a one-track interest in *moral* questions, and was not so much interested in either metaphysics or epistemology. The ideal and eternal world that Plato tried to construct in his later works was unknown to Socrates, for whom reality – and also real knowledge, virtue and happiness – was the empirical world he lived in (Vlastos, 1991, ch. 2).

How could a dialogue about the meaning of concepts such as virtue have practical consequences? Socrates assumed that when people have a better understanding of what e.g. 'friendship' or 'courage' is, they would also be able to be a good friend and do courageous things. *Knowing* what is good automatically leads to *being* good. In meta-ethics, this stance is known as 'motivational internalism': Socrates believed that a judgment that something is good is intrinsically motivating. Plato's student Aristotle was a motivational internalist as well, but only with regard to people who possessed full virtue and practical wisdom. People who were brought up in fine habits would feel the right things and be moved while passing moral judgments. Aristotle is, however, a motivational externalist with regard to people who are not completely virtuous yet. While Socrates would recommend somebody who lacks self-control to get to *know* what is good, Aristotle would advice him to go through a process of emotional habituation. The neo-Aristotelian developmental model presented earlier (see §3.4) made clear that knowing what is virtuous is not sufficient for being virtuous. People must also develop a commitment to possess and to practice virtue. This epistemological difference between Socrates and Aristotle affects the potential use of Socrates' dialectical method as part of an Aristotelian approach to moral education. On a Socratic account, a dialectical enquiry can foster moral knowledge, which is itself sufficient to become a good human being. In an Aristotelian reading, dialogues foster moral knowledge too, but they are only useful if they are proceeded and accompanied by an education of the emotions. Aristotle writes that "...arguments seem [...] unable to turn the many toward being fine and good." (*NE* 1179b5-11). If we assume that Socrates' dialectical approach can foster moral knowledge, but also accept that moral knowledge is not sufficient for full virtue, we have to conclude that Socratic dialogues have a limited (but nonetheless important) role to play as part of an Aristotelian approach to moral education in schools.

However, the question of how Socrates' own approach to dialogue can be part of an neo-Aristotelian approach to moral education will not be dealt with in this chapter. Socrates' approach had one serious disadvantage. While many people listened to the conversations Socrates had with his interlocutors, and while these interlocutors took turns, the dialogues are basically between *two* people. What we are looking for, however, is a kind of dialogue that allows for the participation of a group of people, so that teachers can use this Socratic tool in the classroom. Therefore, focus will be here on a contemporary Socratic approach to dialogue, the so-called 'Socratic method', developed in the 20th century by two Germans: Leonard Nelson and, to a lesser extent, Gustav Heckman. As a preliminary, their method will be described in more detail, which helps to address the question of whether this method can be detached from its Platonic and Nelsonian presuppositions, and be used as part of an Aristotelian education for virtue. An attempt will be made to explain why it makes sense to use the Socratic method as part of a character educational programme in schools. More specifically, the emphasis will be on effects that participating in Socratic dialogues can have on participants' development of practical wisdom.

4.4.3 Leonard Nelson's Approach

In the 1920s, the German philosopher, pedagogue and politician Leonard Nelson took both a practical and a theoretical interest in a Socratic way of doing philosophy. On a practical level, Nelson was convinced that Socrates' approach could help to renew education and politics by creating more reflective and critical citizens. While the unstable Weimar Republic was plagued by an increasingly popular nationalism, he was involved in the foundation of the *Internationaler Sozialistischer Jugendbund* (ISJ/IJB) and the *Philosophisch-Politische Akademie* in 1922, which still organises Socratic conversations today. Before turning to the kind of conversations that he advocated, his justification of the method will be examined. While the Socratic method refers to the founding father of Western philosophy, Nelson justifies it by referring to the ideas of Immanuel Kant and Jakob Fries. In order to make sense of Nelson's Socratic method, we have to turn to the ideas of these philosophers, and more specifically to a 17th-century controversy about the nature, acquisition and limits of our knowledge. This historical detour is necessary to make clear what kind of knowledge a Socratic dialogue is supposed to yield, according to Nelson.

Continental rationalists such as Descartes, Spinoza, Leibniz and others believed that some important truths, such as the existence of God, the immortality of the soul, and truths about our moral duties are known intuitively through reason or can be deductively proved. However, British empiricists, such as Locke, Berkeley and Hume rejected this view, and argued that these ideas can ultimately be traced back to experiences, such as sense perceptions and emotions. In order to formulate the issues between these two schools, Kant employed two distinctions. The first distinction is between analytic and synthetic judgments: a judgment is analytic if the predicate concept is contained in its subject concept; the judgment is synthetic if it adds something new to our conception of the subject. Analytic judgments, such as 'All bachelors are unmarried' are true by definition, they do not report results from observation or experiments, but explain the meaning of a term. The second distinction is between the *a priori/a posteriori* distinction, which is about the way we know a judgment to be true. A judgment is known *a posteriori* if we know it from experience, while it is *a priori* if it is known completely independently of particular experiences.

When the two distinctions are combined, four possible types of judgment appear. The first two are the least controversial. The first kind of judgment is 'analytic *a priori*': if a judgment is analytically true, we do not need to experience anything to tell us what is contained in our concepts. The second kind of judgment is 'synthetic *a posteriori*': if a judgment is known *a posteriori*, the subject and the predicate are 'synthesised' in our experience. A third type of judgments, 'analytic *a posteriori*', does not make sense, since analytic judgments are necessarily true, and since necessity entails apriority (Hanna, 2009). Finally, the fourth kind of judgment is 'synthetic *a priori*'. An important goal of Kant's philosophy was to find out whether and how we can establish such synthetic *a priori* judgments. He wanted to find out how some judgments could provide new information about a subject without having recourse to experience.

For example, the physical knowledge that viruses are the cause of colds can be derived from experience, but the idea that every event has a cause is not based on experience, nor is it part of the meaning of the concept 'event' that it has a cause (Korsgaard, 1998, p.x). The knowledge that everything in the world behaves in a lawlike manner, must therefore be synthetic *a priori*. This makes clear that physics has an empirical part, and a part that is synthetic *a priori*. The same holds for the domain of ethics. Morality is concerned with questions about which behaviour one *ought* to have. According to Kant, these oughts cannot be derived from our experience about how the world is (he agrees with Hume here), but they cannot be derived from the meaning of the word 'ought' by conceptual analysis either. Kantians believe that controversial moral questions cannot be settled by simply analysing the meaning of a concept like 'ought' (Korsgaard, 1998, p.x). So, if moral obligations exist, there must be what Kant called the 'metaphysics of morals', which is the body of *synthetic a priori* judgments about what we ought to do. 'Metaphysics' is the study of the collection of synthetic *a priori* knowledge.

This detour through Kant's ideas was necessary to show that Nelson's Socratic method is a means to retrace the metaphysical presuppositions underlying people's everyday (moral) judgments, leading to synthetic *a priori* knowledge. However, things are more complicated, because Nelson was less influenced by Kant and more by the neo-Kantian Fries (1773-1843). While Kant tried to prove that synthetic judgments are necessary *a priori*, Fries doubted the nature of this 'proof'. In order to defend Kant's critical philosophy against the excesses of transcendental idealism, Fries replaced Kant's ontological justification of *a priori* categories with a psychological explanation, grounding knowledge in universal human psychology (Gattei, 2008, p. 6). Although Fries is often criticised for his psychologisation of Kant, he did not abandon Kant's category of the *a priori*, but insisted that it could be legitimised with the shared experience of human intellects. Certainty would lie not in the connection between mind and world, but in the coherence within human subjectivity (Howard, 2000, p. 45). This was the source of Nelson's idea of the methodological procedure of the 'regressive abstraction'. A group of people could discover synthetic *a priori* knowledge by carefully examining the conceptual

Chapter 4

presuppositions of their everyday experiences. The method is called *regressive* abstraction, because it moves backwards from a judgment that has already been made in concrete circumstances to implicit, more general assumption that have to be made if this judgment is going to make sense (Brune et al., 2005, p. 98).

In several of his writings, Nelson (1970a, 1970b) gives examples of the kind of knowledge that Socratic methods which use the regressive abstraction can yield. For example, when someone says e.g. 'this crime should be punished', Nelson notes that this judgment is neither based on empirical observations nor on the meaning of the concept of a 'crime': the very idea of a violation of a law does not include the idea that a violation should be punished. It is a philosophical (i.e. metaphysical) judgment. The participants in a dialogue can try to retrace what has to be assumed about the foundational principles of morality in order for a judgment to be true. Another example concerns a number of philosophers who meet to discuss the meaning of the metaphysical concept of 'substance'. Nelson (1970a) predicts that the discussion will get bogged down in endless repetitious arguing, in which the sceptics eventually gain the upper hand. However, if one of the sceptics cannot find his coat anymore when he is about to leave, it is not very likely that he will resign himself to the loss because it would confirm his philosophical doubt about the constancy of substance. Just like everybody else who looks for something that is lost, the (implicit) judgment which prompts him to search makes clear that he presupposes that a thing cannot suddenly disappear.

After Nelson's death, Gustav Heckmann (1898-1996) continued Nelson's work by furthering its cause and refining the method. As the approach grew more popular, it was used increasingly outside the original neo-Kantian/neo-Frisian framework, too. But what kind of knowledge did the method track if it is not after synthetic *a priori* judgments? One possibility, previous mentioned, was Plato's claim that the dialectical method recovers knowledge about Forms that have always been in the immortal soul. Another possibility is to place the Socratic method in a pragmatic or social constructivist framework. Dialogues are then a means for groups to 'form common concepts', which enable participants to get a better grip on their interactions with the world (Knežić et al., 2010). However, the risk involved in treating a dialogue as an attempt to achieve consensus about the meaning of a word or phrase is that the 'truth' gets out of sight. For example, after hours of Socratic talking, a group may come up with a definition of a 'professional' as 'somebody attached to a particular study without pay and formal training'. If consensus and truth are identical, this definition would be true, but it goes against the standard use of the word in the (English) language community. This does not automatically qualify the outcome of the dialogue as untrue, but the least the participants will have to do is explain why most people have an incorrect understanding of professionalism. In theory, there is no reason why the Socratic group could not be right, but it seems very unlikely that they are. The best way to preserve the Socratic method as a *critical* theory is to accept that all formed concepts are fallible and provisional. Ideally, we would ask more people, preferably those who seem to have divergent views and are willing to discuss them, to join the dialogue. In that case, we have to be satisfied with something like 'warranted assertability': our judgments gain status when they are warranted through a dynamic, ongoing, self-correcting processes of enquiry. We may move asymptotically near to a 'truth' that will always remain beyond our grasp.

4.4.4 The Hourglass Model

The Socratic method has not only been justified in various ways, but there is also disagreement about the method itself. The following section concerns the elements common to almost all of these approaches. Not only the 'formal' criteria (the procedure which the participants have to follow) will be considered, but also the attitude that participants need in order to commit themselves to these procedures. The method will be explained using the metaphor of the so-called hourglass (or sandglass) model (Kessels, 2001, p. 200). According to the hourglass model, a Socratic dialogue consists of five elements: a question, an example, judgments about the relation between question and example, reasons for the judgment ('rules') and justifications for these reasons ('principles'). I prefer to refer to these as 'elements' of the method instead of as 'steps' or 'levels', because they do not necessarily have to be discussed chronologically.

Figure 1: The Hourglass Model (Brune et al., 2005, p. 98)

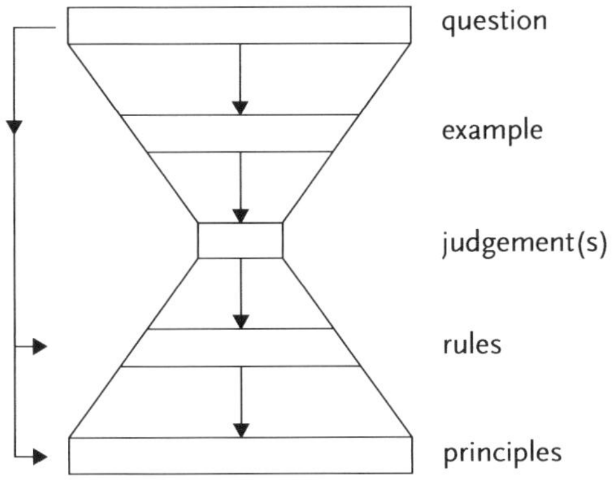

question

example

judgement(s)

rules

principles

Often, a group starts with a question that the facilitator has chosen beforehand (ideally on the basis of a meeting with representatives of the group), or which is chosen by the participants during the meeting itself. For a question to be suitable

Chapter 4

for a Socratic dialogue, it will have to be conceptual, concrete, simple, striking and actual (Kessels, 2001, pp. 143-146). A question is *conceptual* when it can only be investigated by thinking. The question does not primarily address the issue of what is the case or not (facts) but what the participants consider to be good, just, true etc. (meaning). However, it is *concrete* in the sense that the question can only be answered by investigating something that the participants have experienced. This criterion rules out many questions, such as 'Are viruses alive?' or 'Can computers think?'. While such philosophical questions require some hard thinking about the concepts of 'life' and 'thinking', (most) people cannot answer them by appealing to their own experiences.[37] A question would be better *simple* and short, because every concept included in the question is a potential source of conflict, while there is only a limited amount of time available. A question is *striking* if it captures what the participants want to know. A good indication of whether this criterion has been met is when the members of the group, upon hearing the question, react enthusiastically, because they know that it is exactly what is at stake. Finally, a good question is *actualised* in the dialogue if one investigates the very subject one is talking about by reflecting on the behaviour of the participants during the dialogue. For example, if the dialogue is about professionalism, and one of the participants categorises the behaviour of another participant as 'unprofessional', this judgment can become an example which the group can reflect upon to answer the central question.

Once a question has been chosen, the next step is to recall a number of recent situations in which the participants said or did something that can, when investigated further, potentially answer the original question. Suppose that the question is 'What should we expect from a professional?'. One of the participants, a headmaster in a secondary school, might recall a situation in which he had to call a teacher to account because he considered the teacher's conduct to be 'unprofessional'. Typical of a good example is that it is personal, concrete, relevant, simple and closed (Kessels, 2001, pp. 140-141). A *concrete* case is one in which the person who introduces the case (the 'presenter') can talk about it in terms of time, place, people involved, etc. For a case to be *personal*, the contributor must have experienced the story himself. A case is *relevant* when it is related to the question, at least for the case contributor. When he introduces the example, he has to have an intuitive grasp of how his experience is related to the central question. Ideally, the case is *closed*, because dialogues in which the presenter is still involved in a case can trigger in other participants the desire to help the presenter to solve the problem, while the aim is to investigate retrospectively which assumptions the presenter made while acting the way he did. Finally, it is an advantage when a case is *simple*, because the conceptual inquiry can only start when it is clear to everyone what has happened.

When a case has been selected, the participants have the opportunity to ask clarifying questions to the presenter, Marc. The facilitator asks the participants to

---

[37] Such questions can be used in other approaches to philosophise with children. See, for example, Lipman (2003), Lipman et al. (1980) and McCall (2009).

imagine that they are in the situation just described. They are not asked to imagine what they would do *if they were Marc*, but what they would do *if they were in the same situation* as Marc was. They are all asked to formulate a judgment, starting with the phrase 'In this situation, I considered the teacher to be professional/ unprofessional, because y' (where y is the reason). For example, Marc says that his colleague was unprofessional because this teacher criticised another colleague in front of the pupils. He justifies this reason by arguing that professionals should be honest with each other and air their criticism to the colleague privately first. His answer reveals his 'principle' that collegiality and loyalty to one's colleagues are important elements of a professional attitude. Now, it is the facilitator's task to tempt the participants to investigate each others' ideas further. The participants can disagree about different things. For example, they may agree with Marc that the teacher was unprofessional, but for entirely different reasons, or they may disagree with him that the teacher acted unprofessionally in the first place. The purpose of exchanging views is twofold: to elucidate the different convictions, ideas and visions that participants have about the theme (e.g. professionalism), and to critically test the validity of these convictions, i.e. whether they are correct, adequate, true (Bolten, 2003, p. 16).

If a conversation does not include the five elements of the hourglass model, and if the questions and examples put forward do not meet the above-mentioned criteria, there is – strictly speaking – no Socratic dialogue. However, a Socratic dialogue is not necessarily a *good* dialogue when it meets these criteria, because the participants will also need an understanding of and commitment to the method if it is to be successful. Most importantly, those who engage in a Socratic dialogue must acknowledge that it makes sense to search for a true answer to a pressing question together (Van Tongeren, 2000, p. 44). This attitude holds a delicate mean between two extreme attitudes that can both kill the dialogue. Those with dogmatic attitudes assume that there is a moral truth, and are convinced that they know what it is. If they stubbornly refuse to consider the possibility that they may be wrong, a *quest* for the truth does not make much sense to dogmatists. In contrast, relativists deny that there is something like 'the' moral *truth*. Instead, they believe in a plurality of local moral truths. Since each person's moral beliefs are equally true, there is no need to convince somebody of anything.

If one is, however, committed to a shared quest for the truth, one assumes (contra the relativist) that there is a true answer to a question, but (contra the dogmatist) that no participant has a privileged access to it. While participants to a Socratic dialogue are advised to defend (like the dogmatist) their views as long as possible, they should also (like the relativist) have the courage to recognise other perspectives as a challenge to their own. Ideally, a collection of different and seemingly incompatible views function as a catalyst that spurs the participants to look deeper into the matter at hand. However, if there is too much disagreement, the conversation may end in chaos, ending the common quest. If there is too little disagreement, the community of inquiry degenerates into some kind of complacent consensus (Swanton, 2003, p. 269).

Heckmann (1993, p. 3) believed that this common search for the truth can best be sustained if the participants adhere to certain rules. These rules are not constitutive, in the sense that there is no Socratic dialogue without them, but heuristic, in the sense that they help participants, especially those unfamiliar with the method, to remain committed to the goal. Inspired by Heckmann's writings, the German *Gesellschaft für Sokratisches Philosophieren* currently uses the following rules (Kessels, 2001, pp. 157-158). First, participants justify their ideas by referring to their own experiences, not by pointing at what they have read or heard. It is not allowed to rely on authorities. Second, the Socratic dialogue is supposed to contribute to knowledge by self-examination, and this means that if a participant has doubts about the topic under discussion, he should express these concerns. However, if he agrees with the course of the dialogue, he should not feign doubt, as this will only delay the dialogue. Third, participants should make an effort to make themselves understood, but they should also be concise in order to prevent the dialogue from degenerating into a monologue. Fourth, participants should not only focus on the expression of own ideas, but also try to understand the ideas of others. Ideally, every participant relates his own point to his predecessor's by first summarising in his own words what his predecessor has just said. Fifth, participants often have the tendency to talk about a topic in very general, abstract terms. In order to make the conversation more concrete and personal, participants should always be able to illustrate their ideas by relating them to the example that is being examined. Sixth, the enquiry continues (in principle) as long as participants have incompatible convictions. The enquiry will often end because time is up, and not because the group has formulated a definitive answer to the central question. Seventh, to keep track of the insights that the dialogue yields, the facilitator may use all kinds of aids, such as flip-charts, in order to keep track of participants' judgments and arguments.

What is required of teachers who want to supervise a Socratic dialogue? First of all, it is important that they create an atmosphere that puts pupils at ease so they dare talk about their personal ideas. For example, a teacher may want to have the children agree before the conversation starts that everything that is said is confidential and will remain within the four walls of the classroom. He can try to influence the classroom environment explicitly by sharing something personal before they start to examine the pupils' ideas (Elkind & Sweet, 1997). Moreover, teachers can tell the children that they do not have all the answers either, and that adults have fears and insecurities too.

In general, a facilitator should encourage the participants to ask each other questions about more general principles that underlie judgments dormant in everyday opinions, choices and behaviour. He knows the Socratic method and is himself a model of critical thinking during the conversation, by posing questions that are more meaningful than the questions that participants develop on their own, stimulating the inquiry. The two most basic questions that Socrates also posed to his interlocutors are: 'What do you mean?' and 'Is it true what you say?'. They are respectively after the clarification and justification of one's (moral) commitments. Teachers should try not to voice their own opinions, but show a genuine interest in children's ideas and look for pupils who disagree with each other, enabling *them* to critically investigate *each others'* opinions. Teachers can do so by listening carefully and keeping the discussion focused, following up on pupils' responses and inviting elaboration, stimulating the conversation with probing questions, summarising what has been discussed and by posing concrete, simple questions that children can apprehend. As children internalise these rules, the facilitator can gradually keep a lower profile. The facilitator may even become superfluous when he has succeeded in turning the participants into Socratic facilitators, helping each other give birth to their ideas.

4.4.5 Practical Wisdom's Regressive Movement

Before examining how a series of Socratic dialogues can make pupils and teachers practically wiser, a definition of 'practical wisdom' is necessary. In the account of practical wisdom provided in Chapter 3, its role in generating virtuous action and desire in all kinds of circumstances was stressed. However, if we overemphasise its action-guiding feature, we run the risk of treating practical wisdom as a capacity that merely stamps general knowledge of virtue, of ethical principles as such, on specific acts or situations (Dunne, 1997, p. 272). Practical wisdom would then merely help people with well-formed characters to recognise occasions to put their character in action. However, for those who have not reached the level of full virtue yet, the 'forward' movement from character to actions, would ideally be supplemented with a 'backward' (regressive) movement from action to character. This can be called the 'virtue-specifying task' of practical wisdom. By rethinking our virtues and vices after acting in a particular situation, we can change and learn how to act differently in similar situations in the future (see also §3.4.3). Practical wisdom is not only the quality that people need in order to *be* good, but it is also required for people to gain a better understanding of virtue, and to *become* good (Gadamer, 2006, p. 310). If the forward and backward movements of practical wisdom are combined, practical wisdom turns out to establish a dynamic circle between virtue and action.

This circle can be illustrated with two examples. Firstly, imagine that you, a young but respected teacher from a family of teachers, want to leave your job because you have become sceptical about the possibility of really educating pupils.[38] You have to teach so many classes and have been under so much stress that you do not feel inspired anymore. You like how teaching is part of your life, but now really consider quitting. However, your team leader is still satisfied with your work, and you know that your family would be very disappointed if you were to leave the profession. You have a rough understanding of courage, so you perceive this moment as a situation that calls for a courageous response. But the question is: which response is the courageous one? Secondly, suppose you are grading papers and you read one written by Peter, who is struggling to get a C in your course.[39] It is decently written and coherently organised, and it has no major misunderstandings of key concepts. It is a B- paper, but it is by far the best work Peter has done in your course. Next, you turn to one written by the Mary, the smartest girl in class. It is well written and organised, and it demonstrates fine comprehension. A solid B+, perhaps even an A-. But Mary could definitely have written a much better piece of work. Which grades do you give these two pupils? You have a rough understanding of justice, therefore, you perceive this as a situation that calls for a just response. But the question is: which response is the just one?

While practical wisdom can be of help in these situations to find out what the morally appropriate response is, making a decision and reflecting on it can also increase one's understanding of the virtues involved. In the examples, both teachers started with a 'rough' understanding of courage or justice. This will include the idea that courage is needed in dangerous situations, and that justice has something to do with a fair distribution. Using practical wisdom to examine carefully the particulars of the situation will also illuminate what the still vague concepts of 'courage' and 'justice' mean in these concrete situations. In the first situation, a courageous person should find a mean with regard to the emotion of fear. This raises the question: what is the pertinent fear here? Is it the fear of having to tell his parents and colleagues that he has decided to pursue a path contrary to their expectations? Or is it the fear of suffering through the attempts to do more than just transferring knowledge and skills to his pupils? In either case, the question is how the teacher decides what is cowardly and what is reckless to do in relation to these fears. In the second situation, justice requires you to treat both pupils fairly, i.e. they should both be rewarded in accordance with certain standards. But what are these standards? Do you give the papers the grades they actually deserve, evaluating them as if you did not know who wrote them? Or should you recognise individual differences, and take pupils' efforts and the quality of their past work into account?

The oscillation between virtue and action enables us to see something about practical wisdom more clearly. On the one hand, we can describe a good, happy life as a virtuous life, and identify a number of virtues, such as 'generosity', 'friendliness' or 'honesty', which are defined as the best ways to deal with certain

---

38 Adapted from Higgins (2011), p. 131.
39 Derived from Schwartz & Sharpe (2006), p. 377.

spheres of human experience. If we describe virtues in this formal way, they remain rather vague, 'uninstructive' and 'meaningless' (Higgins, 2011, p. 131; Gadamer, 2006, p. 311). It is the task of practical wisdom to find out what these virtues mean in the concrete circumstances of everyday life. However, these concrete actions can inform us about our general moral orientations. When we put our character into action, our actions will have effects on ourselves and others, and by reflecting on the feedback we get, we can learn something about the specific content of virtues and vices, and obtain a more detailed account of what a happy, flourishing life consist of. As our understanding develops, we will approach new situations differently than we did before. This will result in new experiences, which will, if they accumulate and gradually become habitual, change our character in the long run (Dunne, 2011, p. 18; Higgins, 2011, p. 132; Nussbaum, 2001a, p. 306). While the kind of character people have acquired over time enables them to approach situations in a certain way, a person can only be called 'practically wise' if he also has a kind of attentive receptivity that helps him notice something of the 'newness' of each situation, and a willingness to inform and reform his more general moral principles. Alluding to Kant's famous phrase that 'thoughts without content are empty, intuitions without concepts are blind', we could say that actions without virtue are unguided, but that virtues without experience are meaningless.

4.4.6 Teachers' Practical Wisdom

After discussing the Socratic method and the movement that practical wisdom makes between virtue and action, focus turns to the question of how Socratic dialogues can improve participants' practical wisdom. While it is obvious that Socratic dialogues can be explicitly about moral issues, these last sections will show that participation in a dialogue is itself morally educative, regardless of the topic discussed. The movement that participants make in a dialogue between a conceptual question and a concrete example gives them an opportunity to practice practical wisdom, i.e. the kind of judgment that mediates between general virtue and particular circumstance.

How this works will be illustrated by an example, in which Emma, a student at a college for teacher training, encounters a problem.[40] She knows how to maintain order but wonders how to 'connect' with some pupils while doing her teaching practice. When she raises the issue in a meeting with fellow students, they offer her some advice, such as walking round the classroom, making time to talk to pupils individually, etc. Moreover, Emma's supervisor advises her to look at what the scientific literature about social and communicative skills has to say about her problem. Both her fellow-students and her supervisor provide Emma with practical recommendations about how to tackle the problem, but these tips and tricks do not offer Emma any insight into the *cause* of the problem. Before Emma

---

40 The example is adapted from Kessels (2000), chapter 6.

can start thinking about how to *solve* it, the first problem seems to be to *find out* what her problem is. Emma says that she wonders how to 'connect' with pupils, but is it clear what this means? In Emma's case, there does not seem to be a discrete problem already clearly discernible as such. Teachers often find themselves in a predicament, a "point of intersection of several lines of consideration and priority that, thought pulling in different directions, are interwoven tightly in a complex web" (Dunne, 2011, p. 22). Sometimes, teachers are faced with a situation, where they cannot simply 'solve the problem', but have to unravel different strands, which may possibly only introduce greater tangles. The nature of Emma's problem implies that she does not only need to think about the efficiency of the means – as if the end is already determined – but she will also need to deliberate about why 'connecting' is important and what would count as the 'best' outcome in the particular situation.

An additional problem with the social scientific literature is that it is formulated in *general* terms, which hold for *all* kinds of problems and situations. For example, pedagogues may have found that teachers who create 'exciting and modern thematic units' connect better with pupils than those who do not. But what do Emma's pupils consider to be 'exciting' and 'modern'? Do these labels fit Emma's personality? Somehow, she will have to translate the general knowledge into her own specific situation. What Emma needs is an idea of what it means to 'connect', and what this means *for her* with these pupils in these concrete situations. Ideally, she would arrive at a better understanding of what it is she wants to achieve in her work, which concrete circumstances she is in, what kind of person she is herself, and how she can achieve her goal, taking the circumstances and her own specific character into account. It is not a technical or scientific kind of knowledge, but a practical kind of deliberation that can help Emma to realise the goods of teaching in this particular situation.

In one way or another, Emma would have to try to explore questions like: 'What does it mean to connect with pupils?', or 'Why do I want to connect? One possible answer to the second question may be that she wants to know how the pupils are doing. In that case, 'being connected' means something like 'being personally involved' with pupils. If we continue to ask why this involvement is important to her, the answer may be that she is concerned about the pupils' well-being. Another possible answer is that Emma wants to connect in order to be able to check whether the pupils have learned something. If she is after the latter, an interesting question would be whether Emma can *ever* know for sure that her pupils have learned something. Can we say that children who are able to reproduce the answer that the teacher wants to hear have 'learned' something? Or should the pupils also be convinced of these answers? If they do, how do you check this? Would it not be better for Emma to accept that she cannot connect with all pupils in this way?

4.4.7 Practice-oriented Moral Enquiry

Emma could learn much by considering these questions all by herself. Socratic dialogues, however, offer a more structured and critical method for Emma and her colleagues to examine how ends and everyday actions are related. According to Sherman (1989, p. 30) dialogues have several advantages. First of all, they help people to listen to and identify the viewpoints of others. Exchanging experiences, ideas and arguments prevents them from falling into the all-too-human trap of self-deception, neglecting certain unfavourable aspects of our characters. Moreover, participants in a dialogue will be confronted with different ways of reading a situation and different questions to pose. This may lead them to interpret circumstances in a less one-sided way and enable them to look at the circumstances with increased insight and clarity. Finally, a shared enquiry establishes the means for consensus, but is also a means to identify differences that cannot be solved. This is particularly important for teachers who work closely with others who are similarly committed to pupils' virtue and well-being.

In a dialogue, Emma could provide an example in which she did (not) connect with pupils. For example, she may recall a situation in which she taught a history lesson about ancient Greece. The pupils were not bored, but they did not look very enthusiastic either, until Emma started to talk about Greek mythology, in particular about the god of victory, Nike. Pupils suddenly realised that *Nike* is also a famous brand, and some pupils took of their shoes and put them on the table for Emma to have a look. Emma explains that she felt relieved and was very happy when she saw that the pupils smiled and laughed. At that moment, she believed that she really connected with them. When asked why she believed this, she answers that the pupils made a connection between the teaching material and their own lives. Part of the history class fitted their daily experience. The other participants in the dialogue may have different views on this. For example, one of her colleagues, Derek, may point out that Emma's class turned into a chaos, which precisely *prevented* pupils from connecting to the class subject. While Emma made a connection with the class when pupils realised that *Nike* has Greek origins, they became so occupied with their shoes that they lost interest in Greek mythology. Other participants can join in and agree or disagree with what Emma and Derek have said. They can continue talking about the questions whether Emma connected to the pupils, why 'connecting' would be an important ingredient of teaching, and whether 'connecting' is a goal in itself or only a means to achieve something else.

When Emma and her colleagues discuss these issues, they do not simply engage in conceptual analysis, but reflect on their own and others' practical experiences. The concrete example about the history class provides the group with experimental 'data', the material from which the group tries to derive a common concept of 'connecting' they can all subscribe to. This is the 'backward' or 'regressive' movement from particular experiences to more general understanding. As the concept of 'connecting' becomes more meaningful to the participants, they may start to perceive their work differently, recognising situations as an occasion for a 'connection', knowing when and how to make a connection, and keeping the point and purpose of connecting with pupils in mind. This is what we call the forward (or 'progressive') movement from generalised knowledge to concrete situations. When teachers practice moving back and forth between the general question and the particular example in a Socratic dialogue, they can become a person of judgment, which involves a "perceptiveness in reading particular situations" and "flexibility in one's way of possessing, being informed by, and 'applying' general knowledge" (Dunne, 2011, p. 18). The Socratic dialogue offers teacher a place, an environment, in which they can practice the kind of non-technical, non-scientific wisdom that they need in order to know how 'good teaching' can be realised in practice, and also to refine the idea of 'good teaching' by reflecting together on the details of particular problematic situations.

This example makes clear that the Socratic method is an interesting method for teachers and teacher trainers to conduct practice-oriented research about moral-educational issues. Unfortunately, philosophers often treat the ethics of education as an inferior kind of applied philosophy. The term 'applied' implies that professional philosophers do fundamental philosophical research, which can be applied later to solve moral quandaries in a variety of professional domains. However, with regard to moral issues, 'practice-oriented research' is a kind of research that is conducted by professionals working in the field and which can be facilitated by philosophers. This kind of research is still a 'theoretical' activity in the sense that teachers acquire a rational understanding of what they are doing (Carr, 2000, p. 63). Teacher trainers and future teachers can organise Socratic dialogues to articulate and explain the pre-theoretical reasons that motivate their actions. While such conversations may not yield general philosophical insights or valid social-scientific knowledge, it can contribute to a kind of experience-based *practical* wisdom with which teachers can improve educational practice (Bondi et al., 2011; Higgins, 2011, pp. 111-142). On a pessimistic note, however there is a difference between the secure context of a dialogue and daily teaching practice The challenge is to make sure that the kind of practical wisdom that participants acquire is not immediately overshadowed by institutional and authoritarian pressures that seduce people to act contrary to what is morally required (Swanton, 2003, p. 269). If a school management decides to have a group of teachers participate in a series of Socratic dialogues, it would also have to make up its mind about the external structural conditions to support the dialogical process once the series has come to an end (see Achterbergh & Vriens, 2009, ch. 10 and 11).

4.5 Conclusion

Our examination of role modelling, the (narrative) arts and Socratic dialogues provide us with a better understanding of what moral education in schools looks like from a virtue ethical perspective. An important lesson is that these strategies are not far removed from the practice of teaching as it exists today. Most teachers use arts in their classes, all parties involved accept that teachers are role models to children, and teachers frequently have conversations with pupils and colleagues about things like responsibilities, unprofessional behaviour and children's wellbeing. To the extent that teachers and schools elaborate and specify an approach to moral education, 'character education' can change from a haphazard, implicit by-product into a considerate and more systematic teaching method. The moral dimension can be made more explicit if teachers take (or receive) more time to think through what they do, instead of giving way to the urge to invent all kinds of new strategies.

The cultivation of children's virtues in schools does not have to put an even heavier burden on teachers who are already overburdened. As teachers understand how role modelling, arts and dialogue are related to virtues such as compassion, integrity and practical wisdom, they can also start thinking about what else they want to educate pupils for, and whether there are ways in which these goals can be achieved more effectively. So, the increased understanding of the moral dimension of their work enables teachers to make *choices*. This means, on the one hand, that teachers gain the freedom to decide what they, individually and collectively, want to achieve. On the other hand, freedom comes with responsibility: teachers will need to develop good professional judgment to determine how the goods of education can be realised in the concrete circumstances of everyday teaching, and how they can justify their choices to pupils, parents and the wider public.

One way in which teachers can achieve a greater understanding of the moral dimension of their work is by doing what I have tried to do in this chapter, i.e. to find out which teaching methods train which morally relevant capacities. It is not always possible to give a clear answer to this question, because teachers can model all kinds of character traits, the arts contain a variety of moral lessons and dialogues can be about virtually anything. Nevertheless, it turned out that compassion, integrity and practical wisdom are involved in these strategies. 'Compassion' was described as the virtue required to deal with the vulnerability of human life, and in particular with the suffering of people who go through undeserved misfortunes. It can be practiced by putting ourselves in the shoes of characters in books, but also by imagining what one would do in a case introduced during a Socratic dialogue. Practical wisdom is an intellectual virtue that puts people's character into action and improves character by reflecting on experience. It can be cultivated through Socratic dialogues, but also by teachers who really model virtues, in the sense that they make clear that they *embody* virtues, and that children should try to acquire these traits themselves. If 'integrity' is understood as the Aristotelian 'unity of the virtues', it is part of the virtue of practical wisdom. This chapter used 'integrity' to refer to two senses in which our lives can be united. Firstly, integrity guarantees that there is coherence in the various virtues and goods of different *practices*, and secondly, it makes sure that someone's life remains in good order over *time*. Reading, telling or writing stories can make one's life more integrated because actual lives and fictional stories share a narrative structure.

Practical wisdom received significant attention in this chapter, because other approaches to moral education have been sceptical about the character educational potential to make pupils critical. In the sections on role modelling and the Socratic dialogue, however, we have seen that character education is seriously misunderstood if it is reduced to mindless habituation. Admittedly, habituation can be understood as a kind of conditioning, but it would ideally be seen as a much more cognitive process. For example, educators can explain to children why they act the way they do by offering reasons from an early age onwards, so that pupils learn that teachers only exemplify certain virtues, and that deliberation is needed to acquire these virtues for themselves. It was emphasised how the intellectual virtue of practical wisdom is not only indispensable for putting character traits in action, but also for revising and refining our moral commitments. We have to admit, however, that practical wisdom does not offer a *radical* criticism of our moral commitments (see also §3.4.5). Questions about the 'why' of virtue are not the questions of a moral sceptic, but of already emotionally cultivated people who have an interest in living well.

This chapter not only illuminates the strengths and weaknesses of character education in schools, it also casts a new light on Aristotelian virtue ethics. We consulted several virtue ethical authors in this chapter, such as MacIntyre, Carr, Dunne, Kristjánsson, Nussbaum, Higgins and Annas, some of whom turned – to my surprise – to other ethical theories for inspiration. For example, Socrates and Kant were discussed in order to understand how practical wisdom can be fostered through dialogue, because Aristotle does not specify how pupils' practical wisdom can be improved through group discussions. In providing guidelines about how a group of people can get together and uncover the emotions, reasons and habits underlying their judgments and actions, the Socratic method *complements* what Aristotle writes about practical wisdom. It helps to realise an Aristotelian ideal in a contemporary educational context. In the section on the arts, Carr and Nussbaum recommended reading stories that illustrate how the formation of one's character and one's happiness are not completely in one's own hands, but depend on others and some luck. The Greek tragedies stress the tragic dimension of human life that is largely absent in Aristotle's work. In this way, the picture of the self-complacent Aristotelian paragon of virtue was *corrected*. These examples make clear that Aristotelian virtue ethics cannot do all the work in moral education.

Finally, it may have been surprising that hardly any empirical research was consulted when dealing with the question of how virtue can be cultivated in schools. Why? The truth is there is hardly any empirical research about what works and what does not. If empirical research is scarce because social scientists have difficulties conceptualising 'role modelling' or the 'Socratic method', this chapter was hopefully of help. But still, the teaching methods involve so many interventions, and the desired outcomes are so complex that it is extremely difficult to measure their effectiveness. In medicine, it already requires much time and effort to determine whether ibuprofen significantly decreases people's headaches. Imagine the difficulties social scientists encounter when they want to know whether Socratic dialogues increase participants' practical wisdom, or whether role modelling helps pupils to acquire a more virtuous character. Another complicating factor is the measurement of moral development. While there are all kinds of questionnaires to measure people's level of moral reasoning and their self-reported moral emotions, it is much more difficult to measure the *long-term* influence of certain educational strategies on pupils' virtues and actions. Ideally, social scientists would follow a group of subjects for a long time and make detailed observations of their actions and emotional reactions in a wide range of normal situations.

Chapter 5
Virtue and Human Flourishing

5.1 Introduction

Although most teachers recognise that they somehow contribute to the character formation of pupils, many of them are in the dark about a number of things. It is sometimes unclear what an education in the virtues precisely entails (the 'what'). For example, if character education is a matter of educating virtues, which virtues are then most important? What is a 'virtue' anyway? How do children morally develop? These issues were discussed in Chapter 3. In addition, teachers do not really know how they can do character education best (the 'how'). For example, they may not be familiar with the philosophical and social scientific literature about the purpose and effectiveness of teaching methods, and ill-informed about the abundant (online) materials that have been developed to implement character education in schools. The question of how virtue can be 'taught' in schools was the subject of Chapter 4. Now, there are some questions left about why the education of virtue would be desirable (the 'why'). Will it increase children's school performance? Will all behavioural problems in schools be solved? Does it help pupils to become better democratic citizens? This lack of clarity induces us to deal in this chapter with the question: what is the point of paying attention to virtue in the classroom?

While moral education is also a matter of didactical skills, curriculum and teaching methods, it would be foolish to start using methods or acquiring skills if teachers do not have a proper idea about its point and purpose (Carr, 1991, p. 8). Ideally, they can also give reasons to themselves and others, such as parents, colleagues and policymakers why the moral education of children is nothing to worry about, or (more positively) why it is indispensable for their well-being. It is important that they are able to give an explanation, because many people, especially in the United States, have concerns about teachers interfering with

Chapter 5

the moral education of their children. When the questions why the education of virtue matters has been sufficiently clarified, it is to be hoped that teachers will be motivated to take character education, understood as a broadly Aristotelian education in the virtues, more seriously.

Basically, the thesis defended in this chapter is that character education is crucial to a flourishing life as a human being. This means that cultivating children's virtues is essential to the promotion of their well-being or happiness. The relationship between virtue and flourishing, and the connection between 'flourishing', 'well-being' and 'happiness' will be explicated along the way. First, the ways in which many teachers approach the question what character education is for will be examined (§5.2). This examination makes clear that the thesis advocated in this chapter is far from self-evident. The contrast between the way moral education is understood today and the Aristotelian framework (§5.3) means that we will have to go beyond an exegesis of Aristotle's ideas on virtue, education and happiness. In other words: explaining why character education matters according to Aristotle is not enough. In §5.4 and §5.5, the ideas of two neo-Aristotelians are described, compared and evaluated, in order to see whether they can solve the problem with moral education in contemporary society, while staying true to the Aristotelian heritage.

5.2 Teachers' Understanding of Morality

While talking with teachers in schools about moral issues as a Socratic dialogue facilitator, it became apparent that teachers recognise that they contribute to the character development of pupils, but when asked to articulate what this task entails, and why it is morally desirable to perform it, they seem confused. Some have argued that this confusion is not limited to teachers. For example, Haydon (1999, p. 47) notes that "as a society we are deeply confused about the very idea of morality". Teachers and others give two kinds of answers: morality and moral education are either conceived of as a personal choice, or as part of government's attempts to create a shared public moral understanding. How the two perspectives can be related will be explained below.

5.2.1 Private Virtue and Public Morality

The first story one is likely to hear is a personal one. Teachers will explain that they value virtues such as honesty, care or patience, and that they try to embody these values when they deal with pupils and colleagues. However, these teachers do not claim to *know* that the virtues they value *are* moral qualities that *all* pupils should acquire. They value them because it is their opinion, and not because there would be something in the 'nature' of honesty that they could appeal to in order to convince others that all pupils should be honest, or that all teachers should be an example of the virtue of patience.

In education, this kind of 'subjectivism' has been observed by several authors. For example, Best (1996, p. 82) noted that subjectivism about value judgments is "surprisingly persistent". In discussions, teachers will often say 'Oh, that is just my value judgment', and look as if they are convinced that this is all there is to say about moral values and virtues in education. "Just utter the magic words: 'these are my values'", Higgins (2011, p. 24) writes, and any normative discussion will be brought to a crashing halt. Moreover, Haydon (1999, p. 47) noticed that there are tendencies towards what he calls the 'personalisation' of morality, i.e. towards the idea that morality comes down to individual choice or how the individual feels about it. Furthermore, Klaassen (2002, p. 155) empirically investigated the views that teachers have of their pedagogical responsibilities. After interviewing 15 Dutch high school teachers and 34 elementary school teachers, it was concluded that many teachers adopt a neo-liberal point of view and consider moral values as "...lying largely in the domain of personal choice". They take morality to be relative to purely personal belief or conviction. Teachers seem to be afraid that, as soon as they start talking about moral issues, they will indoctrinate children by influencing their ideas about what is wrong and right. As a consequence, some teachers avoid this uncomfortable aspect of teaching and refrain from mentioning the intrinsic educational merit of values and norms. They do not teach moral virtues explicitly and generally avoid moral discussions in class (Klaassen, 2002, p. 155).

Not only teachers think about morality this way. The idea that judgments about what is morally good and bad depend on an individual's preferences is ubiquitous. Many people will say that when you value something, e.g. generosity, this value can only be 'true' in the sense that *you* want to value it. Values are regarded as things we 'make up', as projections of our preferences onto a world which is itself value-neutral (Appiah, 2009, p. 154). Moreover, we believe that everybody is entitled to their own viewpoint on moral matters and that everyone has the right to choose the kind of life and the best moral code that one prefers – provided that one's preferences do not prevent other people from realising theirs. One of the worrying consequences of this subjective understanding of morality is that the truth or falsity of moral claims depends on the subject who utters these judgments. Moral expressions may still be used to represent moral facts, but these are not facts about an 'external moral reality' but about the internal psychological state a subject is in. As no reference is made to more objective reasons, which are somehow independent of people's preferences, it seems impossible to determine whether somebody expresses his or her *real* preferences. On a subjectivist reading, people can only be guilty of a moral fault if they are self-deceived and do not act on what they claim to be their deepest convictions. While 'authenticity', i.e. acting on convictions that people consider to be *their own,* is a great good, the problem is that we might end up in a situation in which one judgment can be both right and wrong according to the idiosyncratic moral outlook of several agents. Even contradictory judgments could be true, as long as they all truly express agents' preferences. It will hardly be surprising that this precludes a rational dialogue about a question such as what children should be morally educated for. On the subjectivist model, 'moral communication' is the exchange of expressions of attitudes and feelings. By expressing these preferences, people can try to influence the emotions of others they disagree with or invite them to share their preferences.

An account of teachers' understanding of moral education is not complete without taking a second voice, one which emphasises the public aspect of morality, seriously. As already mentioned, the freedom to choose and live the kind of life one wants is not unrestrained, but limited by certain rules and, in liberal societies, by certain rights. When teachers are asked about their moral educational task, they also mention the importance of teaching pupils about elementary rules and liberal rights, and some corresponding civic obligations virtues that are needed if pupils are to be capable of and willing to observe these rules and rights (Steutel & Spiecker, 1996). This public component of moral education is often called 'civic education' or 'citizenship education'. While these are contested notions, most political philosophers agree that their goal is to sustain a 'flourishing liberal democracy', distinguished not only by its procedures, but also by certain values or ideals. These values or ideals include justice, freedom and respect for personal autonomy (White, 1996) and equality, self-governance, stability and collective cooperation for the common good (Faulconer, 2004, p. 47).

There is also consensus that the health and stability of liberal democracies do not only depend on the values and ideals that citizens (profess to) cherish, but just as much on citizens' qualities and attitudes (Kymlicka, 2001). Patricia White (1996) calls these 'democratic dispositions', or 'civic virtues'. Citizenship education is desirable because it would be impossible to attain liberal democratic ideals without a broadly virtuous citizenry (Faulconer, 2004, p. 12). Although authors sometimes identify different civic virtues or interpret the 'same' virtues differently, most of them mention justice, tolerance, loyalty/allegiance to or identification with fellow-citizens, public reasonableness or deliberation, obedience to the rule of law and respect for rights. Empirical research affirms that teachers consider respect and justice to be important virtues (Van Oudenhoven et al., 2007).

5.2.2 Beyond the Split Model

The private and public answers to the question why certain character traits are to be promoted in pupils, are two sides of the same (liberal) coin. If people cultivate certain civic virtues that help sustain a liberal democracy, this guarantees certain individual rights which are designed to enable people to live the kind of life that they want, and cultivate the virtues that they highly cherish. In a liberal society, people are free to develop a 'conception of the good life', i.e. a conception of a life that is successful and pleasing – according to people's own standards and viewpoints. This freedom is an important achievement, but a sharp division between conceptions of the good life on the one hand and a public morality of citizenship on the other can have some undesirable consequences. When the subjective nature of private morality sinks in with teachers, they will realise that they cannot rationally persuade pupils to cultivate certain virtues, and that the only thing left for them to do is to make a strong emotional appeal to pupils to share their view. However, as this is not acceptable, the more usual response is to abandon all moral education – except for some kind of citizenship education required by law. If this happens, the education of virtue in schools is reduced to the education of civic virtues, and the cultivation of other (non-civic) virtues becomes a private affair (of the family, church etc.) which teachers should not interfere with, particularly not in public schools.

With regard to the contents of anything that goes beyond a bare minimum, an attitude of "agnostic neutrality" is being adopted (Carr, 1999, p. 36). Provided others are not harmed, all forms of moral life are equally important (and therefore equally unimportant) and no specific virtues can or should be taught. Teachers who engage in character education anyway are believed to 'bother' pupils with their subjective preferences, prevent children from thinking for themselves, and restrict their burgeoning autonomy. This attitude undermines the possibility of *any* real education in values, whether these values are moral, spiritual or aesthetic. For example, with regard to arts education, Carr (1999, p. 36) has argued that:

> "if all forms of literature, painting and music are to be regarded as qualitatively on the same level, as equal candidates for attention or praise, then any form of instruction that attempts to go beyond merely acquainting people with available alternatives is ruled out of court – since, of course, teaching genuine appreciation is more or less distinguishable from persuading or indoctrinating others into one's own subjective point of view."

What Carr points out is that when aesthetic value is relative to one's personal opinion, teachers cannot engage in arts education in the sense that they help pupils to understand the difference between works of art that have more or less quality. In his view, the same holds, *mutatis mutandis,* for moral value. As a consequence, teachers are likely to restrict their conversations to topics about which they believe that rational debate *is* possible, i.e. the "realm of means", or the "realm of measurable effectiveness" (MacIntyre, 2003, p. 30). For example, they mainly talk about the ways in which discipline can be maintained or how pupils can be motivated to do their homework, and far less about the *purpose* of discipline or homework. This lack of 'philosophical' discussion is very unfortunate in a pluralistic society that is marked by much controversy over the question of what the purpose of (moral) education is, and how (moral) education can contribute to people's flourishing.

Since the 1980s, several neo-Aristotelians have argued that this 'split' model of morality and moral education has had some severe drawbacks, and suggested that a virtue ethical approach to moral education has the potential to correct these mistakes or even to replace the liberal model altogether. In their view, no strict division can be made between 'private' and 'public' morality. For example, teachers can be 'neutral' in the sense that they do not mention their political, religious or moral views, but can they separate their professional 'role' as a teacher and their identity as a human being? When dealing with the meaning of role modelling in moral education (§4.2), it was noticed that all kinds of 'public' actions and reactions reveal teachers' 'private' characters. This illustrated that professional and private identities are intertwined, and the moral aspect of teaching has to do with the kind of moral character a teacher has – in and outside school. From this point of view, a question like 'which moral virtues should teachers embody?' makes perfect sense. However, if one insists on a separation of public and private morality, this question either means 'which civic virtues should a teacher embody?' or 'which character traits do teachers want to embody?'. This first question is very narrow, and the second has no moral strings attached. While it would be too quick to conclude that there is currently no room for teachers to support children in finding a substantial conception of the good life, liberals insist on teaching children to differentiate between their public and private moral identities (Steutel & Spiecker, 1996, p. 164). However, stressing the *continuity* between private and public morality (which is something else than dissolving the whole distinction) raises two interesting questions, one of which will be pursued in more detail in the rest of this chapter. Firstly, can civic virtues also be interpreted as the applications of the intellectual virtues and virtues of character in a political community? Secondly, is 'private morality' necessarily subjective, or does it have a similar kind of objectivity as the civic virtues? In this chapter, only the second question will be addressed. But before we do so, it is first suggested that it makes sense to develop something like a 'virtue ethical citizenship education' too (see Collins, 2006).

Liberal political philosophers conceive of civic education as something instrumental: it is a means to help the political system flourish. For example, the influential liberal political theorist William Galston (2006, p. 332) wholeheartedly subscribes to the idea that "civic virtues are to be understood as instrumentally or functionally valuable." Despite the fact that such authors are unwilling to admit that virtues are really to change people's characters, it remains unclear why it would be good for people, as human beings, to be good citizens. The question whether civic virtues are also intrinsically valuable, i.e. whether they are part of a conception of human flourishing, is another matter altogether. Galston wants to keep the two issues separate because he believes that they can and will clash: he argues that the contribution that moral education makes to the flourishing of individuals often points in another direction than the effect it has on the stability and vitality of the society in which these individuals live. As a consequence, Galston (2006, p. 333) is not in favour of a more substantive and 'demanding' kind of civic education to be provided for by families, civil associations, religious communities or professional organisations. Galston is probably right that there can be tensions between people's ideas about what a good life is and which kind of moral education they want for their children, on the one hand, and what is required of them in virtue of their membership of a liberal democracy, on the other hand. We should certainly not underestimate the value of a liberal society, or turn a blind eye to possible threats to its stability.

However, can it not be precisely *because* we care about a liberal democracy that it would be better to think of the civic virtues as naturally following from an education in the other virtues? From an Aristotelian point of view, educating one's children to be temperate, practically wise, just and courageous "...cannot but conduce to their individual welfare as well as that of any society of which they may be members" (Carr, 2006b, p. 452). Without the virtues, one would be less well off as a human being, both individually *and* as a member of society. When we succeed in spelling out what this more comprehensive moral education entails, the civic virtues would simply be a part of an intrinsically valuable character. Or, alternatively, there may be no separate class of 'civic' virtues, but only a civic aspect to all the virtues. The civic virtues would then be the application of all the intellectual virtues and virtues of character in a political community. What will need to be investigated is how the civic virtues are part of an answer to the question what is good for human beings, while we also continue to maintain some kind of distinction between 'humans' and 'citizens'. In other words, it could be attempted to find out whether virtues can have both a civic *and* a personal aspect.

As already announced, most of this chapter will be dedicated to the discussion of a second question, i.e. whether private morality is necessarily subjective, and if it is not, which consequences this may have for moral education. What would a non-subjective 'private' morality look like? Carr (1991, pp. 4-5) and other virtue ethicists have suggested that there are general but objective criteria of moral right and wrong, good and evil, which form a "template" upon which the contours of moral life of individuals and communities can be modelled. Aristotelian virtue ethicists generally believe that human beings share a common nature that inclines us to experience pleasure, fear, anger and all kinds of other emotions, and that virtues are the moral qualities essential to deal with these experiences best. Although a virtue such as 'courage' can be interpreted differently by different people or in different societies, it is difficult to imagine a human community where courage is not needed or valued at all. If we look at virtue from this more objective perspective, we can start to see why virtue would have to lie at the heart of moral education. The remainder of this chapter will be a clarification of what it means to say that character education is necessary if children are to flourish as a human being.

5.3 Aristotle on Human Flourishing

If we want to know why the education of virtue is desirable, an obvious first candidate to turn to is Aristotle, the founding father of virtue ethics. He is, however, certainly not the only one having provided an explanation of why the virtues are good to have (Brown, 2008). For example, deontologists understand virtues as traits that cause people to do the right things, e.g. those acts the maxim of which can be universalised. In addition, utilitarians understand virtues as traits that tend to cause people to maximise the good, e.g. the satisfaction of the desires of all people involved. Aristotelian virtue ethics does not justify virtues in terms of right acts or the consequences of the acts. So, we may ask how Aristotle does justify the virtues. We will see in more detail that he argues that the exercise of the virtues contributes to an agent's flourishing as a human being.

5.3.1 Eudaimonia

Ethics, as viewed by Aristotle, is an attempt to find out the highest and final good. He insists that ethics is a practical discipline that is not only after knowledge of the good, but that theoretical enquiries eventually aim at the improvement of human life and action. We are only interested in the question what is good for human beings because this enquiry could enable us to realise this good in our lives. Though many ends in life are only means to further ends, Aristotle assumes on the opening page of the *Nicomachean Ethics* that our aspirations and desires must have some final object or pursuit. But what can it be? Aristotle starts with the idea that people have different views of which kind of life is best for human beings, but that we can nevertheless sort out which of these answers makes most sense. The difficulty of this inquiry is not so much to compile a list of items that contribute to a good life. Most people agree that health, pleasure and friendship are on this list. The more controversial issue is whether some of these ingredients are more desirable than others. In order to find this out, Aristotle uses three criteria that the highest good must meet: it is desirable for itself, it is not desirable for the sake of some other good, and all other goods are desirable for its sake.

He calls the kind of life that meets these criteria *eudaimonia* ('happiness') or *eu zên* ('living well') (see also §3.2.1). Although Aristotle does not elaborate on the etymology of *eudaimonia*, the Greek term *eudaimōn* is composed of two parts:

eu means 'well' and *daimon* means 'divinity' or 'spirit'. To be *eudaimōn* means roughly to be 'blessed', to be 'god-like', or to 'have a good spirit in you'. In modern English, *eudaimonia* is often translated as 'happiness', 'flourishing' or 'well-being'. However, the problem with these terms is that they can be taken as answers to the question what *eudaimonia* is. Aristotle's initial statement should be treated as a rough outline whose details can only be filled in when the nature of the specific virtues is established. So, even if we translate *eudaimonia* in this chapter as 'flourishing', we should keep in mind that it simply means 'the best possible life' (Ackrill, 1980, p. 24). Nothing could be more ordinary than that we are after the best thing we can get in our lives as human beings. It would even be irrational to go for any lesser good than the greatest available (Lawrence, 2006, p. 37).

According to Aristotle, health, wealth and other goods contribute to happiness, but they do not *constitute* it. So, what constitutes happiness? Aristotle specifies *eudaimonia* by referring to the specific function or characteristic task (*ergon*) of a human being. This is what has become known as the 'function-argument'. An important part of this argument depends on the distinction between different parts of the 'soul', the central notion in Aristotle's metaphysical biology (see also §3.2). The soul manifests its activity in certain 'faculties' or 'capacities', which correspond with stages of biological development. There is a faculty of nutrition and growth (typical of plants), one of movement and appetite (typical of animals), and one of reason (typical of humans). According to Aristotle, the human soul has an irrational element which is shared with the animals, and a rational element (*logos*) which is typically human. This rational element exists partly in a pure form, and is partly mixed with the emotions and desires that arise from the irrational element. Next, Aristotle argues that the *good* of a human being must have something to do with what a human being *is*. Generally speaking, a 'virtue' is a quality that enables something – an object, a living thing – to perform its characteristic function well. For instance, the virtue of a knife, whose function is to cut, is its sharpness, and the virtue of a watch, whose function is to indicate the time, is its accuracy. Likewise, Aristotle writes about the qualities that people need in order to function well as human beings: the *ergon* of a human being is *logos*, both in its pure and mixed form, and the excellences of these rational capacities are the character and intellectual virtues. The virtues of character are the human dispositions to deal properly with these desires, and the intellectual virtues are the excellence of the purely rational part of the soul.

After having argued that humans are rational animals, and that the activity of our rationality can be in accordance with its virtue, Aristotle goes on to claim that *eudaimonia* consists in this kind of rational activity (*NE* 1097b22–1098a20). Usually, Aristotle is interpreted here as saying that man's highest virtue is a life of theoretical activity, but Ackrill (1980 p. 27) has pointed out that the function argument refers to *all* virtues, including practical thought and action guided by reason. It is only in Book X of the *Nicomachean Ethics* that Aristotle comes up with new arguments to prefer a life of theory above a life of action. Even if we agree with Aristotle that a theoretical life is most desirable, the question remains whether this is possible, given the fact that man is a sort of compound creature. Ackrill (1980, p. 33) concludes that contemplation and virtuous action are both valuable, but he admits that this raises the question of how they should be combined in the best life for humans. Aristotle does not attempt to answer this question, and Ackrill suggests that this has to do with Aristotle's anthropology and theology. The kind of answer that Aristotle gives to the question of what life is best for man is based on the nature of man, but since human nature is a mysterious combination of 'something divine' and much that is not divine, the best life for man is also difficult to specify. It remains a "curious feature" of Aristotle's system that no coherent account can be given of how the competition between the intellectual virtues and virtues of character is to be regulated (Williams, 1972, p. 60).

We know now that *eudaimonia* consists of virtuous rational activity. What is yet unclear, however, is what this 'consists of' means. Is virtue a necessary and sufficient condition for *eudaimonia*? By framing the question in terms of 'conditions for', we run the risk of treating virtues as preliminaries that we have to cultivate *in order to* be happy. A comparison with the game of golf can make clear that this language only clouds the nature of *eudaimonia* (Ackrill, 1980, p. 19). Golfers do not put in order to play golf in the same way as they buy clubs in order to play golf. Rather, putting is a *constituent* or *ingredient* of golfing. Likewise, we do not acquire, cultivate and exercise virtues in order to live a happy life; a happy life consists in virtuous activity. This means that 'living well' does not consist of being in a certain state or condition, but in doing something, i.e. those activities that actualise the excellences of the rational part of the soul over a lifetime.

However, Aristotle argues that in order to be happy one must possess some goods external to the soul as well, such as friends, wealth, power, good birth, children and beauty (*NE* 1099a31-b6). Does this not undermine the central thought that virtue is constitutive of happiness? Aristotle would reply that one's virtuous activity will be, to some extent, diminished or defective without an adequate supply of external goods, because someone who has no friends or children, who is powerless, weak and ugly will not be able to find many opportunities for virtuous activity in his life, and whatever he accomplishes will not be recognised by others. Although living well requires some good fortune, Aristotle insists that the highest good does not come to us by chance. True, some things that are conducive to *eudaimonia* depend on our childhood, before we even have the opportunity to influence these factors. But later, once we start to realise that the choices we make influence who we become, we share in the responsibility for acquiring and exercising the virtues.

5.3.2 Some Vexed Questions

We turned to Aristotle because the question of why an education in the virtues is desirable needs to be answered if teachers are fully to understand character education. Aristotle's theory about the relationship between virtue and flourishing, has been briefly discussed, which leaves the question whether this Aristotelian line of reasoning about human nature, function and well-being can still make sense to modern people like us. While the core idea that acquiring virtues enables people to live a flourishing life is intuitively appealing, two elements need to be reformulated or revised in order to provide a convincing justification for those interested in or applying character education in schools. In short, Aristotle's virtue ethics is problematic because it presupposes a biology which is both essentialist and teleological.

It is essentialist, in the sense that it defends a taxonomy of natural kinds, within which human beings are classified as rational animals. This taxonomy is problematic, because it is unclear whether 'natural kinds' exist at all (Dupré, 2006), and whether Aristotle's characterisation of human beings is correct. Are they really as rational as Aristotle takes them to be? The other problematic presupposition, which will be discussed in more detail in this chapter, is how to conceive of the idea that (human) nature has an intrinsic *telos*, end or purpose. True, we still use teleological language, in and outside science, e.g. when we say things such as 'Kidneys are for purifying blood' or 'Teeth are for chewing food'. However, Aristotle did not limit teleological explanations to parts of living organisms; he believed that whole organisms, including animals and human beings have a final cause, that for the sake of which they are done or made.[41] In *After Virtue*, MacIntyre (2003, pp. 52-53) has showed that science and philosophy abandoned Aristotle's teleological framework during the Enlightenment period. As a consequence, modern people are left with two things: on the one hand, a certain normative content for morality and, on the other hand, a neutral view of human nature as it actually is. Against this background, Hume's famous claim that, without further reason, 'oughts' cannot be deduced from what 'is' makes perfect sense. After all, the Aristotelian link between 'is' and 'ought', a notion of human-nature-as-it-could-be-if-it-realised-its-*telos*, is not credible any more.

The vexed question is whether we can retain the normative character of Aristotelian virtue ethics while abandoning the idea that human nature has a purpose. Can there be a viable neo-Aristotelian approach to ethics and moral education without an appeal to a kind of nature that is already well-ordered and waiting to be perfected? This chapter focuses on the work of two prominent neo-Aristotelians who do not ground morality in nature in a naive way, but who still think teleologically, in the sense that they endorse the idea that people can conceive of ends to direct themselves toward. But if we accept that nature as such does not reveal to us what is good, what is the source of our beliefs about what

---

41 See §3.2.1 for the Aristotelian distinction between the material, formal, efficient and final cause.

Chapter 5

kind of life is worth living? The examination of the ideas of Kristján Kristjánsson and Alasdair MacIntyre will enable us to do two things at once. One the one hand, to find out whether their neo-Aristotelian justifications of the virtues can offer a solution to the subjectivism we encountered in contemporary education. On the other hand, to consider whether Kristjánsson and MacIntyre manage, each in their own way, to reformulate Aristotle's pre-modern heritage in such a way that their interpretations still qualify as 'Aristotelian'. My hypothesis is that, despite some disagreements, their ideas can be combined in such a way that it provides a strong antidote to the prevailing neutrality concerning moral education in schools. However, Aristotle's *metaphysical* teleology will have to be rejected.

5.4   Interlude: Teaching 'Happiness'

Before examining the ways in which neo-Aristotelians justify the education of virtue, we should note that the idea that schools contribute to children's happiness or well-being is currently very popular. According to Suissa (2008, p. 575), the idea of teaching happiness "has received considerable attention recently in Britain" and according to Kristjánsson (2010a, p. 296) it is "gradually establishing itself as an independent approach to education". In my home country, the Netherlands, teaching happiness first received attention in 2009 after a teacher, Theo Wismans, introduced happiness lessons ('gelukskunde') at Eijkhagen College, the secondary school he teaches at. These happiness lessons put us in an awkward predicament: if an education in the virtues is desirable *because* virtues enable people to live a happy life, and schools are already teaching happiness in schools in other ways, why should we still promote character education? What is its added value?

However, when one examines the rationale for paying attention to happiness in schools, it seems that character educational projects and happiness programmes have something different in mind. When reading through the websites dedicated to these happiness lessons, a number of reasons are given for why happiness is a highly needed school subject. Happiness should be taught in school, it is argued, because it can teach children how to deal with stress, conflicts, fear and sadness. Moreover, it can make them feel good, boost their self-confidence, make them emotionally healthy and more creative. For example, in an interview with pupils who followed the lessons taught by Theo Wismans, one girl said that she has learned that 'life is better when you look at the bright side of life'. The classes are primarily supposed to increase children's psychological well-being. Moreover, there is evidence that happiness lessons improve pupils' results (Boerefijn & Bergsma, 2011). Often, educationalists who advocate the implementation of happiness classes substantiate their claims by drawing on 'positive psychology', an approach to psychology that has its origins in the late 1990s. Its point of departure is a focus on "positive human functioning" and on "effective interventions to build thriving in individuals, families, and communities" (Seligman & Cikzentmihalyi, 2000). Positive psychology can be seen as the social scientific study of human happiness. Recently, teachers and pedagogues interested in happiness have turned to it for a justification of their practices.

A first difference between Aristotelian 'character education' and happiness lessons is that 'happiness' is assumed to be a moral notion by the former, while it is not by the latter. 'Moral' is understood here in a very broad sense as not only being interested in your own well-being, but also in that of others. This difference is illustrative of the moral gap in most of the literature on 'emotional intelligence', 'social and emotional learning' and 'positive education'. "Positive features are considered to be achievable merely on the grounds of cleverness and efficiency without regard for any moral constraints." (Kristjánsson, 2010a, p. 297). The problem is, in short, that children could, e.g. be very happy and cruel at the same time. Those in favour of happiness lessons may argue that children who experience less stress, conflict, fear or sadness will be more likely to have better friends and will be less inclined to hurt people. According to the broaden-and-build theory of positive emotions, there is indeed a link between the experience of positive emotions and people's resilience and flourishing, their capacities for cultivating virtues, and their capacities to build relationships (Fredrickson, 2001, 2003). In this way, happiness classes can contribute to children's moral education, too.

This response is, however, problematic for a number of reasons. If happiness lessons have a positive effect on moral behaviour, it is surprising that happiness teachers do not emphasise the relationship between happiness and virtue, and when they do mention it, the relationship is not intrinsic but more of a welcome bonus. In addition, if 'promoting moral behaviour' is taken on board as one of the goals of happiness lessons, happiness becomes a *means* to promote moral behaviour. From a Kantian perspective, it would make sense to argue that happiness contributes to our motivation to meet moral duties, but from an Aristotelian point of view, happiness (and not moral duty) is the goal for the sake of which we do and value everything. We can conclude that if happiness and virtue are somehow related in happiness lessons, it is not because virtue is a constituent of *eudaimonia*, but because 'happy' people are expected to do virtuous things.

A second difference concerns the issue of whether happiness is something subjective or objective. Today, philosophers and psychologists interested in 'happiness' fall roughly in three categories (Tiberius & Plakias, 2010; Haybron, 2008). Firstly, proponents of a *hedonist* approach understand happiness as 'positive affect' or 'pleasant experiences', however shallow or fleeting these experiences are. Methods to measure people's happiness include physiological measurements and online measures in which subjects are beeped at random intervals and asked to report their current hedonistic state. Secondly, happiness can also be equated with a favourable attitude towards one's life as a whole. This *life satisfaction* approach does not have external standards that have to be met before a life goes well. It is a subject's own norms or values that count to determine whether he is satisfied (Tiberius & Plakias, 2010, p. 411). Understanding happiness as life satisfaction is, however, more objective than hedonism, since it does not focus on the experiences of a single person at a given moment, but on people's overall judgment. Moreover, peer informant reports can be used to measure life satisfaction, too. Thirdly, happiness is understood by *eudaimonists* as being related to vital human needs (Ryan & Deci, 2001) or people's possibility to actualise and develop their capabilities. On this account, pleasure is not so much related to what we want, but to what we need. Eudaimonists refer to empirical research which shows that the pleasure from self-actualisation or relating to other people are valued more than physical pleasures.

Those who teach happiness classes think of happiness mainly in terms of hedonism (they seek to make pupils feel good) or life satisfaction (they want pupils to acquire a positive attitude towards life). On both interpretations, children are considered to be authoritative with regard to their own happiness. An Aristotelian education in the virtues has, however, most in common with what is called the 'eudaimonistic' interpretation of happiness, even though it is more interested in the perfection of human rationality than in the fulfilment of all kinds of needs. One major disadvantage of the hedonism and life satisfaction views is that they do not take into account that people can be systematically deceived about their happiness (Kristjánsson, 2010a, p. 301). The disadvantage of a more eudaimonistic or Aristotelian approach to happiness is, however, that it creates too large a gap between happiness and subjective experience (Tiberius & Plakias, 2010, p. 410). It leaves open the possibility that pupils say they are happy, while virtue ethics says they are not, because they have not acquired the necessary virtues.

This excursion to existing happiness classes and the implicit assumptions about the subjective and morally neutral nature of happiness made clear that there are a number of rival educational approaches that aim at happiness, but that an Aristotelian approach to moral education distinguishes itself by forging a strong link between happiness and virtue. Aristotle has argued that a life that goes well consists of the rational cultivation of emotions, such as fear, anger, indignation, sadness, etc., according to the doctrine of the mean. Despite the differences between a positive psychological and character educational understanding of happiness, the two can benefit from each other's perspective. On the one hand, Aristotelians help happiness teachers to understand the relationship between happiness and virtue better by emphasising that virtue is not just a welcome corollary but a central ingredient of happiness. On the other hand, happiness teachers point out to Aristotelians that it is important to fix 'happiness' to what people like or care about.

5.5 A Common Human Nature

5.5.1 Biological Teleology

Before turning to Kristjánsson's and MacIntyre's attempts to reformulate Aristotelian teleology without appealing to his metaphysics, it should be mentioned that there is an influential current in contemporary Aristotelian scholarship that insists on the relevance of biological teleology to virtue ethics. Interestingly, these authors agree with Aristotle that human nature has an intrinsic purpose and disagree with any strict division between facts and moral values (Brown, 2008). Note, however, that the distinction between 'fact' and 'value' does not equal the Humean distinction between 'is' and 'ought'. While such naturalists want to show that there is no yawning gap between biological facts and moral values, they do not want to prescribe people how they ought to live or behave.

A good example of a philosopher of education that defended a kind of naturalism is David Carr. For example, Carr (1991, pp. 5-6) admits that several different interpretations of the virtue of courage can be found in different societies, but that courage is a virtue because human beings, who share a common physical or biological nature, need it. The idea that the flourishing of an organism is tied to the satisfaction of needs that are characteristic to a species, had already been developed in more detail by Philippa Foot (2001, 2002). She argued, for example, that moral virtues are related to what human beings are and what they do, in a similar way to how owls need to see in the dark in order to live a life characteristic of owls. These views have much in common with the ideas of Anscombe's husband Peter Geach (1977, p. vii), who famously remarked that "Men are benefited by virtues as bees are by having stings". What these authors share is the idea that virtues lead to a flourishing life for human beings *as a biological species*. They are naturalists in the sense that they believe that ethical evaluations are grounded in and can be derived from natural facts.

The advantage of this kind of virtue ethics is it avoids the danger of sliding into a kind of relativism that says that what counts as virtue and vice is relative to the rules and conventions of a community. It considers virtues to be desirable to any human being, regardless of its allegiance to particular communities it is a member of. However, the problem with this approach is that it is questionable whether biology has much positive to say about ethics. In addition, the human nature it refers to is a totally different kind of nature to the one that Aristotle had in mind. This has consequences for the moral conclusions that Carr, Foot, Geach and other virtue ethical naturalists can draw from the facts of human nature. For example, it runs the risk of using human 'flourishing' in some kind of deflationary sense, e.g. in a Darwinian sense, as bare survival or reproduction. Even when flourishing is slightly more substantial than this, including moral ideals such as friendship or justice, the justification of more specific – and more meaningful –

moral judgments seem to be beyond the reach of this kind of biological teleology.

While Kristjánsson has many affinities with these 'naturalists', his ideas will be discussed separately because he is less interested in the relationship between biology and ethics. He believes that there is much more to learn about human virtue from psychology than from zoologists studying the behaviour of bees or owls (Kristjánsson, 2006b, p. 10). Particularly, his idea is that the conceptual and empirical study of human emotions can illuminate our notion of a good life.

5.5.2 Feasibility Constraints

Kristjánsson, a relatively new but already well-respected member of the neo-Aristotelian family, has focused on the contribution that psychology can make to our understanding of the virtues. Throughout his oeuvre, Kristjánsson (2002, 2006b, 2007, 2010b) discusses a large number of virtues in detail, such as justice, generosity, agreeableness, friendship and emulation, practical wisdom and the 'self-conscious virtues' of shame and 'pridefulness' (i.e. dispositional pride). For each of these virtues, he has tried to show that it is (1) morally justified to (2) teach (3) these psychologically realistic virtues.[42] These virtues are intrinsically related to a flourishing human life, which Kristjánsson refers to with the traditional Greek concept of *eudaimonia*. In this chapter, we will focus less on its meaning, and more on Kristjánsson's ideas about the best method to find out what it is, and in particular what contribution the social sciences can make to our understanding of it.

A good way of introducing his ideas is to compare them with Nussbaum's, with whom he shares some – but not all – basic ideas. Like Nussbaum, Kristjánsson argues that the point of cultivating the above-mentioned virtues is that they enable its possessor to choose well in spheres of human experience that figure in more or less any human life. For example, courage is the virtue to deal with the fear of important damages, temperance is the best way to deal with our bodily appetites and their pleasures, and mildness of temper is the right attitude towards slights. According to Nussbaum (1993), this 'thin account' of each virtue informs us about the stable disposition one needs to act appropriately in that sphere of (emotional) experience. She notes that there are usually various competing 'thick' specifications of what these virtues mean in real life. Her thin and still empty conception of the virtues admits of many concrete 'fillings'. While Nussbaum (1993, pp. 247–249) argues that it is the ethicist's job to search for the best further specifications by comparing particularistic accounts of the virtues in the name of an "objective human morality of virtuous action", most of what Kristjánsson writes about the virtues is on this still general but more objective human morality. He is less interested in the (arbitrary) cultural specifications of these virtues, and more in the features of humanness and human morality that *lie beneath* all local traditions.

This difference also explains why the two authors use another method to determine what a good life consists of. Nussbaum's account of the human good is

---

42 See Sanderse (2011) for a review of Kristjánsson's approach to the psychology, development and education of the virtues.

based on a critical investigation of people's self-interpretations and self-evaluations, which can, in her view, best be discovered by studying people's narratives, literature and history (see §4.3). Kristjánsson is, however, rather sceptical about the veracity of people's self-interpretations and emphasises the potential benefits of often untapped psychological sources. In his view, it is a pity that philosophers often disregard social-scientific research about what makes people 'happy', what they consider to be 'just', or how they see their 'selves'. He is convinced that psychological research does not only contribute to a better understanding of the origins or development of virtue, but can also be substantially relevant to moral and educational issues.

In order to understand how psychological research can influence the answers to moral questions, Kristjánsson's (2006b, p. 127) ideas about the so-called 'belief in a just world' (BJW) are illustrative. On the basis of psychological research, this BJW theory concludes that people have a basic, intrinsically motivated desire to believe that the world is a just place (Lerner, 1980). The widespread occurrence of this desire can be explained in terms of children's realisation that the immediate satisfaction of their desires can and should be delayed in favour of long-term gain. It can be worth delaying the satisfaction of some desires, because in the end some universal force of justice, order or stability would guarantee that everyone gets his/her due anyway. This belief can be recognised in various figures of speech, which often imply a negative reprisal of justice, such as: 'You got what was coming to you', 'What goes around comes around' and 'You reap what you sow'. How can facts about whether people have or do not have this belief have evaluative consequences? Does this make justice a more important virtue? Or does the theory clarify its meaning? What matters to Kristjánsson is that research on the BJW theory suggests that people do have all kinds of justice-based emotions, universally, from childhood, and that these emotions can therefore be cultivated into the virtue justice. Provided that the BJW theory is correct, it shows that the education of the virtue of justice is *possible*. It shows that pupils have emotions at their disposal which educators can seize and help to transform into the complex virtue of justice. This criterion can also be formulated negatively: if most people, in particular, children, do *not* have the emotions needed to be educated according to a moral theory, it does not make sense to promote the corresponding virtue – which is, after all, nothing but the dispositional version of that emotion. This means, in short, that virtues should only be cultivated if it can be explained which emotion(s) they are a cultivation of. This can be read as an incentive for ethical theories and approaches to moral education to develop an adequate moral psychology.

While approaches that lack this do not immediately have to be rejected, ethicists who manage to muster (empirical) support to show that people have the motivational structures that they prescribe have an advantage. When discussing Owen Flanagan's principle of minimal psychological realism in §3.3.4, we saw that the risk of not taking these motivational structures into account is that it becomes unclear how the virtues that a theory advocates can come to bear in people's actual lives. As a consequence, moral and moral educational theories can "fail to grip us" (Flanagan, 1991, p. 26). Flanagan refers to Bernard Williams (1985), who has argued elsewhere[43] that there is no direct route from human nature to morality, but that psychology can, nevertheless, contribute to a correct view of morality by limiting the possible content of what could be regarded as a system of *human* morality. In this sense, psychology constitutes some feasibility constraints on the practical realisation of virtue.

5.5.3 Wise and Experienced Judges

However, we may doubt whether there are really that many theories of moral education that fail this psychological feasibility test. It does not seem to rule out that much. However, Kristjánsson has an arrow left in his quiver: there is a second way in which psychology contributes to a substantial justification of moral theories that already meet the criteria of psychological realism. In order to understand this, we need to discuss the work of J.S. Mill, to whom Kristjánsson turns in order to explain his position. The central Millian idea that Kristjánsson takes as point of departure is the claim that "the sole evidence it is possible to produce that anything is desirable is that people do actually desire it." (Mill, 2001, p. 35). This claim is not uncontroversial. Mill has been accused of either making a mistake by confusing 'desirable' and 'desired' or of committing a fallacy, since it cannot logically follow from the fact that something is desired that it is also desirable. However, what Mill wanted to express is the basic idea that desirability is an empirical matter: we learn that something is desirable by experiencing and contemplating our desires (Rachels, 2004, p. 87).

The problem is, however, how to distinguish between desires that indicate morally praiseworthy things and desires that do not. It seems that some contemplation is necessary to find out which desires are desirable. Kristjánsson recognises this as he does not take just anyone's desires seriously. When we want to know what *eudaimonia* is, he argues in a Millian fashion that especially those who have been properly educated and have experienced life in every respect should be consulted. To the verdict of the so-called "wise and experienced" judges who have experienced different ways of living, there can be no appeal, because Mill (2001, p. 11) is confident that these wise people will prefer a life that consists of a combination of physical, intellectual and moral pleasures as opposed to a purely sensual life.

But is Mill not too confident? Why would someone who was until recently uncommitted to virtue (stage 1) but moved on the stage of (lack of) self-control (stage 2 or 3) prefer the former to the latter? Is this necessary? Or can someone regret his moral development and wish he lived the life of a hedonist? Mill (2001,

---

43 See the concise chapter called 'Moral Standards and the Distinguishing Mark of Man' in his *Introduction to Ethics* (Williams, 1972).

p. 9) is clear: "no intelligent human being would consent to be a fool". He even considers it to be "an unquestionable fact" that those who are acquainted with a moral and a hedonistic lifestyle will prefer a life in which they can use their higher faculties. This shows the extent to which Mill shares Aristotle's optimism about human nature. They are both confident that people are rational creatures who will naturally value a life of which the moral and intellectual virtues are important features. By appealing to Mill, Kristjánsson also inherits the Aristotelian and Millian optimism that humans will, once they have a choice, prefer the exercise of the moral and intellectual virtues to the pleasure involved in the use of the 'lower' faculties. Hence, Mill's famous dictum that "it is better to be a human being dissatisfied than a pig satisfied; better to be Socrates dissatisfied than a fool satisfied". To return to the question of how psychology can contribute to a substantial justification of moral theories: on Kristjánsson's account, psychology can contribute to the moral justification of *eudaimonia* when it investigates the desires of competent judges, who are the final authority of *eudaimonia*.

However, psychology cannot determine *who* these people are. To Kristjánsson, the simple fact that a large number of people have converged upon the same moral view is *as such* not a reason for giving that view a constitutive role in the justification of moral virtues or principles. He emphasises that one cannot assume that those 'people' – who, in current psychological research, are more often than not only first-year psychology students – constitute wise and experienced judges. Moreover, Kristjánsson (2010b, p. 192) writes very critically about the 'rampant hedonism' that permeates Western societies, so he would probably not want to include Paris Hilton and others who are only after the immediate satisfaction of their sensual desires either. At the same time, Kristjánsson wants to avoid the haughty outlook that philosophers can discover moral truths by means that are in principle unavailable to lay people. His writings suggest that we should first have psychologists investigate whether a large number of people converge upon the same moral view, provided that the research is conducted in accordance with the best available standards. After psychological research has surveyed people's views, observed their behaviour, or subjected them to experiments, further scrutiny by laypeople and philosophers can correct the resulting picture, e.g. by showing that the data raises questions, is inconsistent or even completely wrong.

This 'compromise' method, which Kristjánsson (1996, ch. 7) calls 'critical naturalistic revision' does not seem to differ essentially from Aristotle's dialectical method. In the *Nicomachean Ethics,* Aristotle first surveys what is already known or familiar to us, such as the popular conceptions of 'happiness' or 'friendship', and goes from there to resolve tensions in the set of popular conceptions in such a way that he preserves as many of the starting-points as possible, while not giving equal weight to all. In Aristotle's view, surveying people's beliefs about ethical issues is only the first phase of ethical enquiry, but it is, nevertheless, a very important task not to be underestimated. Information about our moral views, emotions and behaviour enables moral philosophers to start from somewhere; without it, moral enquiry could not even get off the ground. "Instead of levelling the unsurely built edifice of opinion in order to build knowledge afresh, he [Aristotle] repairs and develops the existing structure by locating its foundation and ensuring that the higher floors are indeed supported by it." (Salmieri, 2009, p. 335). Likewise, we can conclude that it is a waste to treat psychology as a science that lists people's views, maybe interesting in itself, but not because they can substantially contribute to philosophical reflection. Moral philosophers who systematically ignore the results from psychological research are likely to make less progress, because they lack an important source of information about people's beliefs, emotions or values. Psychologists can contribute to finding new and unexpected beliefs that may otherwise have been overlooked, and that can spur philosophers on to refine or adapt their theories even further.

5.5.4 Mapping the Moral Terrain

Aristotle writes in the books on friendship that "we may see even in our travels how near and dear every man is to every other" (*NE* 1155a20). Kristjánsson would not mind using this phrase as his motto, since an important theme in his work is the idea that people share certain emotions in virtue of their common moral-psychological make-up. Regardless of what people value, and regardless of the specific moral conflicts that may divide them, they all share basic emotional experiences and, from a certain point in their development onwards, a commitment to certain basic virtues that are needed if they are to flourish as human beings. What we can learn from Kristjánsson's perspective is that the pluralism of particular moral outlooks, which we often assume to pervade our societies, may not be as deep as we imagine. Moral conflicts are often about the different interpretations of virtues that everyone subscribes to (e.g. 'What is just?') and less about the question of which character traits count as virtues and which do not (e.g. 'Is justice a virtue?').

Nussbaum's metaphor of a 'terrain' can be illuminating: the general account of central human moral experiences and the corresponding virtues form a *map* of the terrain, which guarantees that when several people are discussing where to go, they are roughly talking about the same area. Affirming the commonalities may result in a real interest in what others have to contribute to an even better and more comprehensive understanding of 'the good'. There will still be moral conflicts, but a discussion will not proceed after first having settled what the common moral experiences are that both parties have different opinions about. When we argue – possibly long and hard – with others about friendship, justice or generosity, Kristjánsson teaches us that we should keep in mind that these discussions are often about the further specifications of a more general account of virtue.

For example, with regard to friendship, there are general criteria of mutual benefit and well-wishing, mutual enjoyment, mutual awareness, a shared conception of the good, and some form of 'living together' that must be met (Nussbaum, 1993, p. 256). While there will be disputes over the meaning of 'benefit', 'well-wishing', 'enjoyment' and other elements of this description, it offers some minimal requirements that any conception of friendship must meet in order to prevent people from coming up with completely arbitrary accounts of friendship. Admittedly, Kristjánsson's account *underdetermines* such specifications in the sense that it leaves room for a wide variety of interpretations. However, this implies that a general account of virtue somehow determines the various interpretation of this virtue anyway. When different specifications are compared, some interpretations may have to be eliminated, and a smaller plurality of accounts can remain (Nussbaum, 1993, p. 256). Thus, a moral theory that observes certain limits in order to ensure that the specifications of the good life we come up with are human does not have to be incompatible with a pluralism of moral values and ideals. It is only incompatible with a view that 'anything goes'. Kristjánsson's objective normative picture reminds us that ethics is a collective human enterprise, but it comes at a cost. Although Kristjánsson discusses some practical solutions, his interest in the objective side of virtue makes his writings too indeterminate to be meaningful to people living in a particular time or place. What we still need within such contexts is a 'thick' or 'rich' language for which his theory does not provide. As will become apparent in the next section, MacIntyre is more interested in the diversity of and rivalry between different accounts of the virtues.

5.6 A Variety of Ethical Worlds

Another way of dealing with the Aristotelian teleology is not to focus on the biological or psychological commonalities of the human beings whose flourishing we are concerned with, but more on its social and historical aspects. An important spokesman of this approach is MacIntyre, who is unsympathetic to the idea that "there is some concept of human virtue or good that might be identified, at last in principle, as applicable to something conceivable as human nature as such, irrespective of social circumstance." (Carr, 1991, p. 105). Instead, he has argued in several influential works that there is no direct access to the 'facts' of human nature or the meaning of morality except through the membership of forms of social life. However, as MacIntyre's work spans five decades, his ideas have developed over time. For example, while he believed in *After Virtue* that practical philosophy can do without Aristotle's discredited metaphysical biology, he recognised in *Dependent Rational Animals* (1999) that an Aristotelian ethics cannot be sustained without an understanding of the nature of the being that asks about the good. Since we are, in particular, looking for a critical alternative to Kristjánsson's justification of the virtues, we will restrict ourselves to a discussion of his early work. The reader should keep in mind that the actual differences between the (later) MacIntyre and more naturalistic Aristotelians are not as big as this section suggests.

5.6.1 Virtues in Practices and Life Narratives

In order to understand why MacIntyre thinks that character education is necessary if people are to flourish, we need to distinguish between three domains. Virtues enable people to (1) function in social practices, to (2) construct an individual life narrative and, to (3) improve their tradition.

In the domain of social practices, several functions of the virtues can be distinguished. First of all, the virtues enable members of practices to achieve goods internal to them. Practices are forms of activity, such as architecture, politics or games, which are typically human, coherent, complex, socially established and cooperative (MacIntyre, 2003, p. 187). According to Macintyre, it is only inside these 'ethical worlds' that people *qua* architects, politicians or chess-players encounter 'thick' notions of what human flourishing is (Higgins 2011, p. 50). For example, a chess player can achieve the goods that belong to chess, such as analytic skill, strategic imagination and competitive intensity only when he has also acquired the virtues that make him willing and able not to cheat (honesty), to defend his position in the face of a strong opponent (courage) and wait for his turn (patience). While struggling to meet the standards of excellence internal to practices, people's conception of what these standards are is likely to change, too. Consequently, practices do not merely enable its practitioners to *attain* the virtues. People will never be fully educated in the sense that they reach a point at which they are ready to leave the practice. Practices offer room for people to do exactly what the name 'practice' implies: to *practice* and systematically develop virtue.

The practice as a whole, whether it is a fishing crew, a chess club or group of researchers will also benefit from such morally aspiring practitioners, too. The virtues enable practitioners to maintain the integrity of a practice, especially while it is being confronted with institutional expediency (Higgins, 2011, p. 49). The problem of 'institutional expedience' has to do with MacIntyre's distinction between 'practices' and 'institutions', and in this context, between 'internal goods' and 'external goods'. For instance, science is the practice that is housed in the institution called 'university'. Ideally, universities sustain science by acquiring the necessary funds and distributing money, power and status (the 'external goods') to the practitioners. While institutions are of vital importance to the flourishing of practices, their power can and often does corrupt. For example, scientists can come to believe that publishing in journals with high impact factors is a goal in itself, instead of the truth of what is published. Those who follow the news know that this logic frequently seduces scientists to invent data or manipulate experiments. When fraud is discovered, it may or may not mean the end for someone's career, but it will definitely undermine the public's trust in the practice of science. Another example is sport. Recently, it turned out that in e.g. Italy, Belgium and Turkey, football players and referees were bribed to 'fix matches', i.e. to let a team intentionally lose or win a game, in order to guarantee financial gain for those who gamble on a particular outcome. Alternatively, there are the doping scandals associated with the *Tour de France*. In football, cycling and other games, sportsmen, coaches and sports doctors need basic virtues such as honesty, courage and justice to ensure that those who participate in the practice can succeed in their shared attempt to pursue the internal goods of a practice.

Now, different people engage in all kinds of practices: some work as scientists, some are active in politics, some play an instrument in an orchestra, and some incorporate all of these activities in a single life. In the domain of individual life narratives, the virtue of integrity helps people to answer questions like 'what is my good as a human being?' and 'what place should each practice have in my life as a whole?'. Take the life of Julien Sorel, a character in Stendhal's novel *The Red and the Black*, who is ambitious when it comes to martial life, but works as a priest.[44] These seemingly incompatible activities require of Julien to tell a story about how he thinks that the kind of loyalty and courage that he needs to risk his life in secret service can be squared with the kind of compassion that he needs as an acolyte in the Catholic church. The role of integrity in the process of making one's life a narrative unity was discussed before. Chapter 4 made clear how the virtues that people need in several practices can be synthesised into a single character, and it was examined why it would be morally desirable to do so. Moreover, we already saw in the section on situationism (§3.3) that few people genuinely possess a virtue in the sense that "they manifest it in very different types of situations". (MacIntyre, 2003, p. 205). This is not a refutation of MacIntyre's conception of virtue. Quite the contrary: the experiments that situationists refer to only highlight MacIntyre's thesis that people's lives are nowadays often fragmented into a variety of segments (work vs. leisure, private vs. public, personal vs. corporate), each with its own norms and modes of behaviour. As a historian, MacIntyre has showed that is *possible* to think differently about virtue and character by describing an era in which another conception of selfhood prevailed, and as a philosopher he has argued why this Aristotelian alternative is to be *preferred* to a liberal individualist conception of selfhood.

5.6.2 Virtues and Moral Enquiry in Traditions

The third domain that MacIntyre has in mind is a 'community'. It enables us to determine whether the story that an individual agent tells about his or her

---

44 The example is derived from Appiah (2009), p. 171.

good as a human being makes sense, by critically comparing it to a conception of 'a good human life' that prevails in a larger socio-historical setting. Within a community, an ethos of a particular culture and age, one finds "...a hierarchy of fundamental goods guiding its sense of what is worth striving for in a human life." (Higgins 2011, p. 52). To MacIntyre, it is obvious that a vision of the good life and the virtues that constitute human flourishing is relative to time, place and culture. For example, to an army general living in fifth-century Athens, having a good character means something else than for a 13th-century nun or a 17th-century farmer. The phrase 'the good life for men' only makes sense if we understand its meaning as being determined by the social setting people live in. However, the idea that virtues are rooted in and educated within practices of a particular community is not without its problems: other virtue ethicists have charged him with moral relativism (Carr, 2003a, p. 189; Carr & Steutel, 1999, p. 247; Nussbaum, 1993, p. 243). Does MacIntyre not reduce moral criteria to the arbitrary conventions of a local community, internal to the traditions and practices of each local society or group?

MacIntyre's (2003, p. 220) position has to be understood in contrast to the standpoint of 'modern individualism', according to which we can always question the merely contingent social features of our existence. According to MacIntyre, we are born into social settings like a family, a city and a nation, and we cannot just leave behind their rightful expectations and obligations. However, he goes to great pains to show that individuals are not necessarily stuck in the communities that they happen to find themselves in as they mature: "The fact that the self has to find its moral identity in and through its membership in communities [...] does not entail that the self has to accept the moral limitations of the particularity of those forms of community." (MacIntyre, 2003, p. 221). There is nothing good about local communities as such; they even involve the risk of being corrupted by narrowness, complacency and prejudice (MacIntyre, 1999, p. 142). Communities are a starting point for individuals, who can use the community's moral and intellectual baggage to search for a more universal good. This means that a community is only valuable if it somehow facilitates encounters and conversation about what the good life for human beings entails. But how can a transition be made from a particularistic to a universal notion of the good?

Part of the answer can be found in MacIntyre's notion of a 'living tradition', which he defines as: "a historically extended, socially embodied argument, and an argument precisely in part about the goods which constitute that tradition" (MacIntyre, 2003, p. 222). While this description makes it notoriously difficult to determine what counts as a tradition and what does not, his emphasis on the development of the community over time makes clear that its members can participate in arguments about what a good life is, in order to improve the tradition.

As long as the argument in a tradition is ongoing, the tradition is alive, and the answer to the question of what a good life is, is not settled. A final answer to the question what *the* good life for man consists of is ultimately beyond our reach. We are left with a "life spent in seeking for the good life for man" (MacIntyre, 2003, p. 219). When Aristotle's central insight that nature is a well-ordered whole has been abandoned we can only engage in hermeneutical quests for the good life, without any final metaphysical certainty. The human predicament can be compared to the situation of a race of hyper-intelligent beings in Douglas Adams' classic *The Hitchhiker's Guide to the Galaxy*. In the novel, the intelligent beings build a computer, *Deep Thought*, to come up with the so-called 'Answer to The Ultimate Question of Life, the Universe, and Everything'. After seven and a half million years of calculation, the answer turns out to be 42, which leaves everybody behind in amazement. Deep Thought explains: "I think the problem, to be quite honest with you, is that you've never actually known what the question was." Likewise, we could say that traditions that think they have found the answer to the question what a good life is, have not really understood the question in the first place. As soon as the members of a tradition agree that the central questions have been settled, the tradition will become a museum piece, and will soon be defeated by other traditions that adapt to new circumstances.

We have seen that people need the virtues of truthfulness, justice and courage on the level of practices, and integrity on the level of a narrative unity of life. On the level of community, MacIntyre recommends us to become 'moral enquirers'. It is tempting to interpret this 'enquiry' in a purely intellectual fashion, as if we all have to become philosophers advancing arguments to strengthen a theoretical notion of the good life. But MacIntyre (1991, pp. 62-63) argues that moral enquiry has a twofold character. True, one should try to achieve an adequate theoretical understanding of the specific human good, and people need some intellectual virtues in order to do so. But one should also excel in the practical embodiment of that understanding. As moral enquirers we aspire to answer the question: "'What is the good and the best, both for human beings in general and for this specific kind of human being in these particular circumstance here and now?" (MacIntyre, 1991, p. 62). MacIntyre stresses the practical embodiment of our understanding of the good life because he does not want to debar ordinary people, like farmers or fishermen, from participating in the quest for the good. The way in which practitioners engage in a practice is not often recognised as a kind of 'enquiry', but MacIntyre insists that they too continue a tradition through their devotion. Moreover, MacIntyre (1987, p. 33) reminds us that even the smartest philosophers are still members of a community, and that their research and teaching should serve the need of everyone advancing the tradition: they should articulate "... the presuppositions of, the debates within and the challenges, to specific social groups...".

When people advance a particular conception of the good life, either theoretically or practically, they will inevitably come across people who belong to other traditions, especially in a plural society. Can we rationally determine which tradition has a better view of the good life? There seem to be two options. Relativists presuppose that each tradition has its own rational criteria and that there is no neutral rationality available to decide between them when they clash. Absolutists, however, believe that there is a rational standard outside all traditions that can be used to evaluate the various notions of a good life. However, MacIntyre's view cannot be easily classified with the help of this scheme. On the one hand, he clearly rejects absolutism: there is no tradition-independent access to the good life. On the other hand, he rejects relativism too, since he claims that it is possible to transcend a tradition and search for 'the good'. In the opening chapter of *Whose Justice? Which Rationality?*, MacIntyre (1988, p. 7) presents his solution. It is:

> "...a conception of rational enquiry as embodied in a tradition, a conception according to which the standards or rational justification themselves emerge from and are part of a history in which they are vindicated by the way in which they transcend the limitations of and provide remedies for the defects of their predecessors within the history of that same tradition."

The core idea is that while there are no timeless and universal standards of rational justification, these tradition-dependent standards can be improved, first of all internally. Moreover, MacIntyre does not rule out the possibility that it is also possible, at least in theory, for members of different traditions to engage in serious attempts at mutual understanding, gaining an increasingly richer and clearer picture of moral life. Thereby, MacIntyre holds on to the idea that there is a notion of 'moral truth' as the final aim of moral enquiry (Carr, 1991, p. 106). He circumvents the problem of relativity by discussing the possible synthesis of different rival traditions.

In MacIntyre's view, controversies between traditions process characteristically in two stages. On the first stage, "each tradition characterizes the contentions of its rival in its own terms" (MacIntyre, 1988, p. 166). This can either mean that reasons are given why the rival contentions are refuted, or why something can be learnt from the rival tradition. MacIntyre estimates that the former will more often be the case, and the latter will only apply to marginal questions. The second stage is only reached when the members of the traditions have a clear view on why their own tradition has certain limitations, and the question has been addressed of whether the rival tradition may provide resources to transcend these limitations. This kind of dialectical process between traditions is very difficult, since it requires a "rare gift of empathy and intellectual insight" to reconsider one's own position from the perspective of another tradition's position (MacIntyre, 1988, p. 167). One can only really say that another tradition is better or worse, when one *knows* the other tradition. According to MacIntyre, we cannot really 'know' another tradition from the outside, but have to become a member of that tradition as well.

Simply judging another tradition from your own point of view is not very useful; these judgments only become interesting once we have adopted the other tradition's point of view, and have tried to see the other tradition as a challenge to our own. The *external* progress of a tradition, its progress compared to how other traditions fare, depends on people who are at home in several traditions. MacIntyre (1988, p. 347) takes this 'being at home' very seriously: one has to "become a child all over again" and learn the moral language and the other parts of the other tradition as a 'second first tradition'. One of the few MacIntyrean heroes who managed to belong to two traditions is Thomas Aquinas, who united two rival large-scale intellectual traditions (the Aristotelian and Augustinian) at the University of Paris in the thirteenth century. If we want to follow Aquinas's example, MacIntyre recommends us, first, to be member of a tradition and then try to engage with other traditions. There is no point at all in flirting with other traditions if there is no stable marriage with a first tradition to start with. For most of us, having a subjectivist understanding of morality, justifying one's moral judgments from the point of view of a tradition is already a huge achievement.

5.6.3 Educating Virtue in a Plural Society

We started this chapter with the problem that teachers have difficulties explaining why cultivating certain character traits would be morally desirable. However, while examining the justification of the education of virtue, the specific responsibilities that parents, practitioners and the wider public have towards children's moral education were not discussed. Throughout his work, MacIntyre suggests that activities and enquiries that *benefit* from the education of a new generation have to *contribute* to this education too. Most obvious is the function that practices, as 'schools of excellence', have to subordinate children's morally uncommitted desires to the pursuit and production of goods that are internal to these practices (Knight, 2007, pp. 152-154). Leaving the development of a specific MacIntyrean approach to moral education to others[45] focus here will be on the more general implications of MacIntyre's analysis of modernity for moral education.

If one assumes, like MacIntyre does, that there is no social-historical neutral conception of moral life, and that children need a substantial moral education into the virtues, moral education can only be pursued in rich educational contexts in which the authorities are at home in practices and communities and know how to promote particular moral and intellectual virtues. But are today's schools

---

45 See, e.g. Higgins (2011), and for a critique, consult Katayama (2003) and Vokey (2001).

the kind of miniature communities within which teachers have a shared opinion about the virtues to be taught? MacIntyre's answer is negative. Because of the sharp division between private and public morality and the relegation of private morality to the domain of the subjective (see §5.2), teachers hardly quarrel over specific interpretations of or approaches to moral education. They do not even fully understand the whole point of morally educating children in the first place. Questions like 'Why are virtues important?' or 'Why should we cultivate virtues?' are dodged. Since teachers are afraid to indoctrinate pupils, they limit themselves to the education of *civic* virtue. For example, while Halstead & Pike (2006) are generally positive about citizenship education, they warn that if moral education is reduced to citizenship education in the future, we are left with a very 'impoverished' form of moral education. This warning is in line with MacIntyre's (1999b) point about the "poverty of the shared morality" in modern plural societies.

Under the conditions of profound moral disagreement, the kind of moral education MacIntyre has in mind can only be implemented if there are some "radical changes" in the public school systems of many Western societies (MacIntyre & Dunne, 2002, p. 17). The solution would be a system in which there is a "number of rival and conflicting programmes" that provide moral education from the standpoint of their own specific contending view (MacIntyre, 1999b, p. 118). If there is to be any moral education at all in liberal societies, particularly religious communities or other groups will have to take care of the education of their members themselves, demanding separate schools and trying to find adequate public funding.

For those who live in a country in which most education is public, these implications will sound revolutionary. For example, in the United States, education is mainly provided by the public sector, with both control and funding coming from federal, state and local levels. An estimated 88 percent of pupils attend public schools, and only 9 percent attends so-called 'parochial schools', mostly Catholic primary schools. The remaining 3 percent are either home-schooled or go to a private/independent school. Starting from about 1876, thirty-nine states passed a constitutional amendment to their state constitutions, called 'Blaine Amendments', forbidding tax money to be used to fund parochial schools. In this context, it would be extremely controversial for religious communities to demand equal funding. However, in other countries, such as the Netherlands, private schools do have a constitutional right to be publicly funded. In the Dutch system, there are both 'public' and 'private' schools, the difference being that public schools are controlled by local governments and private ones by independent school boards. The reason why approximately 70 percent of all pupils attend 'private' schools is that *all* school types are publicly funded, provided an independent schools' inspectorate checks whether schools organise their education in compliance with the government's objectives and criteria. This comparison makes clear that

MacIntyre's ideal of rival programmes of moral education is easier to implement in some countries than in others.

Before jumping to conclusions about the difficulties involved in the practical realisability of a MacIntyrean understanding of moral education, we have to question MacIntyre's scepticism regarding the possibility of having a shared public system of moral education in a plural society. Is MacIntyre right in presupposing that there is no shared moral consensus in our societies sufficiently coherent to underpin moral education? While MacIntyre is right that virtue-words such as 'temperance' or 'justice' are indeterminate and open to interpretation, this does not seem to justify the rather extreme conclusion that people do not share *any* interpretation of the virtues they consider to be important. Let us return to MacIntyre's analysis of Western morality. If he is right, most individuals are outside a tradition. They do not seek guidance from the traditions and practices of a community. "All they have as moral resources are commonplace conceptions of the virtues." (Katayama, 2006, p. 334). They are educated under the influences of a variety of social and cultural fragments inherited from different traditions, but detached from the original contexts. As a result, we live in a "conceptual mélange of moral thought and practice", which contains virtue concepts from older traditions alongside modern and individualist concepts such as 'rights' and 'utility' (MacIntyre, 2003, p. 252).

While MacIntyre argues that communities that inherit a moral tradition offer a less fragmented picture of moral life, this neither means that there is a moral vacuum in liberal societies, nor that public schools are completely without moral resources. In the usual, familiar situations, most people actually know what justice, honesty and other virtues require. "Children learn, or mis-learn, how to be just, honest and temperate from parents and teachers in daily, uncomplicated situations long before they start to reflect on what justice, honesty and temperance are" (Katayama, 2006, p. 335). Children can first learn how to be just, honest and brave, before they learn to think about the more specific – and more controversial – meanings that these moral concepts have in different traditions. Below the profound moral disagreements, there seems to be some moral agreement at the surface. There is also some empirical evidence to support this. On the basis of the results of the National Forum for Values in Education and the Community set up in the UK in 1996, Katayama (2006, p. 332) has argued that there is "prima facie evidence for a shared morality in a plural society like ours, based on recognition of certain shared virtues." After several meetings, a poll of about 1,450 adults and consultations with many schools, the forum concluded that it was possible to reach general agreement over virtues such as truthfulness, honesty, justice and integrity. Despite living in a plural society, people seem to agree about a number of basic virtues, which accidentally match MacIntyre's virtue catalogue. A second empirical study showed that there is considerable agreement among teachers about which virtues are important and which are not, regardless of whether these teachers were Catholic, Protestant, Muslim or non-religious (Van Oudenhoven et al., 2007; 2012). Respect, reliability, justice, love and helpfulness were valued highly by all groups. While disagreement about public moral issues, such as abortion, genetic engineering or euthanasia may indeed be pervasive, many people seem to agree about a core set of desirable character traits (Katayama, 2006, p. 331). The disadvantage of this kind of empirical research is, however, that respondents were not asked about their *interpretations* of these virtues. MacIntyre will therefore be the first to note that there will be far more disagreement when people are asked what it means to be honest or helpful in some concrete circumstances.

If we place less emphasis on moral conflicts in our thinking about moral education and accept that our nature as rational animals somehow limits the interpretation of virtue and vice, the development and education of virtue can be a shared practice, even in plural societies. In §3.2 and §5.4, we saw that we can depart, like Nussbaum, from a number of central spheres of human experiences and corresponding virtues that matter to the happiness of all individuals in any society. Furthermore, Kristjánsson regards these virtues as the dispositional version of basic emotions that are shared by all human beings. However, MacIntyre's emphasis on the plurality of moral traditions is not necessarily incompatible with the idea that there is a common human nature. Without different cultural accounts of the good, humans would not be much more than a natural species; but without the recognition that human beings share a psychological make-up, not all of these accounts would be humane. Virtue ethicists with an interest in psychology and those who prefer to explore the potential of history, literature and sociology could be united in their search for a human morality, if it could be shown how different tradition-dependent interpretations specify more general underlying universal features.

5.7 Conclusion

This chapter attempted to help teachers explain to themselves and others what the point is of paying more attention to virtue in the classroom. Although most teachers recognise that they somehow contribute to the character formation of pupils, it is not always clear *why* the cultivation of certain character traits is morally desirable. The Aristotelian answer to this question is that character education enables children to lead a happy, flourishing life as human beings. However, we saw that the link between virtue and happiness is far from evident, both in education and in philosophy. In education, happiness classes receive considerable attention today, but 'happiness' is often understood as a subjective and morally neutral notion. Moreover, teachers have a somewhat schizophrenic understanding of what character education involves. They make a strict division between private and public morality, and treat private morality as something subjective with which they cannot bother children. As a result, they are left with teaching pupils a limited number of civic virtues, while it is unclear how these virtues are related to pupils' overall flourishing, both personally and as citizens of a liberal democracy. As we turned to Aristotle to clarify the relationship between education, virtue and happiness, it became evident that Aristotelian philosophy has problems of its own. For example, Aristotle presupposed a teleological conception of (human) nature, which lost popularity centuries ago. When we, in the twenty-first century, think of the origin of our values, we do not believe anymore that value can be *discovered* in a kind of nature that is already in good order. Instead, we *project* our personal or collective (moral) values onto a world which is itself meaningless.

We examined the work of two neo-Aristotelians, MacIntyre and Kristjánsson, in order to see (1) whether they could justify the education of virtue more objectively while (2) reformulating Aristotle's pre-modern heritage in such a way that it is still acceptable to people living in the 21st century. With regard to the second task, both reject a kind of moral naturalism according to which moral judgments can be derived from facts about humans as a biological species. Even Kristjánsson, who endorses being classified as a 'neo-Millian naturalist', is not, like Foot, interested in the relationship between ethics and biology, but in the ways in which (empirical) psychological research can increase our understanding of human emotions and their relation to virtues. Psychology can, for example, limit the possible content of what could be regarded as a system of human morality. MacIntyre and Kristjánsson are, however, naturalists, in the sense that they consider ethics to be continuous with human nature. Nature may not have an intrinsic purpose, but they both assume that human desires and reason have the potential to be educated in such a way that a good life comes within one's reach.

Despite these commonalities, the authors turn to different sources for inspiration. MacIntyre is interested in the conversations about the good life in a diversity of (past) practices and traditions, while Kristjánsson investigates the contribution that empirical research – about notions like emotions, virtues, character and happiness – can make to obtain a better grasp of *eudaimonia*. These two quests are both open-ended. MacIntyre emphasises the importance of an ongoing dialogue within a tradition, and he mentions the possibility of productive rivalry between traditions. Kristjánsson takes results from empirical research seriously, but considers all scientific and moral theories to be essentially fallible. In the modern, disenchanted world, there is no final metaphysical certainty that our ideas about the good life are correct. The good life for man is a life spent seeking for it – both neo-Aristotelians agree about this.

With regard to the first task, the short answer is that both authors reject subjectivism and other kinds of moral relativism, even though MacIntyre has been criticised by fellow virtue ethicists of having a communitarian and social-constructivist approach to ethics. While Kristjánsson considers a body of experienced and wise judges to be the final arbiter in moral matters, MacIntyre relies on the authoritative masters of a practice and moral enquirers of a tradition. Both authors have shown, albeit in different ways, that it is nonsense to conclude from a moral diversity as such that there cannot be an objective standard to compare or evaluate the evaluative premises in a moral conversation. Kristjánsson has pointed out that even if we are not members of the same tradition, we are still members of the same human race, in virtue of which we share certain emotions and other psychological reactions to a common world. Although an appeal to our common human nature cannot directly adjudicate between two positions in a moral debate, it can inform these debates about what they should be about in the first place, i.e. about virtuous functioning in spheres of emotional experiences.

MacIntyre's virtue theory is less interesting from a moral psychological point of view. His ideas are more helpful when the question is addressed of how different people, living in different social and historical conditions can justify their accounts of what they consider to be virtuous actions and emotional reactions. MacIntyre sees moral development as being initiated in a particular evaluative framework by 'insiders', whereas Kristjánsson talks about moral education in a more 'cosmopolitan' way. To him, it does not really matter who you are educated by, as long as they are experienced and rational human beings. MacIntyre takes differences and conflicts among rational people much more seriously. Combined, these two neo-Aristotelian theories provide an antidote to the ideas that prevail in society at large and in education in particular, i.e. that morality is subjective and a rational standard is lacking to evaluate preferences.

Chapter 6: General Conclusion
Problems, Questions and Prospects

While 'virtue' is not a very popular term in our daily speech, we often say of ourselves and others that we possess (or lack) virtues such as trustworthiness, generosity, justice, patience or wit. These attributions are not merely descriptive; we *praise* people for these moral qualities. While most people will agree that it is important that children possess such virtues, it is far from clear how they can acquire them and what teachers can contribute to the development of children's characters. What does it mean to educate pupils for virtue?

6.1 Aristotelian Character Education

Three central questions were addressed to increase our understanding of an 'education in the virtues'. It was investigated what a virtue is and how it develops, how schools can contribute to this development and why the education of virtue is morally desirable. The aim was, in short, to develop a morally justified and psychologically realistic account that makes clear how virtue can be taught in schools. The kind of 'character education' that has been advocated throughout American history – and which became influential again in the 1990s – is philosophically simplistic, undiscerning and underdeveloped, so we turned to a philosophical theory with a long history and a number of contemporary proponents: Aristotelianism. Aristotle's virtue ethics was treated as a potential source that contains valuable lessons for educational theory and practice, but vigilance was maintained for problems involved in the 'application' of this pre-modern theory to contemporary education. Assembling what has been written about the education of virtue in the previous chapters, it can be concluded that from a neo-Aristotelian perspective, 'character education' consists in the more or less deliberate, more or less comprehensive attempts of teachers to contribute to the ongoing development of moral virtue and practical wisdom in pupils in order to enable them to lead a flourishing life as human beings. Looking at this description, several things catch the eye.

Firstly, the education of virtue has primarily to do with morality in a very basic sense. Teachers educate pupils' virtues by being 'moral teachers', which means that they extend their everyday morality into the nuances of teaching. This may be self-evident to many teachers, and it is very unfortunate that this self-evidence has not always resulted in an understanding of what it really entails and how educational practice can be improved. When schools and colleges for teacher training pay more attention to the character educational aspects of their work, 'character education' can gradually become more deliberate, systematic and comprehensive. However, if character education changes from a haphazard by-product into a more considerate teaching method or school-based approach, teachers should not forget that it is never only a matter of 'teaching pupils a moral lesson'. They cannot make a contribution to children's moral development without being a personal example to them, being honest about their character strengths and flaws and helping individual pupils to find out what it means *for them* to be virtuous.

Secondly, the goal of a virtue ethical approach to moral education is *not* primarily, as most American character educationalists have argued, to promote positive behaviour among adolescents and to diminish socially destructive behaviour (Lockwood, 2009, p. 12). The kind of virtue ethics that was defended in this thesis emphasises the desirability for children to acquire certain dispositional emotions that – when they meet certain criteria such as the doctrine of the mean – are important ingredients of a good life. Admittedly, people who have acquired the virtues are likely to act on them as well, but virtue ethics is not primarily, like modern theories such as deontology and utilitarianism, a theory of right action. An Aristotelian approach distinguishes itself from other approaches to moral education by denying that either reason or desire is a reliable guide to a good life. Virtues are a matter of both heart and mind. Without practical wisdom, people would not be able to recognise occasions to put virtue in action, nor would they be able to improve their understanding of virtue by reflecting on these actions. Yet, without an emotional commitment to the good, practical reason would not be more than an amoral instrument to help people attain their ends, whatever they are. These points have been made before by others, but the neo-Aristotelian account of moral development in Chapter 3 showed in more detail that a developmental story needs to be told if the interdependence of reason and desire is to be understood. Reason and desire are *potentially* morally relevant and can become fully directed towards a good life through a proper education that teaches the two how to work in tandem. Furthermore, the kind of education that can help children become virtuous is not – as rival approaches have claimed – simply a kind of mindless habituation. While character education can be understood as a kind of instrumental conditioning, educators can also learn to verbalise their goals and strategies as they deal with moral quandaries in order to stimulate children's practical wisdom.

Thirdly, virtue ethics illuminated that moral education does not end when teachers have achieved that pupils subscribe to certain values or do not violate the school's rules. While qualitative distinctions between four stages of moral development were made (from being 'morally uncommitted', one can develop via 'lack of self-control' and 'self-control' to full virtue), the development of virtue was presented as an open-ended process. Even people who have acquired virtuous habits of feeling and action will encounter new situations and can do bad things. Moreover, there is, in principle, no end to the further *articulation* of the pursuit to lead a meaningful and happy life. Taken together, this means that there is no point at which people are justified in claiming that they are 'morally educated', if this is taken to mean that there is nothing to learn anymore. When it is part of the meaning of being 'morally educated' that one has the desire to learn and develop continuously, those who air this opinion can be suspected of laziness. This is a valuable lesson to children, as well as, to teachers. For example, the analysis of role modelling made clear that adults have role models too, and that teachers may equally be morally educated by pupils who show e.g. an eagerness to learn from mistakes. In addition, the evaluation of the Socratic dialogue illustrated that teachers can use this method to practice the kind of non-technical and non-scientific wisdom that is needed in order to realise 'good teaching' in a practice that is not only complex, but also ever-changing.

Fourthly, this thesis emphasised that the meaning of the 'education of virtue' is not exhausted by teachers' subjective preferences or the conventions of a dominant culture. It was argued that all pupils need the virtues to be 'happy' – which was interpreted as 'leading a flourishing life as a human being'. This is an important but controversial message, because a diversity of particular moral outlooks is often assumed to pervade our societies. While there is disagreement about public moral issues, such as abortion, genetic engineering or euthanasia, moral conflict may not be as deep as is often imagined, because our discussion of virtue suggested that conflicts are often about the interpretations of virtues that everyone subscribes to, and less about whether a character trait qualifies as a virtue. When teachers are prepared to argue long and hard with colleagues, parents and pupils about the meaning of friendship, justice or generosity, they can keep in mind that these discussions are often about the further specifications of a more objective but still general account of virtue. Affirming the common nature of this quest may result in a real interest in what others have to contribute to an

Chapter 6

even better and more comprehensive understanding of 'the good life'. Admittedly, different people, living in different social and historical conditions have different accounts of what they consider to be virtuous actions and emotional reactions. So, even when morality is saved from relativism by appealing to a common human nature, different tradition-dependent interpretations will still need to be specified if virtues are to be interesting for moral life.

6.2   Six Aristotelian Fusions

It was assumed that an Aristotelian approach can still be of value to issues in contemporary moral education, but the aim of this book was not to sing the praise of Aristotelianism. With the help of several neo-Aristotelians interested in educational philosophy, we also assessed the strengths and weaknesses of Aristotle's heritage. While many educators have labelled their approach as 'Aristotelian' in order to give it an aura of sophistication, several examples in this thesis illustrated that the use of Aristotelian concepts to elucidate contemporary educational concerns is never easy. Aristotle's interpretations of the major notions of this thesis, such as 'soul', 'nature', 'virtue', 'emotion', 'rationality' and 'happiness' turned out to be problematic in some way or another when they were placed in a modern network of moral meanings alien to Aristotle.

A point in case is the notion of 'virtue'. Chapter 3, on the psychology and development of virtue, started with the explanation that ethics is, to Aristotle not primarily about the consequences that our actions have on other people, but about helping people to find out how to live their own life in a way that suits the rational nature of human beings. Moreover, it was pointed out that the notion of moral virtue should not be identified with a particular virtue catalogue, but that virtue (*arete*) means 'excellence', in particular with regard to emotions in a number of spheres of human experience. These two examples show that Aristotelianism can only be made sense of when one oscillates between the modern conceptions of nature, morality, happiness on the one hand, and Aristotle's interpretation on the other.

While reflecting on the typical features of an Aristotelian approach to moral education, it occurred to me that Aristotle fuses several distinctions that are taken to be self-evident today. Below, six of these distinctions are mentioned. Some of them have also been mentioned by Kristjánsson (2007, pp. 176-177), who studied the interconnections between the educational salience of emotions and Aristotle's ideas about emotion and education. Contrary to proponents of cognitive development and care ethics – according to whom moral psychology and development are matters of moral sentiments *or* rational principle – a virtue ethical approach emphasises that emotions have both an affective and a rational aspect that become integrated through a difficult process of moral development. This is the first fusion. In particular, the virtue ethical approach showed how the study of moral education, psychology and development can break out of the Kohlbergian paradigm that dominated these domains for decades.

The second fusion concerns two kinds of moral education, 'habituation' and the promotion of 'critical thinking'. Other approaches to moral education associated character education with the inculcation of patriotic or religious values and virtues. However, they underestimated the critical potential of practical wisdom. Still, an independent practical reasoner cannot automatically be equated with an autonomous person who evaluates conventional morality from an impartial and universal point of view. Questions about the 'why' of virtue are not asked by people outside all evaluative frameworks, but by already morally formed people who have an interest in living well. To use a Wittgensteinian metaphor: habituation is *not* something to be thrown away as one has climbed up the ladder of moral development.

The third fusion relates to the notions of a 'good human being' and a 'good citizen'. While some (liberal) philosophers make a strict distinction between these two and stress the tensions between people's own conception of the good life and what is, more instrumentally, required of them as members of a liberal democracy, Aristotle shows that educating children to be just, courageous, temperate and wise will also be conducive to the society they are member of. From this new perspective, civic education is part of the more comprehensive education of an intrinsically valuable character.

The fusion between 'self' and 'others' surfaced many times in this thesis. This fourth fusion can be interpreted in two ways. Firstly, this book made clear that a 'good life' is not as self-evident as many contemporary ethical theories have assumed it to be, because it depends on the love, care and education that children receive from virtuous adults. As "the early learning of the child is characteristically imperfect learning at the hands of imperfect teachers." (MacIntyre, 1999, p. 84), children's development is rarely a resounding success and will be marked by a number of conflicts. Moreover, we saw that cultivating our own character is not egoistic as our flourishing as a human being is likely to contribute to the good lives of those living in our surroundings. The idea that humans are social animals, however, does not make virtue ethics as impartial and universalistic as modern theories of ethics.

In the fifth fusion, 'nature' and 'morality' are blended. While non-naturalist philosophers separate a value-neutral conception of human nature from a normative content for morality, Aristotle's teleological worldview presupposed that (human) nature has an intrinsic purpose that can be perfected through moral education, which leads to a happy life. While neo-Aristotelians can respect the Humean distinction between 'is' and 'ought', they do believe that it is possible to derive a picture of *good* life for human beings from a description of how human beings *are* constituted, being social and rational animals.

Sixthly, there is a fusion between theory and practice. Aristotle believed that the investigations of moral philosophers should not only yield knowledge about the meaning of 'goodness', but help us to lead good lives. As a philosophical enterprise, this thesis was an abstraction from the practice of teaching, but these abstractions would ideally be made concrete in order to make educational practice more intelligent. The goal is to help practitioners to acquire a more rational understanding of what they are doing.

While these fusions yielded some interesting new insights, Aristotle's metaphysical, psychological and ethical presuppositions caused discomfort too, precisely because they are at odds with some deep-seated modern assumptions. Below, some philosophical controversies can be found that were mentioned in this thesis, but not yet sufficiently addressed or answered. Future research in the philosophy of education could focus on at least the following four problems. First of all, the relationship between Aristotelian virtue and Kantian or Kohlbergian autonomy deserves a closer look. What is the difference between 'autonomy' and an Aristotelian notion of 'independent moral judgment'? Can Aristotelians reformulate this Enlightenment ideal in virtue ethical terms? What can Aristotelians contribute to a better understanding of autonomy? Also of interest would be the relationship between Aristotle's ideal of flourishing or well-being (*eudaimonia*), and obligations towards other people's well-being, an element strongly stressed by utilitarian theories. How is one's own well-being related to the well-being of others? Can attempts to make virtue ethics less particularistic be successful? In addition, the sense in which virtue ethics is 'naturalistic' would have to be investigated further. Does the idea of natural teleology really have to be rejected? How do people's social, psychological and moral natures interact? Finally, the consequences of a virtue ethical interpretation of civic education require more attention. If the Aristotelian education of virtue is compatible with the civic education provided in liberal societies, how exactly are they related? For example, should civic virtues be seen as a separate class of virtues or do all virtue have a personal and a civic dimension?

6.3   Implications for Education, Psychology and Philosophy

This book will end with some general conclusions about the implications that the enquiries into the goal, development and education of virtue have for psychological and educational research, and for moral philosophy.

To educationalists, it must have become clear by now that an 'education in the virtues' is much more than what character educationalists have traditionally taken it to be. This has several implications. While the didactics of moral education do not have to be jettisoned, educationalists interested in moral education should do more than developing hundreds of classroom interventions that are supposed to solve the youth's moral decline. They would be well-advised to learn from or cooperate with psychologists in order to achieve a better understanding of the psychological mechanisms underlying educational practice. Ideally, psychology and education would go hand in hand: when psychologists find out more about the moral aspects of developmental psychology, teaching methods could be adjusted to fit the developmental phase that children are in. Character education has also been criticised for having a simplistic philosophical view of virtue, e.g. because it hardly examines the concept of 'virtue' and the meaning of specific virtues. The Aristotelian moral psychology discussed in this thesis offers enough food for educational thought. When reviewing the social scientific research on role modelling – which is generally considered to be the most obvious way in which teachers morally educate children – it turned out that there are no studies that can either confirm or refute its effectiveness. It is to be hoped that once educationalists have a better grasp of what it means e.g. for teachers to contribute to the children's moral development, they are in a position to improve empirical research. This is of great importance, since Chapter 2 showed that proponents of the three rival approaches perceive character education as an ineffective approach.

To psychologists interested in the psychology and development of morality, the overview of approaches in Chapter 2 will have made clear that 'morality', 'moral education' and 'moral development' are contested notions. Kohlberg's impressive research has yielded an abundance of valuable data, but his philosophical assumptions are problematic, for instance because he assumes that being 'morally educated' means that one can *reason* according to self-chosen principles of *justice*. The study of virtue and character "were pushed to the margins" for several reasons, e.g. because it was not clear how it could be reconciled with the study of moral judgments, or because it was believed that virtues could not provide the solution to the problem that Kohlberg and other post-war scientists and scholars were after, i.e. to "defeat relativism on psychological grounds" (Narvaez & Lapsley, 2009, p. 1). Twenty-five years after Kohlberg's death, psychology may have broken out of Kohlberg's theoretical confines, but this has not immediately led to clarity about the distinctive *moral* aspects of (developmental) psychology. The Aristotelian virtue ethical framework singled out in this thesis provides an alternative and richer account of morality and its development. Admittedly, the situationism debate in Chapter 3 illustrated the various ways in which many people lack self-control or virtue, but social psychological research was not a deathblow to virtue ethics. Therefore, it can continue to encourage psychologists to investigate the conceptual and empirical

Chapter 6

links between emotions, practical reasoning, character traits and actions. Moreover, chapters 3 and 4 provided some clues about the emotions and virtues involved in moral development, such as 'shame' (*aidōs*), 'emulation' (*zelos*), 'compassion' and 'integrity'. Philosophers and psychologists would have to cooperate more in order to specify virtues which can be measured empirically but are not philosophically naive. It will need the lifelong devotion of a 'second Kohlberg', but then someone with more Aristotelian sympathies, to specify a full-blown, virtue ethical alternative to Kohlberg's developmental model.

This thesis has implications for several groups of (moral) philosophers, too. Firstly, I hope that the discussion of the cognitive developmental and care ethical approaches made clear to neo-Kantians and neo-Humeans what a neo-Aristotelian approach to moral education has to offer. It was shown that and how virtue ethics can survive situationism; that moral virtue and practical wisdom are interconnected and need a critical kind of education; and that the education of virtues does not depend on the 'bag of virtues' that a particular teacher happens to value. Secondly, I hope that moral philosophers who already have a (historical) interest in Aristotle become aware of what the Aristotelian tradition means for the philosophy of education. This thesis emphasised that ethics, despite being a theoretical enterprise, has a practical aim, i.e. to *acquire* virtue and actually lead a meaningful life. If this message is brought to their attention, they will hopefully dedicate more time to the development of philosophically persuasive accounts of moral psychology, development and education. Thirdly, there are a handful of ethicists and philosophers of education who have developed, each in their own way, an Aristotelian approach to moral education. The most important ones mentioned in this thesis are Alasdair MacIntyre, David Carr and, currently, Kristján Kristjánsson. Compared to their impressive oeuvres, this thesis is a much more modest attempt to assemble what the virtue ethical tradition has yielded since the late 1980s, preparing the way for research into a number of philosophical controversies that deserve a closer look.

Finally, the thesis contains a lesson that all philosophers may want to take to heart, i.e. that philosophy was in ancient times, and can still be today, a way of life. While we are easily tempted to think of Aristotle as a pure theoretician, and while he did believe that the life of contemplation was the highest, Aristotelian 'theory' must not be opposed to 'practice', because the best life that Aristotle had in mind must still be lived and practiced. What would philosophy look like if its products are not read as doctrinal expositions, but as a set of exercises that are meant to have a practical effect, i.e. to help the authors to progress towards moral virtue and wisdom?

References

Achterbergh, J. & Vriens, D. (2009). *Organizations: social systems conducting experiments*. New York: Springer.

Ackrill, J.L. (1980). Aristotle on eudaimonia. In: A.O. Rorty (Ed.), *Essays on Aristotle's Ethics*. Berkeley etc.: University of California Press, pp. 15-33.

Annas, J. (1993). *The morality of happiness*. New York, Oxford: Oxford University Press.

Annas, J. (2011). *Intelligent virtue*. Oxford: Oxford University Press.

Anscombe, E. (1958). Modern moral philosophy. *Philosophy* 33(124), 1-19.

Appiah, K.A. (2008). *Experiments in ethics*. Cambridge, MA: Harvard University Press.

Aristotle (1932) *Politics* (transl. by H. Rackham). Cambridge, MA: Harvard University Press.

Aristotle (1957). *De Anima* (transl. by W.S. Hett). Cambridge, MA: Loeb Classical Library.

Aristotle (1975). *The Nicomachean Ethics* (transl. by H. Rackham). Cambridge, MA: Harvard UP.

Aristotle (1991). *On Rhetoric* (transl. by G.A. Kennedy). Oxford: Oxford University Press.

Aristotle (2002). *The Nicomachean Ethics* (transl. by S. Broadie & C. Rowe). Oxford: Oxford University Press.

Arnold, M. (1994). *Culture and anarchy* (ed. by S. Lipman). New Haven/London: Yale University Press.

Arnold, M.L. (2000). Stage, sequence and sequels: changing conceptions of morality, post Kohlberg. *Educational Psychology Review* 12(4), 365-383.

Asch, S.E. (1951). Effects of group pressure upon the modification and distortion of judgment. In: H. Guetzkow (Ed.), *Groups, leadership and men*. Pittsburgh, PA: Carnegie Press, pp. 177-190.

Badhwar, N.K. (2009). The Milgram experiments, learned helplessness, and character traits. *Journal of Ethics* 13 (2-3), 257-289.

Baier, A. (1985). What do women want in a moral theory? *Noûs* 19(1), 53-63.

Baier, A. (1986). Trust and antitrust. *Ethics* 96(2), 231-260.

Bandura, A. (1963). *Social learning and personality development*. New York: Holt, Rinehart & Winston.

Bandura, A. (1986). *Social foundations of thought and action: a social cognitive theory*. Englewood Cliffs, NJ: Prentice-Hall.

Bandura, A. (1997). *Self-efficacy: the exercise of control*. New York: WH Freeman.

References

Battistich, V. (2010). School contexts that promote students' positive development. In: J.L. Meece & J.E. Eccles (Eds.), *Handbook of research on schools, schooling, and human development*. New York, NY: Routledge, pp. 111-127.

Bennett, W.J. (1992). *The de-valuing of America: the fight for our culture and our children*. New York: Simon & Schuster.

Best, D. (1996). Values in the arts. In: J.M. Halstead & M.J. Taylor (Eds.), *Values in education and education in values*. London: Falmer Press, 79-91.

Blackburn, S. (2005). *Oxford dictionary of philosophy*. Oxford: Oxford University Press.

Blasi, A. (1980). Bridging moral cognition and moral action: a critical review of the literature. *Psychological Bulletin* 88(1), 1-45.

Blatt, M. & Kohlberg, L. (1975). The effects of classroom discussion upon children's level of moral judgment. *Journal of Moral Education* 4, 129-161.

Blum, L. (1988). Gilligan and Kohlberg: implications for moral theory. *Ethics* 98(3), 472-491.

Boerefijn, J. & Bergsma, A. (2011). Geluksles verbetert schoolprestaties [Happiness lessons increase school performance]. *Tijdschrift voor Orthopedagogiek* 50, 110-121.

Bogdan, R.C. & Biklen, K.P. (2003, 4th ed). *Qualitative research for education: an introduction to theories and methods*. Boston, MA: Allyn & Bacon.

Bolten, H. (2003). Spreken buiten de orde. Radicale reflectie in een socratisch gesprek [Thinking 'out of order'. Radical reflection in a Socratic dialogue]. In: J. Delnoij & W. van Dalen (Eds.), *Het Socratisch Gesprek*. Budel: Damon, pp. 14-56.

Bondi, L., Carr, D., Clark, C. & Clegg, C. (2011). *Towards professional wisdom. Practical deliberation in the people professions*. Farnham: Ashgate.

Bouchard, N. (2002). A narrative approach to moral experience using dramatic play and writing. *Journal of Moral Education* 31(4), 407-422.

Bowditch, N. (2008). Aristotle on habituation: the key to unlocking the Nicomachean Ethics. *Ethical Perspectives* 15(3), 309-342.

Bricheno, P. & Thornton, M. (2007). Role model, hero or champion? Children's views concerning role models. *Educational Research* 49(4), 383-396.

Brown, R. & Herrnstein, R.J. (1975). *Psychology*. Boston: Little & Brown.

Brown, S.R. (2008). *Moral virtue and nature. A defence of ethical naturalism*. London: Continuum.

Brune, J.P., Gromadecki, U., Gronke, H., Jänike, B., Littig, B. Rendez, V. & Ycesoy, S. (2005). The methodology of Socratic dialogue. In: J.P. Brune & D. Krohn (Eds.), *Socratic dialogue and ethics*. Münster: Lit Verlag.

Bucher, A. (1998). The influence of models in forming moral identity. *International Journal of Educational Research* 27(7), 619-627.

Burns, D. P. & Rathbone, N. (2010). The relationship of narrative, virtue education, and an ethic of care in teaching practice. *in Education* 16(2). Retrieved from http://ineducation.ca/article/relationship-narrative-virtue-education-and-ethic-care-teaching-practice on November 21, 2011.

Burnyeat, M. (1980). Aristotle on learning to be good. In: A.O. Rorty (Ed.), *Essays on Aristotle's Ethics*. Berkeley: University of California Press, pp. 69-92.

Campbell, R.L. & Christopher, J.C. (1996). Moral development theory: a critique of its Kantian presuppositions. *Developmental Review* 16, 1-47.

Carr, D.B. & Wellenberg, E.P. (1966). *Teaching children values*. Freeport, CA.: Honour Your Partner Records.

Carr, D. (1991). *Educating the virtues. An essay on the philosophical psychology of moral development and education*. London, New York: Routledge.

Carr, D. (1996). After Kohlberg: some implications of an ethics of virtue for the theory of moral education and development. *Studies in Philosophy and Education* 15, 353-370.

Carr, D. (1999). Cross questions and crooked answers: the modern problem of moral education. In: J.M. Halstead & T.H. McLaughlin (Eds.), *Education in morality*. London: Routledge, pp. 24-43.

Carr, D. (2000). *Professionalism and ethics in teaching*. London, New York: Routledge.

Carr, D. (2003a). *Making sense of education. An introduction to the philosophy and theory of education and teaching*. Abingdon: Routledge.

Carr, D. (2003b). Spiritual, moral and heroic virtue: Aristotelian character in the Arthurian and Grail narratives. *Journal of Beliefs and Values* 24(1), 15-26.

Carr, D. (2005). On the contribution of literature and the arts to the educational cultivation of moral virtue, feeling and emotion. *Journal of Moral Education* 34(2), 137-151.

Carr, D. (2006a). Moral education at the movies: on the cinematic treatment of morally significant story and narrative. *Journal of Moral Education* 35(3), 319-333.

Carr, D. (2006b). The moral roots of citizenship: reconciling principle and character in citizenship education. *Journal of Moral Education* 35(4), 443-456.

Carr, D. (2006c). The significance of music for the moral and spiritual cultivation of virtue. *Philosophy of Music Education Review* 14(2), 103-117.

Carr, D. (2012). *Virtue, practical judgement and emotion in literary and arts education* (PhD thesis, Free University Amsterdam).

Carr, D. & Steutel, J. (1999). The virtue approach to moral education. Pointers, problems and prospects. In: D. Carr & J. Steutel (Eds.), *Virtue ethics and moral education*. London: Routledge, pp. 241-255.

Casebeer, W.D. (2003). Moral cognition and its neural constituents. *Neuroscience* 4, 841-846.

References

Casteel, J.D. & Stahl, R.J. (1974). *Values clarification in the social studies: six formats of the value sheet.* Gainsville: Florida Educational Research and Development Council.

Claus, D. (1981). *Toward the soul.* New Haven/London: Yale University Press.

Cogan, J.J. & Paulson, W. (1978). Values clarification and the primary child. *The Social Studies* 69(1), 20–24.

Cohon, L. (2010). Hume's moral philosophy. In: E.N. Zalta (Ed.), *The Stanford Encyclopedia of Philosophy* (Winter 2003 Edition). Retrieved from http://plato.stanford.edu/entries/hume-moral/#inmo at August 3, 2011.

Colby, A. & Damon, W. (1992). *Some do care. Contemporary lives of moral commitment.* New York: The Free Press.

Collins, S.D. (2006). *Aristotle and the rediscovery of citizenship education.* Cambridge: Cambridge University Press.

Cottingham, J. (2010). Integrity and fragmentation. *Journal of Applied Philosophy* 27(1), 2-14.

Cox, D., La Caze, M. & Levine, M. (2008). Integrity. In: E.N. Zalta (Ed.), *The Stanford Encyclopedia of Philosophy* (Fall 2008 edition). Retrieved from http://plato.stanford.edu/archives/fall2008/entries/integrity/ on November 18, 2011.

Craighead, W. E. & Nemerhoff, C. B. (2001, 3rd ed.). *The Corsini encyclopedia of psychology and behavioural science* (vol. 1). New York: John Wiley & Sons.

Creamer, R.C. & Creamer, J.K. (1978). Values-clarification in the middle school classroom. *Contemporary Education* 49(2), 110-2.

Crisp, R. & Slote, M. (2007). *Virtue ethics.* Oxford: Oxford University Press.

Cunningham, C.A. (2005). A certain and reasoned art: the rise and fall of character education in America. In: D.K. Lapsley & F.C. Power (Eds.), *Character psychology and character education.* Notre Dame, Ind.: University of Notre Dame Press.

Curzer, H.J. (1998). To become good (paper presented at the 20th World Congress of Philosophy, Boston (MA), August 10-15, 1998). Retrieved from www.bu.edu/wcp/index.html on April 26, 2012.

Curzer, H.J. (2002). Aristotle's painful path to virtue. *Journal of History of Philosophy* 40(2), 141-162.

Curzer, H.J. (2005). How good people do bad things. Aristotle on the misdeeds of the virtuous. *Oxford Studies in Ancient Philosophy* 28, 233-256.

Curzer, H.J. (2012). *Aristotle and the Virtues.* Oxford: Oxford University Press.

Doris, J. (1998). Persons, situations, and virtue ethics. *Noûs* 32, 504-530

Doris, J. (2002). *Lack of character. Personality and moral behaviour.* Oxford: Oxford University Press.

Doris, J. (Ed.) (2010). *The moral psychology handbook.* Oxford: Oxford University Press.

Dudzinski, D.M. (2004). Integrity: principled coherence, virtue, or both? *Journal of Value Inquiry* 38(3), 299-313.

Dunne, J. (1997). *Back to the rough ground. Practical judgment and the lure of technique*. Notre Dame, Ind.: Notre Dame University Press.

Dunne, J. (2011). Professional wisdom in 'practice'. In: L. Bondi, D. Carr, C. Clark & C. Clegg (Eds.), *Towards professional wisdom. Practical deliberation in the people professions*. Farnham: Ashgate, pp. 13-26.

Dupré, J. (2002). *Humans and other animals*. Oxford: Oxford University Press.

Elkind, D.H. & Sweet, F. (1997). The Socratic approach to character education. *Educational Leadership*, 54(8), 56-59.

Fairchild, S. (2006). *Character education in the United States: a history of a movement with special attention to the character education inquiry* (PhD thesis, University of Georgia).

Fallona, C. (2000). Manner in teaching: a study in observing and interpreting teachers' moral virtues. *Teaching and Teacher Education* 16, 681-695.

Faulconer, A. (2004). *Civic excellence: citizenship virtue and contemporary liberal democratic community* (PhD thesis, University of Notre Dame).

Festinger, L. (1957). *A theory of cognitive dissonance*. Evanston, IL: Row, Peterson.

Flanagan, O. (1991). *Varieties of moral personality. Ethics and psychological realism*. Cambridge, MA: Harvard University Press.

Flanagan, O. & Adler, J.E. (1983). Impartiality and particularity. *Social Research* 50(3), 567-596.

Flanagan, O. & Jackson, K. (1987). Justice, care and gender: the Kohlberg-Gilligan debate revisited. *Ethics* 97(3), 622-637.

Flanagan, O. Sarkissian, H. & Wong, D. (2008). What is the nature of morality? A response to Casebeer, Railton, and Ruse. In: W. Sinnott-Amstrong (Ed.), *Moral psychology* (Vol. 1). Cambridge, MA: MIT Press, pp. 45-52.

Foot, P. (2001). *Natural goodness*. Oxford: Clarendon Press.

Foot, P. (2002). *Virtues and vices and other essays in moral philosophy*. Oxford: Clarendon Press.

Fowers, B.J. (2012). An Aristotelian framework of the good. *Journal of Theoretical and Philosophical Psychology* 32(1), 10-23.

Fredrickson, B.L. (2001). The role of positive emotions in positive psychology. *American Psychologist* 56 (3), 218–226.

Fredrickson, B. L. (2003). The value of positive emotions. *American Scientist* 91, 330-335.

Gadamer, H.G. (2006, 2nd ed.). *Truth and method*. London, New York: Continuum.

Galston, W. (2006). Signs of progress: the debate over civic education. *Theory and Research in Education* 4(3), 329-337.

Garrett, J.E. (1993). The moral status of 'the many' in Aristotle. *Journal of the History of Philosophy* 31(2), 171-189.

References

Gattei, S. (2008). *Thomas Kuhn's 'linguistic turn' and the legacy of logical empiricism. Incommensurability, rationality and the search for truth.* Ashgate: Aldershot.

Geach, P.T. (1977). *The virtues.* Cambridge: Cambridge University Press.

Gibson, D.E. (2003). Developing the professional self-concept: role model construals in early middle and late career stages. *Organization Science* 14(5), 591–610.

Gilead, T. (2011). Countering the vices. on the neglected side of character education. *Studies in Philosophy and Education* 30, 271–284.

Gilligan, C. (1977). In a different voice: women's conceptions of self and of morality. *Harvard Educational Review* 47(4), 481-517.

Gilligan, C. (1980). Moral development in late adolescence and adulthood: a critique and reconstruction of Kohlberg's theory. *Human Development* 23(2), 77-104.

Gilligan, C. (1982). *In a different voice: psychological theory and women's development.* Cambridge, MA.: Harvard University Press.

Gilligan, G. (2009). *Learning to see in the dark. The roots of ethical resistance* (public lecture at MIT, April 24, 2009). Retrieved from http://mitworld.mit.edu/video/729 on August 8, 2011.

Goldhill, S. (2009). Introduction: why don't Christians do dialogue? In: S. Goldhill (Ed.), *The end of dialogue in antiquity.* Cambridge: Cambridge University Press, pp. 1-12.

Gould, C.S. (1994). A puzzle about the possibility of Aristotelian enkrateia. *Phronesis* 39(2), 174-186.

Griffin, R. (1976). Worries about values clarification. *Peabody Journal of Education* 53(3), 194-200.

Gross, J.J. (2010, 3rd ed.). Emotion regulation. In: M. Lewis, J.M. Haviland-Jones & L. Feldman Barrett (Eds.), *Handbook of emotions.* New York: Guildford Press, pp. 497-512.

Guthrie, W.K.C. (1971). *The sophists.* Cambridge: Cambridge University Press.

Hadot, P. (1995). *Philosophy as a way of life.* Malden, MA: Blackwell

Haidt, J. (2001). The emotional dog and its rational tail. A social intuitionist approach to moral judgment. *Psychological Review* 108(4), 814-834.

Hall, B.P. (1973). *Values clarification as learning process. A sourcebook of learning theory.* New York: Paulist Press.

Halstead, J.M. & M.A. Pike (2006). *Citizenship and moral education. Values in action.* London, New York: Routledge.

Hanna, R. (2009). Kant's theory of judgment. In: E.N. Zalta (Ed.), *The Stanford Encyclopedia of Philosophy* (Summer 2009 Edition). Retrieved from http://plato.stanford.edu/entries/kant-judgment/ on July 3, 2012.

Hansen, D. (2001). Teaching as a moral activity. In: V. Richardson (ed), *Handbook of research on teaching* (4th ed.). Washington: AERA, pp. 826-857

Hardy, B. (1968). Toward a poetics of fiction. *Novel* 2, 5–14.
Hare, R.M. (1952). *The language of morals*. Oxford: Oxford University Press.
Hare, R.M. (1963). *Freedom and reason*. Oxford: Clarendon.
Harman, G. (1999). Moral philosophy meets social psychology: virtue ethics and the fundamental attribution error. *Proceedings of the Aristotelian Society* 99, 315-331.
Harman, G. (2000). The nonexistence of character traits. *Proceedings of the Aristotelian Society* 100(2), 223-226.
Hart, D., & Fegley, S. (1995). Prosocial behaviour and caring in adolescence. relations to self-understanding and social judgment. *Child Development* 66, 1346–1359.
Hartshorne, H. & May, M. (1930). A summary of the work in character education inquiry, part II. *Religious Education* 25(8), 754-762.
Haybron, D.M. (2008). *The pursuit of unhappiness. The elusive psychology of well-being*. Oxford: Oxford University Press.
Haydon, G. (1999). The moral agenda of citizenship education. *The School Field* 10(3/4), 47–54.
Heckmann, G. (1993). *Das Socratische Gespräch: Erfahrungen in philsophischen Hochschulseminaren*. Bonn: Philosophisch-Politische Akademie.
Hekman, S. (1993). Moral voices, moral selves: about getting it right in moral theory. *Human Studies* 16, 143-162.
Hekman, S. (1995). *Moral voices, moral selves: Carol Gilligan and feminist moral theory*. Cambridge: Polity Press.
Higgins, C. (2011). *The good life of teaching. An ethics of professional practice*. Malden, MA: Wiley-Blackwell
Higgins, E. T. (1987). Self-discrepancy: A theory relating self and affect. *Psychological Review* 94, 319-340.
Hilder, M.B. (2005). Teaching literature as an ethic of care. *Teaching Education* 16(1), 41-50.
Hoffman, M. (2000). *Empathy and moral development. Implications for caring and justice*. New York: Cambridge University Press.
Howard, T.A. (2000). *Religion and the rise of historicism*. Cambridge: Cambridge University Press.
Hume, D. (1975). *A treatise of human nature* (ed. by L.A. Selby-Bigge, 2nd ed. revised by P.H. Nidditch). Oxford: Clarendon Press.
Hunter, J.D. (2001). *The death of character: moral education without good or evil*. New York: Basic Books.
Hursthouse, R. (1999). *On virtue ethics*. Oxford: Oxford University Press.
Hursthouse, R. (2007). Virtue ethics. In: E.N. Zalta (Ed.), *Stanford Encyclopedia of Philosophy* (Winter 2010 edition). Retrieved from http://plato.stanford.edu/entries/ethics-virtue on August 29, 2011.

Ibarra, H. (1999). Provisional selves: experimenting with image and identity in professional adaptation. *Administrative Science Quarterly* 44(4), 764–791.

Javidan, M., Bemmels, B., Stratton-Devine, K., & Dastmalchian, A. (1995). Superior and subordinate gender and the acceptance of superiors as role models. *Human Relations* 48(1), 1271–1284.

Jorgenson, G. (2006). Kohlberg and Gilligan: duet or duel? *Journal of Moral Education* 35(2), 179-196.

Kail, R.V. & Cavanaugh, J.C. (2010, 5th ed.). *Human development: a life-span view*. Belmont, CA. Wadsworth.

Kamtekar, R. (2004). Situationism and virtue ethics and the content of our character. *Ethics* 114(3), 458-491.

Katayama, K. (2003). Is the virtue approach to moral education viable in a plural society? *Journal of Philosophy of Education* 37, 325–338.

Kessels, J. (2001). *Socrates op de markt* [Socrates on the market]. Amsterdam: Boom.

Kilpatrick, W. (1993). *Why Johnny can't tell right from wrong*. New York: Simon & Schuster.

Kirschenbaum, H. (1973). Beyond values clarification. In: H. Kirschenbaum & S.B. Simon (Eds.). *Readings in values clarification*. Minneapolis: Winston Press, pp. 92-110.

Kirschenbaum, H. (1976). Clarifying values clarification: some theoretical issues. In: D. Purpel & K. Ryan (Eds.), *Moral education. It comes with the territory*. Berkeley, CA: McCutchan, pp. 3-17.

Kirschenbaum, H. (2000). From values education to character education. A personal journey. *Journal of Humanistic Counselling, Education and Development* 39(1), 4-20.

Klaassen, C. (2002). Teacher pedagogical competence and sensibility. *Teaching and Teacher Education* 18, 151–158.

Klaassen, C. (2010). Teachers and normative perspectives on education. In: C. Klaassen & N. Maslovaty (Eds.), *Moral courage and the normative professionalism of teachers*. Rotterdam: Sense.

Kohlberg, L. (1958). *The development of modes of moral thinking and choice in the years 10 to 16* (PhD thesis, University of Chicago). Chicago, Ill.: Department of photo duplication, University of Chicago Library.

Kohlberg, L. (1963). The development of children's orientations toward a moral order. 1. Sequence in the development of moral thought. *Human Development* 6, 11-33.

Kohlberg, L. (1969). Stage and sequence: the cognitive-developmental approach to socialization. In: D. A. Goslin (Ed.), *Handbook of socialization theory and research*. Chicago: Rand McNally, pp. 347-477.

Kohlberg, L. (1970). The child as a moral philosopher. *Psychology Today* 2(4), 25-30.

Kohlberg, L. (1976). Moral stages and moralization: the cognitive-developmental approach. In: T. Lickona (Ed.), *Moral development and behaviour: theory, research, and social issues*. New York: Holt, Rinehart and Winston, pp. 31-53.

Kohlberg, L. (1981). *The philosophy of moral development. Moral stages and the idea of justice*. San Francisco: Harper & Row.

Kohlberg, L. (1984). *The psychology of moral development: the nature and validity of moral stages*. San Francisco, CA: Harper & Row.

Kohlberg, L., Wasserman, E., Richardson, N. (1975). The just community school: the theory and the Cambridge Cluster School experiment. In: L. Kohlberg (Ed.), *Collected papers on moral development and education*. Harvard University, MA: Center for Moral Education, pp. 1-77.

Korsgaard, C.(1998). Introduction. In: I. Kant, *Groundwork of the metaphysics of morals*. Cambridge: Cambridge University Press, pp. vii-xxx.

Koster, B., Brekelmans, M., Korthagen, F. & Wubbels, T. (2005). Quality requirements for teacher educators. *Teaching and Teaching Education* 21(2), 157-176.

Knežić, D., Wubbels, T., Elbers, E., & Hajer, M. (2010). The Socratic Dialogue in teacher education. *Teaching and Teacher Education* 26, 1104-1111.

Knight, K. (2007). *Aristotelian philosophy. Ethics and politics from Aristotle to MacIntyre*. Cambridge: Polity.

Kraut, R. (2010). Aristotle's ethics. In: E.N. Zalta (Ed.), *Stanford Encyclopedia of Philosophy* (Winter 2011 Edition). Retrieved from http://plato.stanford.edu/entries/aristotle-ethics/#DocMea on January 25, 2011.

Kristjánsson, K. (1996). *Social freedom: the responsibility view*. Cambridge: Cambridge University Press.

Kristjánsson, K. (2002). *Justifying emotions. Pride and jealousy*. Abingdon: Routledge.

Kristjánsson, K. (2006a). Emulation and the use of role models in moral education. *Journal of Moral Education* 35(1), 37-49.

Kristjánsson, K. (2006b). *Justice and desert-based emotions*. Aldershot: Ashgate.

Kristjánsson, K. (2007). *Aristotle, emotions, and education*. Farnham: Ashgate

Kristjánsson, K. (2008). An Aristotelian critique of situationism. *Philosophy* 83(323), 55-76

Kristjánsson, K. (2010a). Positive psychology, happiness and virtue: the troublesome conceptual issues. *Review of General Psychology* 14(4), 296-310.

Kristjánsson, K. (2010b). *The self and its emotions*. Cambridge: Cambridge University Press.

Kristjánsson, K. (2011). The unfortunate seclusion of moral education in an age of virtue ethics: why has psychology not delivered the goods? In: D. de Ruyter & S. Miedema (Eds.), *Moral education and development. A lifetime commitment*. Rotterdam: Sense.

Kupperman, J. (1991). *Character.* New York, Oxford: Oxford University Press.

Kupperman, J. (2009). Virtue in virtue ethics. *Journal of Ethics* 13(2-3), 243-255.

Kymlicka, W. (2001). *Politics in the vernacular: nationalism, multiculturalism, and citizenship.* Oxford: Oxford University Press.

Lawrence, G. (2006). Human good and human function. In: R. Kraut (Ed.), *The Blackwell guide to Aristotle's Nicomachean Ethics.* Malden, MA: Blackwell, pp. 37-75.

Lerner, M.J. (1980). *The belief in a just world: a fundamental delusion.* Plenum: New York.

Lickona, T. (1991). An integrated approach to character development in the elementary school classroom. In: J.S. Benninga (Ed.), *Moral, character and civic education in the elementary school.* New York, London: Teachers College Press, pp.67-83.

Lickona, T. (1992). *Educating for character. How our schools can teach respect and responsibility.* New York: Bantam.

Lickona, T. (2004). *Character matters.* New York: Touchstone.

Lipe, D.L. (1981). *A critical analysis of values clarification.* Montgomery, AL: Apologetics Press.

Lipman, M. (2003). *Thinking in education.* Cambridge: Cambridge University Press.

Lipman, M., Sharp, A.M. & Oscanyan, F.S. (1980, 2nd ed.). *Philosophy in the classroom.* Philadelphia: Temple University Press.

Lockwood, A.L. (2009). *The case for character education. A developmental approach.* New York, London: Teachers College Press.

Louden, R.B. (1984). On some vices of virtue ethics. *American Philosophical Quarterly* 21, 227-36.

Lunenberg, M., Korthagen, F. & Swennen, A. (2007). The teacher educator as a role model. *Teaching and Teacher Education* 23, 568-601.

Maas, S. (2010). *Confrontaties met moreel kritische situaties. Overwegingen, emoties en handelingen van docenten* [Confronting morally critical situations: considerations, emotions and actions of teachers] (PhD thesis, Radboud University Nijmegen). Ede: GVO.

MacIntyre, A. (1987). The idea of an educated public. In: G. Haydon (Ed.). *Education and values.* London: Institute of Education, pp. 16-35.

MacIntyre, A. (1988). *Whose justice? Which rationality?* Notre Dame, Ind.: Notre Dame University Press.

MacIntyre, A. (1991). *Three rival versions of moral enquiry. Encyclopaedia, genealogy, and tradition.* Notre Dame, Ind.: University of Notre Dame Press.

MacIntyre, A. (1998, 2nd ed.). *A short history of ethics: a history of moral philosophy from the Homeric Age to the twentieth century.* London: Routledge & Kegan Paul.

MacIntyre, A. (1999a). *Dependent rational animals. Why human beings need the virtues.* Chicago, La Salle, Ill.: Open Court.

MacIntyre, A. (1999b). How to appear virtues without actually being so. In: J.M. Halstead & T.H. McLaughlin (Eds.) *Education in morality.* London: Routledge, pp. 118-131.

MacIntyre, A. (2003, 2nd ed.). *After virtue: a study in moral theory.* Notre Dame, Ind.: University of Notre Dame Press.

MacIntyre, A. (2006). The end of education: the fragmentation of the American university. *Commonweal* 133(18), October 20, 2006.

MacIntyre, A. & Dunne, J. (2002). Alasdair MacIntyre on education: in dialogue with Joseph Dunne. *Journal of Philosophy of Education* 36(1), 1–19.

Mackie, J.L. (1977). *Ethics: inventing right and wrong.* London: Penguin.

Martelaere, P. de (1997). De voorbeeldige schrijver [The exemplary writer]. In: P. de Martelaere, *Verrassingen.* Amsterdam: Meulenhoff, pp. 155-173.

Matsuba, M.K., & Walker, L.J. (2004). Extraordinary moral commitment: young adults involved in social organisations. *Journal of Personality* 72, 413–436.

Matsuba, M.K., & Walker, L.J. (2005). Young adults' moral exemplars: the making of self through stories. *Journal of Research on Adolescence* 15, 275–297.

May, H. (2010). *Aristotle's Ethics. Moral development and human nature.* London: Continuum.

Mayton, D.M., Ball-Rokeach, S.J. & Loges, W.E. (1994). Human values and social issues: an introduction. *Journal of Social Issues* 50(4), 1-8.

McCall, C.C. (2009). *Transforming thinking. Philosophical inquiry in the primary and secondary classroom.* London, New York: Routledge.

McKinnon, C. (1999). *Character, virtue theories, and the vices.* Peterborough, ON: Broadview Press.

Merritt, M.W. (2000). Virtue ethics and situationist personality psychology. *Ethical Theory and Moral Practice* 3, 365-383.

Merritt, M.W., Doris, J.M., Harman, G. (2010). Character. In: J. Doris et al. (Eds.). *The moral psychology handbook.* Oxford: Oxford University Press.

Meijers, F. (2008). Mentoring in Dutch vocational education: an unfulfilled promise. *British Journal of Guidance & Counselling* 36(3), 237–256.

Milgram, S. (1974). *Obedience to authority.* New York: Harper and Row.

Mill, J.S. (2001). *Utilitarianism and the 1868 Speech on Capital Punishment.* Indianapolis: Hackett Publishing Company.

Miller, C. (2003). Social psychology and virtue ethics. *Journal of Ethics* 7, 365–392

Miller, N.E., & Dollard, J. (1941). *Social learning and imitation.* New Haven, CT: Yale University Press.

Miller, P.H. (2011, 5th ed.). *Theories of developmental psychology.* New York: Worth.

Mink, L.O. (1970). History and fiction as modes of comprehension. *New Literary History* 1, 541-558.

Mischel, W., Shoda, Y., & Rodriguez, M. L. (1989). Delay of gratification in children. *Science* 244, 933-938.

Mulisch, H. (1974). *Voer voor psychologen* [Food for psychologists]. Amsterdam: De Bezige Bij.

Musschenga, A.W. (2001). Education for moral integrity. *Journal of Philosophy of Education* 35(2), 219-235.

Narvaez, D. & Lapsley, D.K. (Eds.) (2009). *Personality, identity, and character: explorations in moral psychology.* Cambridge: Cambridge University Press.

Nelson, L. (1970a). Die Sokratische Methode. In: *Gesammelte Schriften in neun Bänden*, 1. Band. Hamburg: Felix Meiner Verlag.

Nelson, L. (1970b). Von der Kunst, zu philosophieren. In: *Gesammelte Schriften in neun Bänden*, 1. Band. Hamburg: Felix Meiner Verlag.

Noddings, N. (1984). *Caring: a feminine approach to ethics and moral education.* Berkeley, London: University of California Press.

Noddings, N. (1995). *Philosophy of education.* Boulder, CO: Westview.

Noddings, N. (2002a). *Educating moral people. A caring alternative to character education.* New York: Teachers College Press.

Noddings, N. (2002b). *Starting at home: caring and social policy.* Berkeley: University of California Press.

Noddings, N. (2003). *Happiness and education.* Cambridge: Cambridge University Press.

Noddings, N. (2006). *Critical lessons: what our schools should teach.* Cambridge: Cambridge University Press.

Noddings, N. (2008). Caring and moral education. In: L.P. Nucci & D. Narvaez (Eds.), *Handbook of moral and character education.* New York: Routledge, pp. 161-174.

Noddings, N. (2010). Moral education and caring. *Theory and Research in Education* 8(2), 145-151.

Noddings, N. & Slote, M. (2002). Changing notions of the moral and of moral education. In: N. Blake, P. Smeyers, R. Smith & P. Standish (Eds.), *The Blackwell guide to the philosophy of education.* Malden, MA: Blackwell, pp. 341-355.

Nucci, L.P. (Ed.) (1989). *Moral development and character education.* Berkeley, CA: McCutchan.

Nucci, L.P. & Narvaez, D. (2008). *Handbook of moral and character education.* New York: Routledge.

Nussbaum, M. (1993). Non-relative virtues. An Aristotelian approach. In: M. Nussbaum & A. Sen (Eds.), *The quality of life.* New York: Oxford Clarendon Press, pp. 242–269.

Nussbaum, M. (1997). *Cultivating humanity. A classical defence of reform in liberal education.* Cambridge, MA: Harvard University Press.

Nussbaum, M. (1999). Virtue ethics: a misleading category? *The Journal of Ethics* 3, 163-201.

Nussbaum, M. (2001a). *The fragility of goodness. Luck and ethics in Greek tragedy and philosophy.* Cambridge: Cambridge University Press.

Nussbaum, M. (2001b). *Upheavals of thought. The intelligence of emotions.* Cambridge: Cambridge University Press.

Oudenhoven, J.P. van, Pomp, M., Sluis, A.F. & Taroni, I. (2007). *Nederland deugt! Een empirische deugdenanalyse* [The Netherlands is virtuous! An empirical virtue analysis]. Rijksuniversiteit Groningen.

Oudenhoven, J.P., van, Raad, B., de, Carmona, C., Helbig, A.-K. & Linden, M., van der (2012). Are virtues shaped by cultures or religions? *Swiss Journal of Psychology* 71(1), 29–34.

Pamental. M. P. (2010). Dewey, situationism and moral education. *Educational Theory* 60(2), 147-166.

Peters, R.S. (1966). *Ethics and education.* London: George Allen and Unwin.

Peterson, C. & Seligman, M.E.P. (2004). *Character strengths and virtues. A handbook and classification.* Oxford: Oxford University Press.

Piaget, J. (1983). *The moral judgment of the child.* Harmondsworth: Penguin Books.

Pojman, L.P. & Vaugh, L. (2010, 4th ed.). *The moral life: an introductory reader in ethics and literature.* Oxford: Oxford University Press.

Popp, N. &, Portnow, K. (2001). Our developmental perspective on adulthood. In: R. Kegan (Ed) *Toward 'a new pluralism' in Abe/Esol classrooms: teaching to multiple 'closures of mind'.* Cambridge, MA: NCSALL, Harvard University Graduate School of Education.

Power, F.C. (1981). Moral education through the development of the moral atmosphere of the school. *The Journal of Educational Thought* 15, 4-19.

Power, F.C. (1988). The just community approach to moral education. *Journal of Moral Education* 17, 195-208.

Power, F.C. (2007). Anne Colby. In: C. Power, R.J. Nuzzi, D. Narvaez, D.K. Lapsley & T.C. Hunt (Eds.), *Moral education. A handbook* (Vol. 1, A-L). Westport, Connecticut: Praeger. pp. 91-92.

Power, F.C. & Kohlberg, L. (1986). Moral development: transforming the hidden curriculum. *Curriculum Review* 26, 14-17.

Power, F.C., Higgins, A., & Kohlberg, L. (1989). *Lawrence Kohlberg's approach to moral education.* New York: Columbia University Press.

Power, F.C. & Higgins-D'Alessandro (2008). Moral education and the moral atmosphere in the school. In: L.P. Nucci & D. Narvaez (Eds.), *Handbook of moral and character education.* New York: Routledge, pp. 230-247.

Power, F., Nuzzi, R., Narvaez, D., Lapsley, D. & Hunt, T. (2007). *Moral education. A handbook.* Westport, CT: Preager.

Pozdol, M.D. & Pasch, M. (1976). Values clarification in teacher education: an explanation and an evaluation. *Contemporary Education* 47(4), 202-206.

Pritchard, M. (1984). Cognition and affect in moral development: a critique of Lawrence Kohlberg. *Journal of Value Inquiry* 18(1), 35-49.

Rachels, J. (2000). Naturalism. In: H. LaFollette (Ed.), *The Blackwell guide to ethical theory*. Malden, MA: Blackwell, pp.74-91.

Radford, C. (1975). Can we be moved by the fate of Anna Karenina? *Proceedings of the Aristotelian Society* 49, 67-93.

Raths, L., Harmin, M. & Simon, S.B. (1966). *Values and teaching. Working with values in the classroom*. Columbus, Ohio: Charles E. Merrill.

Raths, L., Harmin, M. & Simon, S.B. (1978, 2nd ed.). *Values and teaching. Working with values in the classroom*. Columbus, Ohio: Charles E. Merrill.

Rawls, J. (1971). *A theory of justice*. Cambridge, MA: Belknap Press of Harvard University Press.

Reimer, J., Paolitto, D.P. & Hersh, R.H. (1983, 2nd ed.). *Promoting moral growth. From Piaget to Kohlberg*. Longman: New York.

Rest, J., Narvaez, D., Bebeau, M.J. Thoma, S.J. (1999). *Post-conventional moral thinking: a neo-Kohlbergian approach*. Mahwah, NJ: Lawrence Erlbaum Associates.

Rest, J.S., Narvaez, D., Thoma, S.J., & Bebeau, M.J. (2000). A neo-Kohlbergian approach to morality research. *Journal of Moral Education* 29(4), 381-396.

Ricoeur, P. (1983). *Time and narrative*. Vol. 1 (transl. K. McLaughlin & D. Pellauer). Chicago, Ill: University of Chicago Press.

Rietti, S. (2009). Utilitarianism and psychological realism. *Utilitas* 21(3), 347-367.

Riggio, R.E., Zhu, W., Reina, C. & Maroosis, J.A. (2010). Virtue-based measurement of ethical leadership: the Leadership Virtues Questionnaire. *Consulting Psychology Journal: Practice and Research* 62(4), 235-250.

Rogers, C. (1972). Toward a modern approach to values: the valuing process in the mature person. In: H. Kirschenbaum & S.B. Simon (Eds.). *Readings in value clarification*. Minneapolis: Winston Press, pp. 75-91.

Rokeach, M. (1968). *Beliefs, attitudes, and values. A theory of organization and change*. San Francisco: Jossey-Bass.

Rokeach, M. (1973a). *The nature of human values*. New York, NY: Free Press

Rokeach, M. (1973b). Persuasion that persists. In: H. Kirschenbaum & S.B. Simon (Eds.), *Readings in Values Clarification*. Minneapolis: Winston Press, pp. 65-74.

Rokeach, M. (1977). Age differences in values. In: M. Smith (Ed.), *A practical guide to value clarification*. La Jolla, CA: University Associate, pp. 246-256.

Rokeach, M. (1979). Values education in educational settings. In: M. Rokeach (Ed.), *Understanding human values. Individual and societal*. New York, NY: The Free Press, pp. 259-269.

Rumsey, J.P. (1997). Justice, care, and questionable dichotomies. *Hypatia* 12: 99–113

Ruyter, D. de (2002). The virtue of taking responsibility. *Educational Philosophy and Theory* 34(1), 25–35.

Ryan, K. (1989). In defence of character education. In: L.P. Nucci (Ed.), *Moral development and character education: a dialogue*. Berkeley: McCutcheon, pp. 3-18.

Ryan, K. & Lickona, Th. (Eds.) (1992). *Character development in schools and beyond*. Washington DC: Council for Researching Values and Philosophy.

Ryan, R. & Deci, E. (2001). On happiness and human potentials: a review of research on hedonic and eudaimonic well-being. *Annual Review of Psychology* 52, 141-166.

Rymarz, R. (2010). Religious identity of Catholic schools: some challenges from a Canadian perspective. *Journal of Beliefs and Values* 31(3), 299-310.

Salmieri, G. (2009). Aristotle's non-'dialectical' methodology in the Nicomachean Ethics. *Ancient Philosophy* 29, 311-355.

Sanderse, W. (2011). Review essay of Kristján Kristjánsson's 'Justifying emotions: pride and jealousy', 'Justice and desert-based emotions', 'Aristotle, emotions, and education' and 'The self and its emotions'. *Theory and Research in Education* 9(2), 185-196.

Sanderse, W. (forthcoming). The meaning of role modeling in moral and character education. *Journal of Moral Education*. Retrieved from http://dx.doi.org/10.1080/03057240.2012.690727 on August 30, 2012.

Schaubroeck, K. (2005). Hoe belangrijk is literatuur in de morele opvoeding? [How important is literature to moral education?] *Bijdragen* 66, 432-454.

Schindler, D. L. (1992). On the foundations of moral judgment. In: G.F. McLean & F.E. Ellrod (Eds.), *Philosophical foundations for moral education and character development: act and agent*. Washington, D.C: The Council for Research in Values and Philosophy, pp. 251-279.

Schuitema, J., Dam, G. ten & Veugelers, W. (2008). Teaching strategies for moral education: a review. *Journal of Curriculum Studies* 40(1), 69-89.

Schwartz, B. & Sharpe, K.E. (2006). Practical wisdom: Aristotle meets positive psychology. *Journal of Happiness Studies* 7, 377-395.

Seligman, M.E.P & Csikszentmihalyi, M. (2000). Positive psychology: an introduction. *American Psychologist* 55(1), 5–14.

Shaffer, R.S. & Kipp, K. (Eds.) (2010). *Development psychology. Childhood and adolescence*. Belmont, CA: Wadsworth.

Sherman, N. (1989). *The fabric of character. Aristotle's theory of virtue*. Oxford: Clarendon Press.

Simon, S., Howe. L.W. & Kirschenbaum, H. (1972). *Values clarification. A handbook of practical strategies for teachers and students*. New York: Hart Publishing.

References

Singer, P. & Singer, R. (2005). *The moral of the story: an anthology of ethics through literature*. New York: Wiley-Blackwell.

Slote, M. (1999). Caring versus the philosophers. *Philosophy of Education Yearbook*. Retrieved from www.ed.uiuc.edu/EPS/PES-Yearbook/1999/slote.asp at August 12, 2011.

Slote, M. (2007). *The ethics of care and empathy*. London: Routledge.

Slote, M. (2010a). *Moral sentimentalism*. Oxford. Oxford University Press.

Slote, M. (2010b). Sentimentalist moral education. *Theory and Research in Education* 8(2), 125-143.

Smith, K. (2001). Professional knowledge of teacher educators (paper presented at the AERA annual meeting, April 10–14, Seattle, WA).

Smith, M. (1977). *A practical guide to value clarification*. La Jolla, CA: University Associates.

Snarey, J., Reimer, J. & Kohlberg, L. (1985). The Kibbutz as a model for moral education: a longitudinal cross-cultural study. *Journal of Applied Developmental Psychology* 6, 151-172.

Steele, S.M. (1983, 2nd ed.). Values and values clarification. In: S.M. Steele & V.M. Harmon (Eds.), *Values clarification in nursing*. Connecticut: Appleton-Century-Crofts.

Steutel, J. (1997). The virtue approach to moral education. Some conceptual clarifications. *Journal of Philosophy of Education*, 31(3), 395-407.

Steutel, J. (1998). Virtues and human flourishing: a teleological justification. In: D. Carr (Ed.), *Education, knowledge and truth: beyond the postmodern impasse*. London: Routledge, pp. 129-142.

Steutel, J. & Carr, D. (1999). Virtue ethics and the virtue approach to moral education. In: D. Carr & J. Steutel (Eds.), *Virtue ethics and moral education*. London, New York: Routledge, pp. 3-18.

Steutel, J. & Spiecker, B. (1996). Moral identity and education in a multicultural society. *Studies in Philosophy and Education* 15, 159-165.

Steutel, J. & Spiecker, B. (2000). Authority in educational relationships. *Journal of Moral Education* 29(3), 323-337.

Steutel, J. & Spiecker, B. (2004). Cultivating sentimental dispositions through Aristotelian habituation. *Journal of Philosophy of Education* 38(4), 531-549.

Stohr, K. (2002). Moral cacophony: when continence is a virtue. *Journal of Ethics* 7(4), 339-363

Suissa, J. (2008). Lessons from a new science? On teaching happiness in schools. *Journal of Philosophy of Education* 42(3-4), 575-590.

Swanton, C. (2003). *Virtue ethics. A pluralistic view*. Oxford: Oxford University Press.

Swennen, A., Lunenberg, M. & Korthagen, F. (2008). Preach what you teach! Teacher educators and congruent teaching. *Teachers and Teaching: Theory and Practice* 14(5-6), 531-542.

Taylor, G. (2006). *Deadly vices.* Oxford: Oxford University Press.

Tiberius, V. and Plakias, A. (2010). Well-being. In: J. Doris (Ed.), *The moral psychology handbook.* Oxford: Oxford University Press. pp. 401-431.

Timmerman, G. (2009). Teacher educators modelling their teachers? *European Journal of Teacher Education* 32(3), 225-238

Tobin, B. (1989). An Aristotelian theory of moral development. *Journal of Philosophy of Education* 23(2), 195-211.

Tongeren, P. van (2000). On the beginning of ethics. A propedeutic reading of Book I of Plato's Republic. In: G. de Stexhe & J. Verstraeten (Eds.), *Matter of breath. Foundations for professional ethics.* Leuven: Peeters, pp. 35-44.

Tronto, J.C. (1993). *Moral boundaries: a political argument for an ethic of care.* New York, NY: Routledge

Upton, C.L. (2009). Virtue ethics and moral psychology: the situationism debate. *Journal of Ethics* 13(2-3), 103-115.

Urmson, J. (1980). Aristotle's doctrine of the mean. In: A.O. Rorty (Ed.), *Essays on Aristotle's Ethics.* Berkeley etc.: University of California Press, pp. 157–170.

Verbeke, G. (1990). *Moral education in Aristotle.* Washington D.C.: The Catholic University of America Press.

Veugelers, W. & De Kat, E. (1999). *Moral development at home and at school: division of moral tasks between parents and teachers in secondary schools* (Paper presented at the Annual Meeting of the American Educational Research Association, Montreal, Canada, April 19-23, 1999).

Veugelers, W. & De Kat, E. (2003). Moral task of the teacher according to students, parents and teachers. *Educational Research and Evaluation* 9(1), 75-91.

Vlastos, G. (1991). *Socrates. Ironist and moral philosopher.* Ithaca, NY: Cornell University Press.

Vokey, D. (2001). MacIntyre and the catch-22 of Aristotelian moral education. *Philosophy of Education Archive*, pp. 192-199. Retrieved from http://ojs.ed.uiuc.edu/index.php/pes/article/view/1891/602 on June 19, 2012.

Walker, L.J. (1999). The perceived personality of moral exemplars. *Journal of Moral Education* 28(2), 145-162.

Walker, L.J. & Hennig, K.H. (2004). Differing conceptions of moral exemplarity: just, brave and caring. *Journal of Personality and Social Psychology* 86(4), 629-647.

Walker, L.J., Pitts, R.C., Hennig, K.H. & Matsuba, M.K. (1995). Reasoning about morality and real-life moral problems. In: M. Killen & D. Hart (Eds.), *Morality in everyday life: developmental perspectives.* Cambridge: Cambridge University Press. pp. 371-407.

Webber, J. (2006). Virtue, character and situation. *Journal of Moral Philosophy* 3(2), 193-213.

White, P. (1996). *Civic virtues and public schooling: educating citizens for a democratic society*. New York, NY: Teachers College Press.

Wielenberg, E.J. (2002). Pleasure, pain, and moral character and development. *Pacific Philosophical Quarterly* 83, 282-299. Wielenberg, E.J. (2006). Saving character. *Ethical Theory and Moral Practice* 9, 461–491.

Willemse, M., Lunenberg, M. & Korthagen, F. (2005). Values in education: a challenge for teacher educators. *Teaching and Teacher Education* 21(2), 205-217.

Willemse, M., Lunenberg, M. & Korthagen, F. (2008). The moral aspects of teacher educators' practices. *Journal of Moral Education* 37(4), 445-466.

Williams, B. (1972). *Morality: an introduction to ethics*. New York etc.: Harper & Row.

Williams, B. (1985). *Ethics and the limits of philosophy*. London: Fontana.

Williams, G. (2008). Responsibility as a virtue. *Ethical Theory and Moral Practice* 11(4), 455-470.

Wolf, S. (2007). Moral psychology and the unity of the virtues. *Ratio* 20, 145-167.

Wood, E. & Geddis, A. (1999). Self-conscious narrative and teacher education: representing practice in professional course work. *Teaching and Teacher Education* 15, 107–119.

Wynne, E., & Ryan, K. (1997, 2nd ed.). *Reclaiming our schools: a handbook on teaching character, academics, and discipline*. New York: Merrill.

Yancy, A.K., Siegel, J.M. & McDaniel, K.L. (2002). Role models, ethnic identity, and health-risk behaviours in urban adolescents. *Archives of Pediatrics and Adolescent Medicine* 156, 55-61.

Yancy, A.K. Grant, D. Kurosky, S., Kravitz-Wirtz, N. & Mistry. R. (2011). Role modelling, risk, and resilience in Californian adolescents. *Journal of Adolescent Health* 48(1), 36-43.

Summary

The moral concerns of teachers working in secondary education are diverse. Besides transferring values in separate subjects, enforcing school rules and encouraging critical thinking, there is also a moral concern which most teachers generally recognise as important, but which is at risk of being neglected since it happens in very subtle ways: it is educating pupils' virtues. While the term 'virtue' may not be part of our most people's vocabularies, daily speech is interspersed with virtue terms, such as honesty, patience, generosity, care or responsibility, and many of our actions show whether we have 'character' or not. When we look at this aspect of the practice of moral education, the moral dimension of teaching is about morality in a basic sense: it does not mean 'teaching morality', but 'being a moral teacher', which means extending everyday morality into the nuances of teaching. Teachers' moral character is revealed through all kinds of small decisions and emotional reactions. For example, if the distribution of scarce resources is a matter of justice, the way a teacher divides his attention over a group of pupils tells us something about how (un)just he is.

While many teachers recognise that they have a moral educational task, this recognition has not always culminated in a more profound grasp of why moral education is desirable or how it can best be achieved. One reason is that the truth of moral values and judgments is believed to depend on subjective preferences or arbitrary cultural conventions. When 'moral relativism' sinks in with teachers, they realise that they run the risk of bothering adolescents with their own ideas about right and wrong. Consequently, they often adopt an attitude of neutrality towards the kind of moral education that goes beyond a bare minimum. Additional problems are that some of the traditional sources that used to provide an answer to the question of what children should be morally educated for have gradually lost their influence. In addition, many teachers are not used to thinking (collectively) about the moral aspects of teaching in a professional way, because they are trained as experts in a particular subject, and because schools are organised for coursework. Moreover, moral education is often misunderstood, because it is taken to be an instrument to another (political or economic) end, instead of something that is valuable in itself and therefore worth paying attention to.

When teachers consider themselves to be responsible for the cultivation of children's virtues, but do not have an answer to questions concerning the nature, desirability and implementation of moral education, it can lead to feelings of incompetence and insecurity – which together can be labelled as a kind of 'moral embarrassment'. The aim of this book is to remove this embarrassment by contributing to a better theoretical understanding of an education in the virtues, which will hopefully lead to the improvement of educational practice too. Three central questions are investigated in order to help teachers (and teacher educators) to understand what the 'education of virtue' entails. Firstly, what is a 'virtue' and how does it develop? Secondly, how can schools best contribute to the development of virtue? Thirdly, why is an education in the virtues morally desirable? Answering these three questions contributes to a morally justified and psychologically realistic account that makes clear how virtue can best be taught in schools.

One approach that can help us answer the three central questions is known as 'character education'. While character education has a long history in the United States, a number of educationists explicitly addressed issues about educating pupils for virtue and character in the late 1980s and early 1990s. They promised to solve the youth's moral decline and also wanted to provide an alternative to three other approaches to moral education that were influential in post-war educational theory and practice: values clarification, cognitive development and care ethics. However, the interest of these American character educators remained largely practical. With regard to the philosophical and psychological questions about how we should conceive of the development and justification of virtue, the American character education proponents do not have much to offer. At the same time, all character education advocates mention a single source of inspiration: Aristotle (384-322 BC), the father of virtue ethics – a discipline which has received renewed scholarly attention. While Aristotle is referred to, his ideas are rarely elaborated on. This raises the question of whether Aristotelianism can contribute to teachers' understanding of educating for virtue. What would 'character education' look like if it had the full weight of the Aristotelian tradition behind it? When taking this approach, two things need to be considered. Firstly, because a virtue ethical approach has some difficulties of its own, the weaknesses of Aristotle's pre-modern heritage are evaluated as well. Secondly, we are less interested in Aristotle's philosophy as such, and more in the ways in which contemporary Aristotelians, such as Alasdair MacIntyre, Martha Nussbaum, David Carr and Kristján Kristjánsson, have thought through the Aristotelian heritage in order to make it useful for topical issues concerning education.

Before a neo-Aristotelian virtue ethical approach to moral education is specified in chapter 3, 4 and 5, Chapter 2 starts with a discussion of the three other influential approaches to moral education that in the twentieth century. With regards to values clarification, Kohlberg's cognitive development theory and feministic care ethics, it is examined (a) what their main proponents take to be the goal of moral education, (b) what people go through when they morally develop, and (c) what schools can do to stimulate moral development. It is also investigated how these three approaches conceive of the fourth approach, character education. The chapter enables us to see more clearly the distinctive features and limits of a character educational approach, and it culminates in a number of challenges that virtue ethics will have to meet if it is to be successful in the eyes of the other approaches. In short, they take it to be an approach that inculcates certain character traits that are considered to be morally significant by a particular community or society. By looking at the criticism that is directed at this kind of moral education, a number of major objections stand out. Firstly, the question is raised whether virtues are really the qualities that help us to *act* virtuously. Are people's actions not much more determined by the situation they find themselves in? Secondly, there are worries about the cultivation of virtue in schools. Is it effective? And is it not moralistic to impose virtues on children? Does character education not preclude the training of critical thinking? A third issue is *which* virtues should be taught, in particular in pluralistic societies in which there would be no consensus about what a good life consists of. The subsequent chapters on the development, education and justification of virtue are used to investigate how Aristotelian virtue ethics deals with these objections.

Chapter 3 introduces Aristotle's ideas on moral psychology. First, the role of and relations between emotions, reason and character traits as elements in an Aristotelian theory of action are described. The chapter makes clear that – in contrast to cognitive development and care ethics – a virtue ethical approach goes beyond an easy dualism of desire and reason. Virtue ethics affirms a strong intuition that the other two approaches have difficulties apprehending, i.e. that moral psychology and development are essentially a matter of both heart and mind, and that a developmental approach is needed in order to understand how the two become intertwined. Second, the claims of a number of so-called 'situationists' are examined, who have argued that an Aristotelian understanding of moral and intellectual virtue is empirically flawed. The empirical assumption under attack is disturbingly simple but very fundamental, i.e. the idea that people's actions can be explained and predicted in terms of character traits. An evaluation of their criticism reveals certain meta-ethical assumptions about the psychological realism of moral concepts. It is concluded that the virtue ethical ideal of practical wisdom is not too far removed from what psychological research has revealed about the human cognitive make-up. The chapter closes with a neo-Aristotelian developmental model in order to show that social psychological experiments that make clear that many people are not fully virtuous do not have to be taken for granted. The model shows that and how children, who are yet uncommitted to virtue or lack self-control, can make moral progress. In order to understand how people can morally develop, four levels of moral development are distinguished: (1) being uncommitted to virtue, (2) being committed to virtue, but lacking self-control, (3) being committed to virtue, and having self-control, and (4) being fully virtuous. While the virtue ethical model of moral development presented in this chapter is still sketchy and lacks empirical validity, it offers teachers and theorists a conceptual framework that can help them to look at children's development differently. The developmental account can help us to go beyond Kohlberg's still dominant cognitive developmental paradigm.

Summary

Chapter 4 focuses on the educational means that schools can use to stimulate pupils' moral development. By discussing three 'methods', it is shown that an education in the virtues is continuous with everyday teaching. To the extent that teachers and schools elaborate and specify an approach to moral education, 'character education' can change from a haphazard, implicit by-product into a more considerate and systematic teaching method. The moral dimension can be made more explicit if teachers take (and get!) more time to think through and improve what they already do, instead of giving way to the urge to invent all kinds of new methods to solve the problem. When character education is understood as a more sophisticated attempt to contribute to the development of pupils' virtues through teachers' manner, role modelling becomes all-important. It is investigated what it really means to 'model' certain virtues and what teachers should be a model of. A second method is the moral educational use of the (narrative) arts. It is argued that reading books can be a means to stimulate children's moral development because stories and lives share a narrative structure, but that this is not sufficient to become compassionate. As we are emotionally involved with real people in different ways than with fictitious characters in books, educators should not forget to stimulate pupils' (moral) imagination *in practice* by also having them *do* compassionate things. Finally, it is suggested that Socratic dialogues, more in particular the method of 'regressive abstraction' advocated by Leonard Nelson, are a suitable way for teachers to practice the cardinal virtue of practical wisdom. The oscillating movement that participants in a dialogue make between a conceptual question and concrete examples gives them an opportunity to practice the kind of practical judgment that mediates between a still general conception of virtues like justice or courage and the concrete and changing circumstances.

After the development and education of virtue have been discussed, the question of why the education of virtue is morally justified is addressed in Chapter 5. This why-question is saved for last, because it is in line with the idea that knowledge of the 'why' can be acquired best after one has mastered the 'how' and 'what'. Despite the pervasive relativistic understanding of morality in Western plural societies, the main thesis defended in this chapter is that it makes sense to understand virtues as objective moral qualities that are essential to people's well-being or happiness. Even without reducing virtue to minimal and instrumental virtues promoted through liberal citizenship education. As we turn to Aristotle's teleology to clarify the relationship between virtue and 'happiness' (*eudaimonia*), it becomes clear that the idea that human nature has an intrinsic purpose (*telos*) is problematic. Value is ascribed by humans to nature instead of discovered in a kind of nature that is already in good order. We examined the work of two neo-Aristotelians – MacIntyre and Kristjánsson – in order to see whether they could justify the education of virtue more objectively while reformulating Aristotle's pre-modern heritage in such a way that it is still acceptable to people living in the twenty-first century. These two neo-Aristotelians advocate a different kind of Aristotelianism. Kristjánsson is more interested in the relation between ethics and psychology, and he focuses on the shared emotions that underlie the virtues, while Macintyre, who is interested in the sociology and history of virtue, emphasises moral differences and conflicts. Combined, their work shows that there is no direct route from nature to morality, but that virtue ethics does place some limits on what can be regarded as a system of *human* morality.

In Chapter 6, some of the conclusions of the preceding chapters are assembled and elaborated on. The challenges formulated in Chapter 2 are revisited to determine what a neo-Aristotelian approach makes clear about *moral education*. From a neo-Aristotelian perspective, 'character education' consists in the more or less deliberate, more or less comprehensive attempts of teachers to contribute to the ongoing development of moral virtue and practical wisdom in pupils in order to enable them to lead a flourishing life as human beings. Moreover, the question is addressed what the themes explored in this book disclose concerning the viability of an *Aristotelian* approach. While reflecting on the typical features of an Aristotelian approach to moral education, it occurred to me that Aristotle fuses several distinctions that are taken to be self-evident today, such as 'reason' and 'emotion', 'habituation' and 'critical thinking', a 'good human being' and a 'good citizen', 'self' and 'other', 'nature' and 'morality', and 'theory' and 'practice'. While these fusions yield some interesting new insights, Aristotle's presuppositions continue to cause discomfort too, precisely because they are at odds with some deep-seated modern assumptions. This book ends with some general conclusions about the implications that these enquiries into the goal, development and education of virtue have on moral enquiry and social-scientific research.

Samenvatting

Leraren in het voortgezet onderwijs zijn op allerlei manieren met moraal in het onderwijs bezig: via de overdracht van waarden in aparte vakken, het opleggen en handhaven van schoolregels en het bevorderen van kritisch denken via discussies. Maar 'morele vorming' heeft ook nog een andere betekenis – één die echter vaak over het hoofd wordt gezien, omdat het op een zeer subtiele manier gaat. Dit is de vorming van de deugden van leerlingen. Toegegeven, het begrip 'deugd' is geen vanzelfsprekend deel van ons dagelijkse taalgebruik. Toch is de taal vergeven van (on)deugden. We zeggen bijvoorbeeld regelmatig van anderen dat ze (niet) eerlijk, geduldig, vrijgevig, zorgzaam of verantwoordelijk zijn. Als morele vorming wordt begrepen als een geleidelijk proces waardoor kinderen zich zulke goede eigenschappen eigen kunnen maken, dan wordt duidelijk dat de morele dimensie van lesgeven iets heel basaals is. De morele taak van leraren bestaat niet zozeer uit het 'onderwijzen' van deugden, maar primair uit een 'goed mens' zijn, en dat niet alleen in privésituaties, maar ook op school. Of leraren 'karakter' tonen of niet wordt duidelijk door kleine dagelijkse beslissingen en emotionele reacties in de omgang met leerlingen, collega's en ouders. Bijvoorbeeld, als het verdelen van schaarse goederen een kwestie van rechtvaardigheid is, dan zegt de manier waarop een leraar zijn aandacht verdeelt over de groep iets over hoe (on)rechtvaardig hij is.

Hoewel veel leraren erkennen dat ze in deze zin een moreel-vormende taak hebben, heeft deze erkenning nog niet geresulteerd in een goed *begrip* van de wenselijkheid of implementatie van morele vorming in het onderwijs. Een achterliggende oorzaak is dat men er vaak vanuit gaat dat de waarheid van morele waarden en oordelen afhankelijk is van persoonlijke voorkeuren of willekeurige culturele conventies. Leraren bij wie dit 'moreel relativisme' doordringt, realiseren zich dat ze het risico lopen leerlingen lastig te vallen met hun eigen ideeën over goed en kwaad. Het gevolg is dat een neutrale houding wordt ingenomen ten opzichte van morele vorming die substantiëler is dan wat minimaal vereist is. Daar komt bij dat traditionele bronnen die een antwoord boden op de vraag waartoe leerlingen moreel gevormd worden geleidelijk aan invloed ingeboet hebben. Verder denken leraren nog te weinig collectief en op een professionele manier na over de morele aspecten van hun werk, omdat ze zijn opgeleid als experts op een bepaald kennisdomein, en omdat het schoolcurriculum in vakken is opgeknipt. Bovendien wordt morele vorming vaak verkeerd begrepen, omdat het wordt opgevat als een middel tot een ander (politiek of economisch) doel, in plaats van als iets dat op zichzelf waardevol is en daarom aandacht verdient.

Wanneer leraren zich verantwoordelijk achten voor de overdracht van bepaalde deugden, maar geen antwoord kunnen geven op vragen over de precieze aard, wenselijkheid en implementatie van morele vorming, leidt dit tot ervaringen

Samenvatting

van incompetentie en onzekerheid die illustratief zijn voor wat met de term 'morele handelingsverlegenheid' wordt aangeduid. Het doel van dit boek is om deze verlegenheid weg te nemen door bij te dragen aan een beter theoretisch begrip van deugd- en karaktervorming, dat – op zijn beurt – hopelijk leidt tot een verbetering van de onderwijspraktijk. In dit boek staan drie vragen centraal die leraren (en lerarenopleiders) inzicht kunnen geven in de betekenis van morele vorming vanuit een deugdethisch perspectief. De eerste vraag luidt: wat is een 'deugd' en hoe ontwikkelen deugden zich? De twee vraag is: hoe kunnen scholen het beste bijdragen aan de ontwikkeling van deugden? De derde vraag, tenslotte, is: waarom zou karaktervorming moreel wenselijk zijn? De beantwoording van deze vragen draagt bij aan een moreel onderbouwde en psychologisch realistische benadering van morele vorming die duidelijk maakt hoe deugden het best in scholen 'onderwezen' kunnen worden.

Een stroming die op deze vragen ingaat, is bekend onder de naam *character education*. Hoewel deze benadering in de Verenigde Staten een lange geschiedenis heeft, stonden er in de jaren '80 en '90 van de twintigste eeuw een aantal pedagogen op die noties als 'deugd' en 'karakter' weer in het onderwijs centraal wilden stellen. Ze beloofden daarmee niet alleen een aantal prangende maatschappelijke problemen op te lossen, maar wilden ook een alternatief bieden voor drie andere benaderingen die invloedrijk waren in de naoorlogse theorievorming over ethiek en onderwijs, te weten: *values clarification* ('waardeverheldering'), *cognitive development* ('cognitieve ontwikkeling') en *care ethics* ('zorgethiek'). De interesse van de Amerikaanse karaktervormers is voornamelijk praktisch; met betrekking tot de filosofische en psychologische vragen over de ontwikkeling en rechtvaardiging van deugden hebben ze weinig te bieden. Wel verwijzen de voorstanders van deze benadering naar dezelfde inspiratiebron: Aristoteles (384-322 v.Chr.), de grondlegger van de zogenaamde 'deugdethiek', een ethische theorie die sinds de jaren '60 opnieuw in de belangstelling staat. Hoewel aan Aristoteles wordt gerefereerd, worden zijn ideeën nauwelijks uitgewerkt. Dit roept de vraag op wat Aristoteles' theorie kan bijdragen aan een beter begrip van karaktervorming. Hoe ziet *character education* eruit als we haar vanuit de Aristotelische traditie doordenken? Bij dit onderzoek moeten twee punten worden aangestipt. Ten eerste is de Aristotelische deugdethiek filosofisch niet onomstreden. Dat betekent dat ook de zwakke punten van Aristoteles' premoderne theorie aan de orde komen. Ten tweede zijn we niet alleen in Aristoteles' theorieën geïnteresseerd, maar vooral in de manier waarop hedendaagse Aristotelici, zoals Alasdair MacIntyre, Martha Nussbaum, David Carr and Kristján Kristjánsson, in de afgelopen dertig jaar de Aristotelische erfenis bruikbaar hebben gemaakt voor actuele kwesties rond opvoeding, vorming en onderwijs.

Voordat een neo-Aristotelische benadering van de filosofie, psychologie en pedagogiek van de deugd verder wordt uitgewerkt in hoofdstukken 3, 4 en 5, behandelt Hoofdstuk 2 de drie eerdergenoemde benaderingen. Voor waardeverheldering,

Samenvatting

Kohlbergs cognitieve ontwikkelingstheorie en de feministische zorgethiek is onderzocht (a) wat hun voorstanders als het doel van morele vorming zien, (b) welke ontwikkeling mensen doormaken op weg naar dat doel, en (c) hoe scholen het beste aan dit proces kunnen bijdragen. Ook is onderzocht hoe deze benaderingen aankijken tegen de vorming van deugden. Het hoofdstuk maakt duidelijk wat de belangrijkste kritieken zijn, en op welke vragen de deugdethiek een antwoord moet geven, wil ze in de ogen van de drie alternatieve theorieën geslaagd zijn. Ze zien karaktervorming als een benadering die bij kinderen van jongs af aan deugden inprent die waarde hebben binnen een specifieke gemeenschap of samenleving. Drie kritiekpunten keren regelmatig terug. Ten eerste is het de vraag of deugdzame karaktertrekken er wel toe leiden dat mensen ook deugdzaam *handelen*. Bepaalt bijvoorbeeld de situatie niet vaak wat mensen uiteindelijk doen? Ten tweede worden er twijfels geuit over de bijdrage van scholen aan de vorming van het karakter van kinderen. Werkt dat eigenlijk wel? En is het niet te moralistisch om kinderen deugden op te leggen? Sluiten deugdenonderwijs en het bevorderen van kritisch denken elkaar niet uit? Ten derde is het onduidelijk wat de zeggingskracht van de deugdethiek is in een pluriforme samenleving waarin geen overeenstemming lijkt te bestaan over de betekenis van een 'goed leven'. Welke deugden moeten er dan centraal staan? In hoofdstukken 3, 4 en 5 wordt geprobeerd een antwoord op deze tegenwerpingen te formuleren.

Hoofdstuk 3 introduceert de Aristotelische morele psychologie. Allereerst worden de functie van en samenhang tussen emoties, verstand en karaktertrekken als elementen van een Aristotelische handelingstheorie besproken. Daaruit wordt duidelijk dat de deugdethiek – in tegenstelling tot een cognitieve ontwikkelings- of zorgethische benadering – voorbij gaat aan een strikt dualisme van verstand en verlangen. Ze bevestigt juist een sterke intuïtie waarmee de andere benaderingen moeite hebben, namelijk dat moraal idealiter een kwestie van zowel het 'hoofd' als het 'hart' is, en dat een ontwikkelingsperspectief nodig is om te begrijpen hoe ze op elkaar ingrijpen. Vervolgens worden de claims van enkele 'situationisten' onderzocht, die beweren dat de Aristotelische opvatting van 'deugd' empirisch problematisch is. De empirische aanname die ter discussie staat is verontrustend simpel en fundamenteel, namelijk het idee dat handelingen verklaard en voorspeld kunnen worden in termen van karaktertrekken. Een analyse van de kritiek maakt duidelijk welke meta-ethische aannames situationisten maken over het psychologisch realisme van morele concepten. Geconcludeerd wordt dat een deugdethisch ideaal van praktische wijsheid niet te ver verwijderd is van wat psychologisch onderzoek heeft opgeleverd over hoe mensen feitelijk in elkaar zitten. Het hoofdstuk wordt afgesloten met een neo-Aristotelisch ontwikkelingsmodel om te laten zien dat men zich niet hoeft neer te leggen bij onderzoek waaruit blijkt dat veel mensen weinig moreel ontwikkeld zijn. Het model laat zien dat en hoe kinderen die de zin van moraal nog niet inzien of nog weinig zelfcontrole tonen, zich verder zouden kunnen ontwikkelen, en welke morele emoties daarbij in het spel zijn. In het model, dat een open einde heeft, worden vier fasen van morele ontwikkeling onderscheiden: (1) er is geen commitment aan een deugdzaam leven, (2) er is een commitment aan een deugdzaam leven, maar een gebrek aan zelfcontrole, (3) er is een commitment aan een dcugdzaam leven, en men controleert zichzelf, en (4) men is deugdzaam en praktisch wijs. Hoewel het deugdethische ontwikkelingsmodel in dit hoofdstuk schetsmatig blijft en empirisch niet gevalideerd is, helpt het om de morele ontwikkeling van kinderen anders te zien dan in het dominante maar eenzijdige paradigma van Kohlberg.

Hoofdstuk 4 bespreekt drie pedagogische 'methoden' die scholen kunnen inzetten om de ontwikkeling van het karakter te stimuleren. Belangrijk inzicht daarbij is dat het 'onderwijzen' van deugden eigenlijk een bestaande dimensie van het dagelijkse lesgeven betreft die echter vaak onderbelicht blijft. Maar wanneer leraren en scholen deze dimensie thematiseren, kan 'karaktervorming' veranderen van een toevallig en grotendeels impliciet nevenproduct in een meer doordachte en systematische onderwijsmethode. Dit gebeurt pas als leraren de tijd nemen (en krijgen!) om te doordenken waarmee ze eigenlijk dagelijks bezig zijn, in plaats van toe te geven aan de neiging om het probleem met nieuwe werkvormen te lijf te gaan. Als karaktervorming wordt begrepen als de meer systematische en verfijnde poging om via de houding van leraren bij te dragen aan de morele vorming van leerlingen, dan wordt de voorbeeldfunctie van leraren een centrale notie. In dit hoofdstuk wordt onderzocht waarvan leraren een voorbeeld willen en moeten zijn, en wat het precies betekent om op moreel gebied een 'voorbeeld' te zijn. Een tweede methode die aan de orde komt, is het moreel-vormende gebruik van narratieve kunsten, zoals proza, poëzie en toneelspel. Beargumenteerd wordt dat het lezen van boeken weliswaar de morele groei kan bevorderen, namelijk omdat fictieve verhalen en de levens van mensen een narratieve structuur delen, maar dat dit niet toereikend is om meelevend te worden. Omdat we op toneelspelers of fictieve romanpersonages emotioneel anders betrokken zijn dan op echte mensen, moeten opvoeders niet vergeten om de morele verbeeldingskracht van kinderen ook *in de praktijk* te oefenen. Ten derde wordt onderzocht in hoeverre Socratische dialogen, en in het bijzonder die volgens de 'regressieve abstractie'-methode van Leonard Nelson worden gevoerd, een geschikte manier zijn voor leraren om de kardinale deugd 'praktische wijsheid' te oefenen. Het blijkt dat de beweging die deelnemers aan zulke gesprekken maken tussen een algemene, conceptuele vraag en concrete ervaringsvoorbeelden hen in staat stelt om het soort praktische oordeelsvermogen te oefenen dat nodig is om een koppeling te maken tussen een nog algemeen geformuleerde deugd als 'rechtvaardigheid' of 'dapperheid' enerzijds en de concrete en wisselende omstandigheden in de klas anderzijds.

Nadat de ontwikkeling en cultivering van deugden in school aan de orde zijn gekomen, staat in Hoofdstuk 5 de vraag centraal waarom karaktervorming moreel wenselijk is. Deze waarom-vraag is tot het laatst bewaard, omdat eerder is beargumenteerd dat onderzoek naar het 'waarom' het meeste vruchtbaar is als men het 'hoe' en 'wat' van de deugd al beheerst. De belangrijkste stelling van het hoofdstuk is dat deugden, ondanks een relativistische opvatting van moraal in pluriforme Westerse samenlevingen, wel degelijk als objectieve morele kwaliteiten begrepen worden die essentieel zijn voor het welzijn en geluk van ieder mens. En dat zonder morele vorming te reduceren tot minimale en instrumentele burgerschapdeugden. De poging om de relatie tussen deugd en 'geluk' (*eudaimonia*) te begrijpen door te rade te gaan bij Aristoteles' teleologie blijkt echter problematisch, omdat men er tegenwoordig niet vanuit gaat dat de (menselijke) natuur een intrinsiek doel (*telos*) heeft. Waarde kennen mensen aan de natuur toe, in plaats van dat we haar ontdekken in een natuur die zelf al geordend is, goed in elkaar zit. Daarom wordt vooral ingezoomd op de manieren waarop twee hedendaagse Aristotelici – MacIntyre en Kristjánsson – met de Aristotelische teleologie omgaan. Kunnen zij de vorming van deugden objectief rechtvaardigen, en tegelijk Aristoteles' erfenis zo herformuleren dat ze voor moderne mensen aanvaardbaar is? Beide auteurs staan een ander soort Aristotelianisme voor. Kristjánsson is meer geïnteresseerd in de relatie tussen ethiek en psychologie, en focust op de gedeelde emoties die aan deugden ten grondslag liggen, terwijl MacIntyre door zijn sociologische en historische invalshoek meer de morele verschillen en conflicten benadrukt. Hun gezamenlijke werk maakt echter duidelijk dat wat moreel wenselijk is niet direct uit de 'menselijke natuur' af te leiden is, maar dat er wel grenzen zijn aan wat nog een *menselijke* moraal genoemd mag worden.

Tenslotte worden in Hoofdstuk 6 de belangrijkste bevindingen van de voorgaande hoofdstukken bij elkaar gebracht. Wat heeft een Aristotelisch perspectief opgehelderd over de betekenis van *morele vorming*? Samenvattend kunnen we zeggen dat morele vorming als 'karaktervorming' bestaat uit de meer of minder weloverwogen en meer of minder uitgebreide pogingen van leraren om bij te dragen aan de continue ontwikkeling van morele deugd en praktische wijsheid bij kinderen, om hen daardoor in staat te stellen een gelukkig leven als mens te leiden. Verder wordt teruggeblikt op de vraag wat de onderzochte thema's duidelijk maken over de levensvatbaarheid van een *Aristotelische* benadering. Kenmerkend voor Aristoteles is dat begrippen die in de moderne tijd juist scherp van elkaar worden gescheiden bij hem juist versmelten, zoals 'rede' en 'emotie', 'habituatie' en 'kritische reflectie', een 'goed mens' en een 'goede burger', 'zelf' en 'ander', 'natuur' en 'moraal', en 'theorie' en 'praktijk'. Terwijl zijn genuanceerde ideeën van deze schijnbare tegenstellingen nieuwe inzichten opleveren, blijven Aristoteles' aannames vaak wat ongemakkelijk, juist omdat ze op gespannen voet staan met diepliggende moderne veronderstellingen. Het boek sluit af met enkele algemene implicaties die dit onderzoek naar het doel, en de ontwikkeling en vorming van deugden heeft voor ethisch en sociaalwetenschappelijk onderzoek.

Curriculum Vitae

Wouter Sanderse was born on March 5, 1982 in The Hague, the Netherlands, and he grew up in the province of Zeeland. After secondary education, he studied international business communication at the Radboud University Nijmegen. As an exchange student, he studied journalism and media at the University of Sunderland, England. After graduating in 2004, he started to study philosophy with the financial support of the Thomas More foundation. He continued his studies, specialised in ethics and graduated in 2007 on a master's thesis entitled 'Dealing with moral value conflicts in a pluralistic society'. During his final year, he did a work placement at the Dutch daily newspaper *Trouw*.

In September 2007, he started working as a junior researcher at the Department of Ethics of the Radboud University Nijmegen, under supervision of prof. dr. Paul van Tongeren. He continued his research at the University of Edinburgh (Scotland), the University of Iceland and the University of Rochester (NY, USA). He combined his research and teaching responsibilities with a part-time job as coordinator of the Centre for Ethics (until June 2010), and as secretary of the university's ethical committee (until January 2012). After he followed a course to become a Socratic dialogue supervisor, he started organising courses about 'moral education' to help teachers in secondary education to understand better the extent to which teaching is a moral enterprise (www.morelevorming.nl). Moreover, he organised the conference 'Excellent Education' for a hundred school leaders and teacher trainers at the Fontys Teacher Education Institute.

His current research interests are on virtue ethics and the philosophy of education, more in particular on professional ethics and moral education. In his PhD thesis, he investigated what a neo-Aristotelian virtue ethical approach can contribute to teachers' understanding of moral education, and what the relative strengths and weaknesses of virtue ethics are, compared to other approaches, such as cognitive development, care ethics and values clarification. In his work, he integrated insights from philosophy, psychology and pedagogics to develop a account of how morality may be taught in schools that is both morally justified and psychologically realistic.

Printed in Great Britain
by Amazon